DATE DUE

D0966452

Provoking Theater

Published by
Smith and Kraus, Inc.
177 Lyme Road, Hanover, NH 03755
www.smithkraus.com

First edition: September 2003
9 8 7 6 5 4 3 2 1

Cover and text design by Freedom Hill Design, Reading, Vermont
Layout by Electric Dragon Productions, Montpelier, Vermont
Cover and frontispiece photo by Ken Reynolds. Kama Ginkas, 1995.

Library of Congress Cataloging-in-Publication Data
Provoking theater : Kama Ginkas directs / by Kama Ginkas and John Freedman.
p. cm. — (career development book)
Includes index.
ISBN 1-57525-332-1
1. Ginkas, Kama—Interviews. 2. Theatrical producers and directors—Russia
(Federation)—Interviews. 3. Theater—Production and direction—Russia
(Federation) I. Freedman, John, 1954– II. Title. III. Art of theater series.

PN2728.G55A3 2003
792'.0233'092—dc21
2003057250

PROVOKING THEATER

KAMA GINKAS DIRECTS

by
Kama Ginkas
and
John Freedman

CAREER DEVELOPMENT SERIES

Smith and Kraus

KAMA GINKAS is one of the most celebrated theater directors in Russia today. His Moscow productions of *K. I. from "Crime," The Black Monk, The Lady with the Lapdog, The Happy Prince* and many others have established a new aesthetic standard in his homeland and have toured the world to acclaim. The miraculous survivor of a Jewish ghetto in Lithuania as a child during World War II, Ginkas nearly abandoned the theater in Leningrad in the 1970s — his challenging, independent style was such that he rarely could find work in the Soviet Union. But a move to Moscow in the 1980s, followed by perestroika and the changes it brought, signaled a drastic change in his fortunes and thrust him into the international spotlight. A professor of theater at the Moscow Art Theater School, he primarily works out of Moscow's Young Spectator, or New Generation, Theater (TYuZ), whose artistic director is his wife, the director Henrietta Yanovskaya. He made his American debut with multiple projects in 2003.

•   •   •

JOHN FREEDMAN has written or edited and translated nine books about Russian drama and theater, including *Silence's Roar: The Life and Drama of Nikolai Erdman* and *Moscow Performances: The New Russian Theater 1991–1996*. He has been the theater critic of *The Moscow Times* since 1992 and frequently contributes to the *New York Times* and other periodicals.

CONTENTS

Preface vii

1. Russian Theater Is Not a Time-Killer:
   Five Monologues and a Dialogue 1

2. A Russian Director from Lithuania with a
   Jewish Accent 19

3. The Director as Alpha and Omega 33

4. Meyerhold, Stanislavsky, and Others 67

5. The Pathology of the Actor 90

6. We Play Literature: Chekhov, Pushkin, Dostoevsky,
   Shakespeare, and Others 138

7. Digressing and Surviving 202

8. Provoking the Spectator 233

9. The Theater of Biography 259

10. Joseph Brodsky and Crossing Borders 304

Index 321

PREFACE

"The violin is not an easy instrument to play," Kama Ginkas deadpans in chapter 9 of this book. "You must hold the bow and move it lightly so that it does not make sawing noises."

There we have it: the acerbic wit, the incisive drive for honesty, the fascination with how things are done, and even an echo of the cathartic release (the thought of those ripping, sawing squeals) that characterize the art of this renowned and paradoxical director from Russia. Ginkas is passionate about theater, and this is a passionate book about those who make it and those who watch it. It is a book about theater that acquires meaning because it takes risks and makes demands.

Ginkas in conversation (this book is culled primarily from thirty-five hours of interviews taped throughout the year 2000) reminds me of the productions he stages: He is intense, funny, exact, and exacting. Ginkas does not just talk when he talks about theater, he whispers, shouts, smiles, and laughs. He carries on dialogues with himself as if he were a single actor playing every part in a play. He is excited by the thoughts running through his head, and he throws himself fully into them. He often leaps up and acts something out — showing *exactly* what he means — obviously not satisfied that words are enough. He wants his listener to see what he is after, but more important, it would seem, he wants to get it right for himself.

Provoking Theater collects the thoughts of a director who has spent thirty-five years as a professional working on getting it right. Make no mistake, getting something right for Ginkas is a process, not a goal, and so this book is full of inconsistencies and contradictions. This is one of the strengths of Ginkas's art, and it is one of the virtues of this book. It is what gives them both the aroma of life.

Provoking Theater is the testament of a survivor, literally and figuratively. It is the remarkable tale of an infant miraculously surviving the Holocaust and living to become an artist whose life and art are inextricably intertwined. It is also the tale of a director who rarely could work for the first fifteen years of his career because his theatrical vision did not suit the style or content required of Soviet artists.

Ginkas was born in Kaunas, Lithuania, on May 7, 1941, six weeks before Hitler's forces swept across the Baltic states toward the western border of the Soviet Union. For a while, his family was forced to live in a Jewish ghetto. When word reached his parents that the Nazis were about to begin exterminating children, they escaped. Like so many Jewish fugitives during World War II, Ginkas was sheltered from the SS forces by various people, including a Lithuanian actress and a nun at a Catholic hospital. Of the thousands of people who lived in the Kaunas ghetto at one time or another, Ginkas was one of only about a half-dozen children who survived. No wonder that Ginkas's mother used to tell him that he was "alive in spite of Hitler," and that Ginkas himself admits to having lived a life in defiance of the forces around him.

Ginkas's brush with mindless extinction encrusted a vivid mark on his art. In *K. I. from "Crime"* (code for "Katerina Ivanovna from *Crime and Punishment*" — meaning the character of the drunken Marmeladov's widow in Dostoevsky's novel), the figures of three forlorn children both abused and loved by their dying mother cannot help but call up images of children abandoned to fate. In *The Execution of the Decembrists,* based on actual documents pertaining to the grisly, botched execution of the rebels from Russia's high nobility who ineptly tried to overthrow the tsar in 1825, Ginkas created a harrowing and often hilarious primer of the business and psychology of killing and dying. In *Pushkin. Duel. Death,* a group of Alexander Pushkin's friends gather after his death and engage in gossip to try, in vain, to achieve a consensus about who their murdered friend had really been. These shows feature a Ginkas trademark: humor and horror mixed inextricably. The result is a powerful, very personal kind of theater that is liable to hit a spectator like a fist in the solar plexus. It is not uncommon to see Ginkas's spectators in tears at the end of a show. I have seen people run from the hall in hysterics — only to come back after regaining composure to watch the performance to the end.

Ginkas not only escaped literal extinction as a child, he fought back extinction as an adult artist. Following his professional debut in 1967, he had rare opportunities to ply his trade until the early 1980s because his uncompromising kind of art did not suit the requirements of the Soviet age. Ginkas enjoyed (if that is the proper word) a brief stint as the chief director of the Young Spectator Theater in the Siberian city of Krasnoyarsk from 1970 to 1972. But he has told me the story of one Communist Party official who so hated his shows that he used to kick the theater's posters when walking by. Needless to say, Ginkas did not last long in Krasnoyarsk, and he spent the next decade barely scraping out an existence in Leningrad mounting infrequent productions that were often crippled or closed down by the censor as soon as they opened. As if having Ginkas's case in mind, the Russian novelist and short-story writer Mark Kharitonov described this era, the 1970s to the mid-1980s, as "a dead and killing period in our history, a viscous, suffocating time that crippled many lives and was ruinous for culture."* Thinking his career was over, Ginkas in 1979 created a one-actor show he never really expected anyone to see. Most of the rehearsals took place in his apartment, and later he and his actor both admitted they were so fed up they each wished the other would quit. The production was called *Pushkin and Natalie* and it changed Ginkas's life. Not only did it help him discover a style that he continues to develop today, but a few out-of-the-way, semipublic performances came to the attention of some people with the power to help Ginkas find work. Among them were Oleg Yefremov, the actor and artistic director of the Moscow Art Theater, and Nina Drobysheva, a popular actress at the Mossoviet Theater in Moscow. And so, in the early 1980s, Ginkas moved from Leningrad to Moscow. His productions there of Sergei Kokovkin's *Five Corners* (1981) and Ibsen's *Hedda Gabler* (1984) at the Mossoviet Theater and Nina Pavlova's *The Club Car* (1982) and Alexander Galin's *The*

---

*From the essay "A Hostage of Eternity" (Zalozhnik vechnosti) in Mark Kharitonov, *Izbrannaya proza* (Moscow: Moskovskii Rabochii, 1994): 258.

Toastmaster (1986) on the main stage of the Moscow Art Theater are now considered classics.

Another major turn for the better took place in 1986 when Ginkas's wife, Henrietta Yanovskaya, a major artist in her own right, was named the artistic director of Moscow's Young Spectator Theater, also known in English as the New Generation Theater. This is the period when the first tentative freedoms of perestroika began touching Soviet society. Coming twenty years after his debut, it marked the first time Ginkas would have a stable, professional home base. It also marked the beginning of his rise to prominence. His powerful trio of Dostoevsky adaptations —*Notes from Underground* (1988) followed by *We Play "Crime"* (1991) and *K. I. from "Crime"* (1994), the latter two based on the novel *Crime and Punishment* — were landmarks in Moscow theater. For a decade, Ginkas frequently mounted shows in Finland where he also taught at the Helsinki Academy of Arts. His Finnish productions included several dramatizations of prose: Chekhov's *Ward No. 6* (1988), Dostoevsky's *Crime and Punishment* (1990), Dostoevsky's *The Idiot* (1993), and *Life Is Beautiful* (1995), based on Chekhov's story, "The Lady with the Lapdog." His Helsinki production of *Macbeth* (1997) is one of his masterpieces.

The second half of the 1990s and the beginning of the new century witnessed Ginkas's flourishing as a star both in Russia and abroad. His Moscow productions for this period included two works Ginkas himself had written based on historical documents during his long, frustrating years of semi-unemployment: *The Execution of the Decembrists* (1995) and *Pushkin. Duel. Death* (1999). He also dramatized more works of Chekhov's prose, *The Black Monk* (1999) and *The Lady with the Lapdog* (2001), as well as staging several conventional plays, Alexander Pushkin's *The Golden Cockerel* (1998), Oleg Bogayev's *The Russian National Postal Service* under the title *Room of Laughter* (1998), and Oscar Wilde's *The Happy Prince* (2000). Ginkas's stunning production in 2001 of *The Polyphony of the World,* a musical mystery by the composer Alexander Bakshi, was arguably the crowning achievement of what, by that time, had become an exceptional career.

Provoking Theater is a record of Ginkas's thoughts on his art and, to a lesser extent, his life up to and including his production of *The*

Happy Prince, which premiered in late October 2000. But neither Ginkas nor I wanted merely to explain or describe his productions. Nor were we interested in writing a book of memoirs. No matter how fascinating the blend of biographical fact and legend — it often makes for gripping reading — the purpose of this text is always to pursue Ginkas's unique, uncompromising approach to theater. When talking about his teacher, the great director Georgy Tovstonogov (1913–1989), Ginkas states that Tovstonogov never taught anyone anything; it was up to his students to learn from him what they could. This impresses me as an apt commentary on Ginkas's book. Ginkas never attempts to delineate any system; he offers no formulas, no point-by-point programs, no paint-by-number schemes. Yet when we follow his wending thoughts, his leaps of fancy, and his winding digressions, we easily perceive the method in his creative madness. We feel the presence of a master creator, and he makes the process of creation tangible.

In working with me, Ginkas invariably engaged me as an actor and a spectator wrapped in one. Going into the project, I set myself the task of staying out of view as much as possible. Thus the genre of questions and monologues. But Ginkas will not abide neutrality or lack of involvement. He used me, cajoled me, and bullied me. He embarrassed me, confused me, brought me to tears, and, most often, delighted me. I believe the lively nature of our communication remains imbedded in the text. The reader will feel Ginkas coming off the page to make personal appeals to reason or, more to the point, to the emotions. One of Ginkas's favorite words is *physiology* — he seeks, through art, to affect people as fire and ice do flesh. Ginkas's voice in this book does that.

I have sought to retain in English the energy, the tempo, and the style of the original conversations Ginkas and I had in Russian. At times there is a biblical nature to Ginkas's speech. This, understandably, comes out strongly in chapter 9 in his discussion of his ancestry and his brush with death. Paradoxically — and everything about Ginkas is paradoxical — this chapter may contain some of the book's most valuable theatrical insights, although there is less in it about theater per se than in other chapters. This is the place, along with his reminiscences of growing up in Lithuania in chapter 2, where we see art emerging from biography, style emerging from experience. But see, also, the story of

Ginkas's father's funeral in chapter 6, and the important role the telling of that tale played during the rehearsals of his production called *K. I. from "Crime."* Or consider his eloquent explanation in chapter 7 why he has never staged a production about the Holocaust. (As proof that Ginkas is nothing if not predictable in his unpredictability, he opened a show called *Dreams of Exile* as this book entered the final stage of preparation. *Dreams of Exile,* created with his students at the Moscow Art Theater and based on themes drawn from the paintings of Marc Chagall, marked the first time Ginkas ever had addressed the topic of his Jewish heritage directly in his work.)

The centerpiece of *Provoking Theater* is chapter 5, "The Pathology of the Actor." Here, and in echoes of the topic throughout almost every other chapter, we become privy to Ginkas's almost excruciatingly complex relationship with the actor, to the "material" that lends living flesh to his theatrical imagination. His insights into the nature of the actor, and into the ways one must work with hypersensitive artists whose sole instruments are their bodies and psyches, are astonishing in their depth and scope. His prejudices may be every bit as evident, but I will say this: All directors and actors will find echoes of their own strengths and weaknesses here. They will also discover much practical wisdom that may aid them in utilizing those strengths and weaknesses to good ends.

Finally, the ambiguity of the title, *Provoking Theater,* sounds like Ginkas to me. It is a book by and about a man who always challenges, and sometimes aggravates, those who come into contact with his art, from his actors and his stagehands to his spectators and critics. For me, however, the verbal qualities of the word *provoking* overwhelm the adjectival in relation to Ginkas, as they imply notions of prompting, causing, or inducing. This is a book about how one takes raw material and coaxes it into art, about how one provokes one's life, one's surroundings, one's colleagues, and one's self in such a way that art arises from them.

• • •

This book, in a small sense, is a family project. Ginkas's wife Henrietta Naumovna Yanovskaya is present in these pages far more than meets the eye. She has developed as an artist alongside her husband ever since they were married in 1964. She has supported him — and he, her — throughout their parallel lives and careers. Several of the interviews that went into the book were conducted in Henrietta Naumovna's office at Moscow's Young Spectator, or New Generation, Theater. One took place in her living room. One day before a work session I told Henrietta Naumovna that I was encouraged by the progress Ginkas and I were making. With the irony characteristic of both Ginkas and his wife, she said, "Get Kama to talk all you can. I don't know whether it is age or experience, but he has become a very wise man of late." I would like to think that Henrietta Naumovna will be pleased with the result of my work with her husband.

My wife Oksana Mysina is another component in the family circle. Oksana is not only my wife, however; she is also the actress who performs the role of Katerina Ivanovna in Ginkas's production of *K. I. from "Crime."* Some may be suspicious that I have violated an ethical code by incorporating into the book so many of Ginkas's discussions of this show and his work with the actress. To them, I can only say that this production, often regarded as one of Ginkas's most important and still running in repertory, has been performed over two hundred times in fourteen countries and has won honors and acclaim everywhere it has gone. It hardly needs saying that my gratitude for Oksana's contribution to this book is immeasurable.

Another familial link is Daniil Gink, the son of Kama and Henrietta. I came to know Daniil — a playwright whose hit play *Bald/Brunet* I translated into English — before I met his parents. Later, at his father's request, Danya wrote the text for *K. I. from "Crime,"* bringing the family and professional relations full circle.

Several friends and colleagues are especially deserving of thanks. Theodore Shank, the playwright and editor of *TheatreForum,* asked me in early 1997 to contribute to his journal. The resulting piece, "Russian Theater Is Not a Time-Killer," was published in *TheatreForum* no. 12 (1998) and it served as the spark for what was to become *Provoking Theater.* I have incorporated segments of this interview and its introduction into this preface and several of the chapters. I am grateful for Ted's permission to reprint parts of the original interview.

Ken Reynolds, the photographer, has been a friend ever since I met him in Moscow in 1995. At that time he also became the primary photographic chronicler of Ginkas's and Yanovskaya's productions. Ken has read, commented on, and ardently supported the development of this manuscript at every stage. I am thrilled that his photographs — works of art in their own right — form an important part of this book.

Timothy C. Westphalen is a friend and colleague whose clear thinking and incisive mind have been invaluable to my work. He critiqued key portions of the manuscript and selflessly offered his expert advice on literary theory, style, and translation whenever I demanded them. Tim translated the song fragment in chapter 9 and the excerpt from Joseph Brodsky's *A Talk with Heaven's Denizen* in chapter 10.

Robert Olinger, an American student in Ginkas's directing course at the Moscow Art Theater, appeared late in my work on this project. But his deep admiration for Ginkas's work and his willingness to read and comment on the final draft were a great benefit to me.

I wish to thank Sharon M. Carnicke for reading and commenting on the passages about the Stanislavsky system.

My mother, Frances R. Freedman, has not only been a devoted believer in this book, she has been a patient, astute, and critical reader. What a joy to have a mother who knows when and how to tell you what to do — even if you don't always do it.

The five monologues comprising the first half of chapter 1 were drawn and edited from a manuscript that Ginkas published in full as "Why I Love and Hate Theater" (*Pochemu ya lyublyu i nenavizhy teatr*) in the book *Rezhissyorsky teatr: Razgovory pod zanaves veka* (Director's Theater: Conversations at the End of an Age), Vypusk 1 (Moscow: Moskovsky Khudozhestvenny teatr, 1999). This text drew on interviews Ginkas has given to Maria Sedykh, Yulia Marinova, Yelena Gruyeva, Irina Glushchenko, and Lyubov Oves. I am grateful to the publishers for permission to reprint.

Finally, I wish to thank Kama Ginkas. It has been an extraordinary experience, one that grabbed hold of me and still has not let me go.

John Freedman
Moscow, March 2003

1

Russian Theater Is Not a Time-Killer:
Five Monologues and a Dialogue

FIVE MONOLOGUES

ON THEATER

I do not pretend that what I show on stage is life. I do not know life. Nor do I trust those who say they do. I do know some of the games life has played with me. And I try to communicate what I experience when life plays games with me.

Why do I love and hate the theater? Because in the theater every fact, every folly of life acquires meaning and significance. In Dostoevsky's novel *Crime and Punishment,* Katerina Ivanovna died on a dirty sidewalk, and when she went off to the other world it was not on the white ladder I gave her in my show *K. I. from "Crime."* The Decembrists were hung to polkas and gavottes, not to Chopin and spiritual music as in my *The Execution of the Decembrists*. When something befalls us in life, thunder does not resound and violins do not play a sorrowful motif. But that is what happens in the theater. My response to that mingles pain, irony, and affection.

Perhaps I love the theater and make it because in it the games of life are not quite as dangerous. Here you do not have to "kill the old pawnbroker" as Raskolnikov does in *Crime and Punishment,* you can just play at it while still learning something about yourself and people. It is only a game. And yet . . . I play a serious game and I demand total devotion from the participants. I want playing and watching to be as dangerous as falling off a cliff so that, later, when you are rescued, you feel the sense of life returning to you.

My goal is to bypass the artifices of art and to reach inside you to make you, if only for a second, feel reality, the literalness of what is actually transpiring on stage. I want what is happening on stage in my show to become a fact of your life — again, if only it is for one second.

In my production of *We Play "Crime,"* based on Dostoevsky's *Crime and Punishment,* Raskolnikov picked up an ax and laid a live chicken on the floor. Some spectators cringed. You could see them thinking, "My God, are they really going to do that right here?!" In that same show the spectators shuddered when the ax head sunk into a ripe head of cabbage. It was only a head of cabbage, but it did have a nice, juicy pop when sliced open. A few moments later it became quite amusing — all the characters gaily chopped the cabbage into little pieces and chewed it. But there was also a nagging sensation of dread: What if those are brains they are eating?

I have staged productions of Anton Chekhov's *The Lady with the Lapdog* in which no one is hung and no old ladies are chopped up. There is nothing in them but love. Yet, here is what I sought to evoke in that "nothing but": I wanted Anna Sergeyevna's final moment of touching and stroking the rough walls of a boat to make you, my spectators, tremble as you do when caressing someone you love and desire.

Theater exists to allow you to sense the fleeting seconds of your life. As a rule, this is only possible in the pauses, in moments of quiet repose when nothing happens. Only then does real time merge with stage time. That is when you, the spectator, suddenly feel the seconds of your life ticking away. This was first revealed to us by that great "director" Anton Chekhov in *The Three Sisters.* Remember the scene at the beginning of Act Four? Everyone poses to be photographed. The magnesium burns and hisses. Nothing happens. Everything is frozen.

Gurov (Igor Gordin) and Anna (Yulia Svezhakova) in the dramatization of
The Lady with the Lapdog; Moscow, 2001. *Photo by Yelena Lapina.*

Motionless, everyone waits as the magnesium burns and hisses. At this
moment spectators in the hall have goose bumps. Why? What is the
big deal? Nothing is happening! But time is passing . . . The seconds
of *our own* lives are passing and nothing can return them. It is terrifying, horrible. And we get goose bumps.

Then the flash goes off, everyone stands and begins speaking nois-
ily at once. It is just as in life — everyone has already forgotten the
sensation of the moment. Just as it is impossible to spend all your time
thinking about the fact that you will die, it is impossible to draw that
photographic pause out for the two hours that a show lasts.

In the theater, the plot and everything it entails are nothing but a
trap. Everything here is undertaken for one reason only: To put the spectator in motion so that you can stop everything for a second and make
him listen to the sound of time passing.

Art, especially theater, has become so clogged up with intellectual finesse that purity and artlessness have lost their value. These days I understand and cherish an apple drawn well enough to be equal to itself. This is the hyper-realistic approach, where a nail is a nail and nothing more. And yet it is no less important than the eye of a beautiful woman watching you at a close distance. We cannot say what is more important, what is less. In truth, we do not know. We can only verify the facts: This man laughs; this man is dying; this man is combing his hair. This is all we can do.

Someone said the following about my production of *The Execution of the Decembrists*: "What is said is what we see. Nothing more. The result, for some reason, is a production of deep significance." I am pleased if that is true.

THE LIVING MATTER OF THEATER

Theater is flesh despite its absolutely ethereal nature. Theater is resilient. It breathes, it incites. Theater is not words, ideas, or problems. It is flesh. It is an independent being born of intercourse among the director, the actors, the designer, the playwright. It is born of the word and sound, of space and rhythm, of the interactions of objects and live people. It is flesh. With its own personality, its own manner of life, its own temperament. The director's job is to assist in the birthing of this living flesh. This is what real directors do. Everyone else is busy using the stage as a platform for enacting ecological stories or debating issues.

ON ACTORS

Some day I may write a book entitled *The Pathology of the Actor*. Does that sound too harsh? Too offensive? Not at all! Just as there is a pathology of any living being, there is a pathology of the actor, his or her own personal "medical history." After all, we are speaking of a *living* theater, are we not?

I, a director, do not exist if there is no actor. I am manifested through the actor. Who is this being without which I am not?

The actor is an enigmatic entity a priori. A normal person, such as you or I, will not voluntarily undress for a public display as will the actor. From ancient times civilized man has covered himself. He seeks to conceal what sets him apart, to disguise what makes him silly. He does not wash his dirty linen in public, does not thrust himself on others. Those are the behavioral norms. We have learned and assimilated a large number of skills of courtesy. We know how to protect ourselves. We know how not to open ourselves up, or, at least, to open ourselves up only insofar as it is absolutely necessary or proper. Only fools strip down to nothing and parade about, declaring, "Look at me! Look at what I am!" Or actors. The more frankly an actor bares himself, the more open he is, the more defenseless, interesting, unique and, perhaps, pathological, he is, the better he is as an actor.

There is an internal paradox here, perhaps a tragic conflict. On one hand, the actor *wants* to open himself up entirely. On the other he fears doing that more than anyone because he is more vulnerable, more easily hurt than anyone else. He constantly thinks: "Maybe I am not handsome enough, smart enough, talented enough, emotional enough, deep enough. What if my knees are knobby?" Here is the crux of the actor's nature: an uncontrollable desire to "undress" and a dread fear of doing just that. The job of the director and, if you will, one of the goals of the Stanislavsky system, is to eliminate that fear.

Here I must say a word about an actor who would appear to be just the opposite type. This kind of actor never reveals himself. He is a jokester. He is always ready to pull some gag or stunt on stage, to hide behind any mask, disappear behind any deception — anything to avoid having to show his true face. But is this not really just the opposite side of the same coin?

The relationship of a director and actor are those of a male and female. The actor is always the female, regardless of his or her sex, just as the director is always the male. The director proposes the plan of action, makes demands, desires a specific result, makes promises and uses seduction to his ends. At the same time he must be deceptive, must disappoint, must appear to be weak. If the director-male is too crude, he may force the actor-female to shut him out. If he is too patient, he risks letting the actor-female cool toward him. If his caresses are too light, he risks failing to excite her. As with a woman, a director's behavior with an actor must be the perfect one for the specific time and place, whether it is gentleness or rudeness, whether it is aggression or caution. This is not something that can be programmed in advance. The instant one partner senses routine, the love act is over! And what takes place between a director and actor is an act of love. It is a game of love.

Every actor suffers from his own case of "aggravated amnesia," his long and complex "medical history" or, as is usually the case, "medical histories." This, in fact, is the record of his or her subconscious memory of earlier traumas. Anyone may traumatize an actor. But I, the director, am the one who does it most. And I reopen the wounds with every rehearsal. I do this because I am indifferent, I am rude, I am hasty, I lack professionalism, or I am ignorant of this given actor's individuality.

The actor is naked. He is vulnerable. I long ago learned that all the so-called actors' whims, their stunts, their arrogance, their insolence, their big heads, even their boorishness (something you often see in the greater actors) is nothing more than the reflection of their complex natures. Their stunts are always either a self-defense mechanism or a case of their "illness" acting up. As such, the hysterics that actors throw at their directors or their fellow actors, like the costumes they throw at their costumers or the backstage intrigues they weave — these are all the agonizing convulsions that accompany their specific illnesses. (Incidentally, where might I find the book entitled *The Pathology of the Director*? This is a very necessary book. The director may know of his own pathology and may suffer from what he knows. But he cannot analyze it, cannot write a book about it. Someone else is needed for that. Chances are, an actor.)

An actor is an uncommonly sensitive being. The more talented the director, the stronger the magnetic force he is able to project. And the more difficult he makes life for the actor.

The interaction of the actor and the spectator comprises an entire chapter in the "medical history." But long before the actor meets the public, there is an enormous knot of pathological contradictions that must be untangled. Any director who plans to do this must know exactly what the job is that lies ahead. He must understand that, essentially, he will be poking an open wound. Moreover, he cannot do otherwise, for if there are no wounds, there is no actor.

ON THE SPECTATOR

I consciously violate the fourth wall between the actor and the spectator. I consider it an untruth that actors should walk right by and make believe that I, the spectator, do not exist. I like to pretend that a fourth wall exists, to collude with, to tease the spectator. But it is essential to reveal its gaping absence.

I like this game because it reflects the ambivalence of everything — that is, I think I am free, but, in fact, I am locked in a prison; or, I think I am alone, but everybody is looking at me; or, I believe that I exist but it turns out I am playing. I love these theatrical pranks. They give us a true sense of ourselves.

My job is to provoke the spectator, to exist with him in critical, even aggressively playful, situations. It is a striptease: I undress and assume you are doing the same. When I am creating a show, my actors and I bare ourselves to the fullest extent of our talents. We stand naked before you. You, on the other hand, are certain that you are safe on your side of the fourth wall.

That infuriates me. You came to watch a play. Yes, you sit and observe us. But we observe you, too. Everything that is happening on stage is not only about us, it is about you, too.

I admire Velazquez's *Las Meninas* in which you suddenly realize that the painter is watching you observe his characters.

The spectator is uncomfortable. He had thought he was in control. Yes, he was the boss. But not always. That moment of hesitation provides the truest sensation that a person can have of him or herself in this world.

ON MYSELF

I have begun feeling lately as if I am a dinosaur. As if I am still alive but no longer understand the purpose of my tusks, my scratchy fur, my enormous size and weight in tons. Rabbits and frogs scurry about just fine without them. Those of us in my generation have spent our lives proving that theater must be personal and confessional, must have a unique style and form that signal the director's personality, must renounce the primacy of lifelike realism. These days, it seems none of this is of any interest to anyone.

I understand how Meyerhold must have felt in the 1930s. He tried to conform to his age by staging *The Lady with Camellias*. His revolutionary qualities (not only in a social sense but also in an aesthetic sense), the magnitude of his ideas and the fury with which he brought them to fruition — all of this became superfluous. A bourgeois age had dawned. What then was valued was the simple human life with all of its quotidian details. One character speaks with a kind of whisper and another sips tea with his head cocked to the side. These minuscule details were then what people were looking for.

Our age is similar. After the enormous social cataclysms of recent years, spectators prefer that which is unadorned and balanced. They have renewed their affection for the old Soviet films and plays about nice people. They hold in highest esteem the trivial details of life. Directors stage Dostoevsky no differently than they would a typical realistic, lifelike writer. Dostoevsky's intensity, his egocentric qualities, his desire to seek the limits of the human experience beyond the pale of the criminal, his attempt to acquire immortality (even if in the form of leaving a chip of a toenail on the stage) — in other words, everything that makes Dostoevsky what he is — is of no interest to anyone these days.

We are monsters, those of us devoted to personal form and style, to intensity and distinctive content. We soon will be superfluous ourselves.

A Dialogue

What do you see as the purpose of theater?

Theater provides the opportunity for us to live through something if it does not exist in life. Of course, it is an imitation of sorts. Foreigners are apt to call it an "experience." I hate that word. A foreigner comes to Russia and says, "Oh, how interesting!" He even wants to go someplace a little dangerous or stay in some seedy hotel and then go back and tell how he survived. Or maybe he goes to the Sahara Desert. But he is not going to live there. He is not a bushman. It is an "experience." Two weeks. A month even. Or maybe he climbed some great height and almost froze off his foot. A wonderful experience. "Yes, I saw that show, what a wonderful experience, yes, yes, yes." I hate that. Because that is not living. It is just touching. My shows do not just touch you. They intend to grab hold and not let go.

It is often said that a poet in Russia is more than a poet. The same can be said about theater — including what you do specifically. I do not suppose you can tell me how you do it . . . but how do you do it?

I do not know, but this I can say: It is not less than theater and it is not more than theater — it is theater and that is all it is.

I have always felt I must do something significant. To take on global questions. I do not mean philosophy. I mean the problems of existence I meet every second of my life. They are not abstract questions; they are tormenting, truly terrible, sometimes hope-inspiring and occasionally even unexpectedly joyful. That is rarer. Maybe that is why I want to get outside my productions. Even if only for a second. To make contact with what is not theater.

I look for those one or two seconds when, amidst the plot and action, I can catch the spectator off-guard for a split second. When he is not thinking about what is happening with Katerina Ivanovna or Macbeth. In fact, when he is not thinking at all. When he himself suddenly comes face to face with life and death. As a rule, it is not more than a second or two. "Is there meaning to life? Is there no meaning to life?" This is not an intellectual question. It is tangible. But not for long. When Katerina Ivanovna rises up on a ladder and beats her fists against the ceiling in *K. I. from "Crime,"* it is a cathartic moment and the spectator weeps. There have been spectators who have been gripped by hysterical weeping.

You are smiling as if you like that . . .

I am smiling because I achieved what I was after. The spectator identifies very easily with her at that moment. There is no person who has never beaten against a wall. The reason is not important. Some beat against the wall of truth, justice, or meaning. Others do it to be able to write more legibly, stage a theatrical show, get women, be understood by a son, whatever. Everyone knows that two times two is four, but why is it four? There is no person who has not struggled to understand that.

When Katerina Ivanovna has lived a tormenting ninety minutes with us, and we see she cannot break through to truth, justice, or meaning, we realize it is impossible! We will never understand the meaning. It is not even a matter of understanding: We cannot comprehend it, cannot catch it. We latch onto the meaning of life for a second and then fall back into doubt again. We want to know, is there justice or not? I am talking about universal justice. I am not talking about one guy charging me fifty rubles for a chair and another guy offering me forty-five to buy it back. No! Although, the bigger question sometimes arises in such a simple thing. That is the charm of theater. The most important, universal problems are revealed by the simplest things. That is the method by which I do what I do: working through basic, elementary devices.

The simple images you create are what remain in the memory. For example, in *We Play "Crime,"* Raskolnikov chops up a head of cabbage when killing the pawnbroker. I have forgotten a lot of that show but even now, many years later, I remember vividly how he cut that cabbage in half — or how they brought out that live chicken.

That's right. In *The Execution of the Decembrists* people are occupied with a simple task — getting to the bottom of the technology of an execution. Like anything else, an execution has its own technology. You need a wooden beam, a wrench, a rope. What kinds of rope? What kinds of knots? How do you grease them? It is all very simple. But we are talking about an execution — life and death.

In the course of my show many things are strung up and hung before our eyes. They hang sacks, and we feel discomfort. We watch them

A scene from *The Execution of the Decembrists,* written by Kama Ginkas on the basis of historical documents; Moscow, 1995. *Photo by Viktor Bazhenov.*

slip nooses over the ends of the sacks. And we feel that *second*. Then the sacks are strung up and the bench is kicked out from beneath them. The sacks hang. We easily identify with them at that moment.

They bring in five sacks and we perceive them as corpses. But the actors open them up and it turns out to be sacks full of overcoats. They start slamming the coats against the wall as if they were useless rags. And in that second we identify ourselves with those coats. We think, "That's me they're slamming up against the wall!"

When one of the characters takes a wooden hanger with an overcoat hanging on it and breaks it, we feel as though someone is snapping our spine. These are the elements that allow us to identify with what happens on stage.

You ask me how? It is through the most elementary things. Something that is happening right now. This very second. I could not, do not want to, and never would, for example, cut off a chicken's head. That would be a monstrous, criminal act. That is neither theater nor art. But how do you instill in the spectator that sensation — that *real* sensation, not artistic — of fear when the ax swings down and a head rolls? When the ax rises over the chicken's head, the spectator is seized by real fear for a second because no one knows what is going to happen — modern theater is liable to pull any crazy stunt. It turns out to be a theatrical joke. But the spectator was thrown into fear for the chicken. For a mere chicken, which, incidentally, we eat.

The point is, how do you get that fear across? Take the cabbage. We truly feel that ax sinking into the crisp, meaty cabbage. It causes a physiological response in us — and that is what I want. It is not intellectual or psychological. It is physiology. It is beyond our control. If someone sticks our hand in a fire, we will yank it out. It does not matter what we are thinking intellectually at that moment. Even if we did not pull our hand out, the meat would blister up because our physiology would respond. Not my spirit, my intellect or my psychology. My physiology. You ask me how I do it? I am telling you how. This is one of the means.

Are these things that emerge in rehearsal, or do you conceive them in advance when you are outlining the show in your head?

It depends. But theater for me exists largely in this very thing, of catching the spectator off guard. That does not mean the whole show will be like that. It is just a second or two. Our organisms cannot deal with it for any longer than that.

I ask about rehearsals for a specific reason. Because I have never seen a weak acting performance in your productions. There are many talented directors in Moscow, but in any one of their shows I usually see a gradation of success among the actors. I have never seen anything like that in your shows. Which is why, if you will pardon me, I come back to saying "This is not theater." Actors exist so naturally in your shows.

I can explain that on a purely professional level. There almost are no bad actors — or at least I will not let you see them. That is one of the lessons of my teacher, Georgy Tovstonogov. As the director I answer for my actors. It is my fault if an overweight, fifty-year-old actress says she is sixteen years old as she plays Luise in *Love and Intrigue*. She may even do it well, but I have put her in an embarrassing, unnatural situation. I am obliged to give an actor a task that corresponds to his gift. If an actor is capable of playing Bernardo in *Hamlet,* I cannot cast him as Hamlet or Claudius.

Next, you do not force the role on the actor, you reveal the actor — actually, the person, the real person — within the conditions and logic of the part. I believe every person is talented — no, let's say interesting. Every person is interesting. Every one. You must give him the opportunity to reveal himself. There are conditions in which he cannot do that. Let's say I tell you to run 100 meters in 9.8 seconds. You will not be able to. You will look silly. You will be sweaty, ugly, and angry. But you can do something else. My job is to find out what and provoke you to do it. That is the pure technology of how I work. I am a harsh, insistent, patient, and impatient director, but I have given up on enormous numbers of things I wanted to do in my shows. Because I will not force an actor to do what does not come naturally. You try one thing, it doesn't work, you change it. Try another? Change it. Try another? Change it. Try another? Well, it looks like this one works. All that is left is what helps the actor exist in the role naturally.

You mentioned Georgy Tovstonogov. I want to ask not about him personally, but about the tradition of the teacher, which, in Russian theater and Russian life in general, is very rich and highly developed. It is very common in Russia for people to invoke their teacher. Do you feel you exist within a tradition that comes from somewhere and goes somewhere?

Without a doubt. In Russian theater and art there is that natural connection of the *pupil* and the *teacher,* the son and the father. This gives rise to the attempt to overcome dependence, to free yourself of love and the sense of duty — the sense that I am under obligation to my father for giving me life or that I am under obligation to my teacher for making me a director. I would have become a director no matter what. But I would have become a different director. Upon graduating from the institute thirty-odd years ago, I wasted enormous amounts of energy battling with the schooling I received. I am still doing it today.

I do everything possible to exceed its limits. But your schooling sits so deeply in you. It is genetics. It is your backbone. I cannot overcome it totally.

My teacher's son, my friend and classmate Alexander Tovstonogov, once said that in my very first production I began betraying Tovstonogov and began doing shows like Anatoly Efros. He believed that I abandoned my teacher and betrayed him. That could not be farther from the truth. I will be grateful to the end of my days for having had the opportunity to study with Tovstonogov. I always feel that I will never fall. Because my backbone is built. I may have strayed very far from Tovstonogov in what is superficial, but not in what is essential.

Do you follow Western theater?

Much of contemporary Western theater is just like ours and, to a certain extent, worse. Because our level of acting is always high. There are always at least two or three excellent actors even in the worst provincial theater. For whatever reasons neither we nor anybody else will ever hear about them. But they could have been stars. The sincerity with which theater is made in Russia cannot be found anywhere in the West. It is a way to spend time in the West: restaurants, television, bars, sports, shopping, concerts, and theater. For the Russian, theater is not a time-killer. It is and always has been something of consequence.

The legendary nineteenth-century actor Mikhail Shchepkin said something like "the theater is a cathedral." What do you think?

In Russia the poet has always been more than a poet and theater has always been more than theater. This was a totalitarian or autocratic state long before Soviet times. People nowadays have a misguided view of Russian history. In Shchepkin's time, as in Soviet times, people went to the theater so that they, unfree people in an unfree country, could feel some sense of freedom. They did not go to hear some actor express an antitsarist or anti-Stalinist sentiment.

In other words, they did not go for political reasons . . .

Not *only* for political reasons, not *only*. The distinction is important, because they went for that too, but not only for that.

Spectators wanted to share the feelings of the hero without having to answer for them. They came to sympathize a little with the criminal Raskolnikov or that woman in Ostrovsky's *Guilty without Guilt* who bore a child out of wedlock — she, too, was a criminal in some way. Sure, there was something morally wrong there. But through the affinities they felt with the characters, they achieved some sort of absolution. They received a kind of sermon they were in need of. I am not talking about the kind of sermon that threatens us and hounds us and drives us farther from life. I mean the kind that opens up possibilities and makes life possible.

Then there is the matter of confession. There may be a character on stage whose confession takes the form of "To be or not to be? That is the question." The spectator hears that and recognizes it as a question he cannot answer either. He needs to encounter that dilemma. *Not* for the intellectual stimulation. *Not* for the experience of it. *Not* to kill time. But because he does not have the proper words to express it. He cannot formulate it.

But he is a living being. He is not concerned with the problem of killing Claudius or not. No. His problems are of the simplest kind. What is he going to eat tomorrow? Basically, he senses on some vague level that these questions are his as well. He may not be a very sophisticated person, but he can weep together with Hamlet. And when he goes out having wept, he knows he can live another day.

Of course the situation was cruder in Soviet times. Somebody on stage would say something and all of us in the audience would burst into laughter. It was not because the actor had said anything all that funny. But we knew that he had just said something that reflected the genuine reality of life in the Soviet state. We often spoke these kinds of thoughts quietly with a friend in the privacy of our kitchen, but in the theater you could hear those thoughts sitting in the balcony in the middle of a thousand people.

It was a way to achieve a sort of power over one's own life . . .

Freedom, not power! There was no gaining power over your life! I am talking about a fleeting sensation of freedom that lasts only as long as my reaction lasts to something I see or hear on stage. Then there was the feeling we had when we all came out of the theater. We were somehow united. We did not know the people on either side of us and they did not know us, but somehow we were together.

Are you aware of your nationality as a person who makes theater?

Of course. An interview I once gave in Lithuania took its title from a comment I made. Something like, "I am a Russian director from Lithuania with a Jewish accent." I am a product of the Russian school: Russian theater, Russian culture, Russian literature. And so, I am, without the slightest doubt, a director of the Russian theater.

But, the visual side is largely Lithuanian. A person's first impressions are not intellectual, they are more properly visual. In my case, this is the Lithuanian landscape. The Catholic Church and its mass. Organ music. The paintings of Ciurlionis. Lithuanian folk sculpture.

Lithuania is famous for its primitive wooden sculptures that were made from the end of the nineteenth century on into the twentieth century. In a certain sense they are close to African art. They are knife carvings of saints or crèche scenes and are always painted in watercolors. It is a unique form of art. I was brought up with that around me.

But my temperament, my emotions, my manner of living, the fact that I wave my hands around, that I cannot sit still and am always jumping up and moving around — my shows are like that, too, incidentally — that is my Jewishness. It can definitely be sensed in my productions.

You have staged traditional plays, but more often you have staged dramatized prose or even historical documents. Why?

Several reasons. One is all those years when I was unable to work because no one would give me a job. I sat at home and fantasized productions. I did that less often on the basis of plays because a play is fixed and there is less to fantasize. Although they were all done recently,

Ward No. 6 and *Life Is Beautiful* in Finland, or *The Execution of the Decembrists, K. I. from "Crime,"* and *We Play "Crime"* in Moscow, were all devised in my head back then. That was compensation for my inability to work.

Second, especially in those years, there was the challenge of staging a nonplay — "You say x, I say y. You say x, I say y. You say x, I say y. I say y." You cannot just stage that. You must think up something to go with it. That gets my juices flowing. All the forms are obvious in a play where they say, "Hello. Good-bye. How are you? I'm fine. Do you love her? I don't love her anymore, I think I'll leave her." The other is more interesting. The material dictates what you do. It makes you find a form, a new kind of theater.

One more nuance. From my student days I have loved *The Cherry Orchard*. To this day I consider it the greatest and most difficult play ever written. No Shakespeare can compare to *The Cherry Orchard* as regards the difficulty of staging it. In many of the shows I do, I am actually staging *The Cherry Orchard:* Nina Pavlova's *The Club Car,* Alexander Galin's *The Toastmaster,* or Daniil Gink's Dostoevsky dramatization, *K. I. from "Crime,"* if you will. They are all *The Cherry Orchard*. It is a play of genius. I am amazed at the lightheadedness and brazenness of many who dare to stage Chekhov. There is nothing surprising in someone doing Shakespeare. You can do him. I myself did *Hamlet* when I was thirty. Shakespeare has this key that unlocks things no matter what. Chekhov does not. Chekhov is vengeful. Let's say some actress plays Ranevskaya well. But you still cannot watch the show. Somebody plays Arkadina wonderfully. But you still cannot watch. Somebody plays Treplev well. But you cannot watch. Everybody has to play well.

I have never liked contemporary plays, either Russian or foreign. I like Lyudmila Petrushevskaya. I like her a lot. But I was also afraid of staging her, as I am of *The Cherry Orchard*. I have been asked why I do not stage Strindberg. But why should I stage Strindberg if I can stage Dostoevsky? If Dostoevsky is a god, Strindberg is a deacon in some provincial theater. He takes a tiny little piece of Dostoevsky and does it very well. But I can get that from Dostoevsky. Dunya and Svidrigailov add up to all of Strindberg. Everything I want to say is already there in Chekhov, Dostoevsky, and Shakespeare.

Playwrights in the West are sensitive about their plays being done exactly as written. What do you think of that?

It is nonsense. "I've got a period here, it must be staged as a period." Nonsense. Because maybe I can do much more through a comma, and perhaps I can give your text new life. I think, what play have I not rewritten? I do not think there is such a play.

What about *The Cherry Orchard*?

I have not staged it yet.

2

A Russian Director from Lithuania with a Jewish Accent

I was born in Lithuania and, like many Jews, went to a Lithuanian school. Jews quickly assimilate into the culture in which they live. In Africa, they — we — are Africans. In America — Americans. In Lithuania — Lithuanians. In Russia — Russians. In fact, Jews often are more Russian than Russians, more Lithuanian than Lithuanians, more African than Africans. That is a feature of the Jewish race; a race of maximalists in all spheres.

Therefore, I am a Lithuanian. I love Lithuanian literature, language, songs, music, nature, customs, history. I am a Lithuanian patriot; always have been and will be. I am even what you might call a "cautious" Catholic. Obviously, I am not a real Catholic. But I know everything about Catholicism. I respect it and observe it, although I always remain on the sidelines, as it were. That is not me. That would be a lie.

On the other hand, I am a Jew. What does that mean? I know all of the problems that being Jewish entails, inside and out, backwards and forwards. I knew anti-Semitism from my earliest childhood. I was a child of the Jewish ghetto who survived by a miracle. Furthermore, in the early 1950s Stalin was prepared to send all Jews to the so-called Autonomous Jewish Republic of Birobidzhan, that is, to a concentration camp. My parents had already packed our things; I remember the suitcases lined up in the corridor. We were ready to go. Stalin died, however, so that never came about. Throughout my youth and my adult life I have been called a Yid. There have been fights on this topic.

I love Jewish songs. I love and am excited by the Jewish intonation of speech. I am inspired by Jewish faces. I love the way Jews talk, it is very humorous and touching at the same time. I am fascinated by Jewish history, the history of my nation. I am always fascinated to learn whether the latest genius is a Jew or not. Because all geniuses should be Jews. That is the Jewish way.

But I am a Russian director. I studied in the Russian school of theater. I am informed by it and by Russian theater traditions. There is the famous phrase that a poet in Russia is more than a poet. Consequently, an artist in Russia is more than an artist, a director is more than a director, and theater is more than theater. That attitude is a natural part of my makeup. I was educated in that culture, that literature, that theater. I am grounded in the values that Russian culture provides. I would not exchange them for anything. I would have no interest, no desire to do so. The values of Russian culture have remained absolutely unchanging for me.

At the same time, as a resident of Lithuania during the era of the Iron Curtain, I had access to and knew more about European culture than most in the Soviet Union. I especially kept up on contemporary developments in theater. We received information by way of Poland, mostly in the way of journals, magazines, and newspapers. As a result, I knew all the latest developments in the West earlier than anyone else in the Soviet Union. I knew Dürrenmatt. I knew Beckett. I knew Kafka before others did here. I knew Saint-John Perse. I knew Picasso. I knew all the things that were banned and therefore essentially did not exist for people here. I read the articles of Jan Kott before I knew Peter Brook. And Peter Brook staged *King Lear* according to the theories of Jan Kott. So you can see the kinds of currents I was plugged into.

I was considered the "Baltic symbolist" as a student. It was a joke at first, but those being Soviet times, it was not much of a joke later. In other words, I was not Soviet, I was Baltic, which meant Western. And, of course, symbolist was automatically bad. But it was true, because, like many in Lithuania, I had a greater chance of learning what was going on in the West. We received journals from Poland. To a large extent I acquired my craft — let's say, the visual aspect, the view of the human, the methods of expression — from what I saw in photos. I was formed not by Western theater, but by my conceptions of Western theater. I did not see the actual productions. They could not come here. But, even with my bad Polish and German and my nonexistent English, I read and learned what I could from photos. What I could not, I completed in my own imagination. That is why when some shows finally did come here I found them worse than I had imagined them. Some, however, were very powerful.

I can safely say my entire generation — not only in the Soviet Union, but throughout the world — is what it is because Peter Brook staged *King Lear*. I saw it twice in Leningrad as a second-year student. That was not just a view of Shakespeare, but of theater itself, of acting, of humankind, of aesthetics. Everything did a somersault. Planchon brought the Théâtre de la Cité. It turned everything around.

I have many teachers. Picasso's influence is deep and strong. I see theater as I do in many ways thanks to him. Fellini. *La Strada*. *The Nights of Cabiria*. To a large extent I became interested in the character of Katerina Ivanovna for my production of *K. I. from "Crime"* because she reminds me of Gelsomina in *La Strada*.

When I arrived in St. Petersburg to study, I considered myself a European because I had a different store of knowledge. Thanks to my Lithuanian surroundings I had the basic grammar of Catholic culture, which was very different from Soviet culture. Soviet culture, although it was atheistic, was nonetheless a culture of the Orthodox Church.

I am a Russian director of Lithuanian background with a strong Jewish accent. An accent is your genetic code, it cannot be obliterated. My gestures, my movements, my intonations, my eyebrows that jump up and down when I speak, the fact that my emotions forge ahead before my thoughts — all of that is my Jewishness, my national background. As is my inner battle between an extreme emotionalism and an extreme rationalism. That is very Jewish.

Still, I consider the visual aspect of my productions to be Lithuanian. Lithuanian landscapes. Catholic churches, meaning both interiors and exteriors. Lithuanian wood sculpture which I always have loved and always will. In many ways Lithuanian wood sculpture was my greatest teacher in the sphere of the visual arts. It is a stunning, unique art form. You could probably call it a primitive art form, and so I can say that my education in the simplicity of the primitive began very early. I have always loved the primitive in art.

What specifically characterizes this kind of sculpture?

In Lithuania, beginning in the nineteenth century, or maybe even before that, a landowner unfailingly would erect a wooden cross next to his home. Naturally, he would make it himself. This cross might be a crucifix or it might depict a little chapel. In Lithuanian it is a *koplicia*. In Russian it is a *kaplitsa*. That is, a small wooden church in the form of a booth, inside of which was depicted a scene of some sort. It might be a depiction of Christ being removed from the cross or it might be a typical crèche scene of Christ's birth. These are carved wooden sculptures that, as a rule, are situated frontally or almost frontally as was done with paintings of the Madonna or in ancient art. They were made of wood because it was easier to work with and because stone was expensive and wood was cheap. Nobody would do it for you. Each man made his own. Moreover, these sculptures were painted. Red clothes. A yellow face. Blue eyes. A silver lance in the hands of a Roman sentinel. The perceptions of these things were quite naive; the people making them were illiterate. But they modeled their own sculptures after traditional pictures or religious images that they knew. Naturally, the themes were often reminiscent of something indigenously Lithuanian.

These sculptures are absolutely stunning.

One of the more common motifs was the *rupintoelis*. *Rupintoelis* in Lithuanian means "the one who is caring." It is a very tender word. There is no word in Russian or English that has such a gentle, tender connotation. It represents the figure of Jesus Christ in a crown of thorns, sitting on a tree stump. Or maybe it is not clear what he is sitting on. As always, only his loins are draped and he sits with his head resting in his open palm. Rather like Rodin's *Thinker*, only Jesus is not just thinking, he is grieving or lamenting. He is thinking about us in the sense that he is caring about us.

This is a very common sculpture. Lithuanians have especially warm feelings for the *rupintoelis,* this figure of Christ who is caring and grieving for each of us. The image in these sculptures is always very touching, very tender, and very sorrowful. Because Jesus has many cares for each and every one of us.

Further, Lithuanian folk graphic art had a great influence on me. I love medieval art. Giotto or the early Germans or Dutch. This all aided me in overcoming our Soviet upbringing whose keystones were the realistic art of the likes of Repin who created genre paintings, character studies, and psychological portraits. Soviet theater was a psychological, genre theater. My love of a different style — I am not talking about theater here, but about the realm of the fine arts — allowed me to realize it was possible to convey profound thoughts and emotions in means other than the genre scene or psychology.

I am talking strictly about my formative period, of course. In the years since, I have worked under the influence of many different visual impressions. I have traveled a lot and I have studied the painting of the early and mid-twentieth century. I love this period very much and am very much under its sway. But the first lasting influence on me was Lithuanian art.

In the primitive Lithuanian sculptures and graphic art, man is depicted as primitive not because he is stupid or imbecilic, but because he is vulnerable. He is represented in a childlike manner. He is vulnerable in his relationship to the surrounding world. Later I found a description of him in Chekhov — he is, in Russian, a *nedotyopa,* that is a clumsy, inept simpleton. He has one feeling, a one-dimensional brain, one prayer, one request.

In other words, all the complexities of psychology may be expressed in the primitive little flower that Katerina shows the spectators in *K. I. from "Crime"* — "See this here?" she asks. "This is a sign that I am an aristocrat. I danced the mazurka. See this? This flower is the mazurka. This is the mazurka." Obviously that flower is not the mazurka. But for her it is the mazurka.

In Lithuania there is a famous hill that once was painted by Mikolajus Ciurlionis. It is called the Hill of Crosses and is located near the provincial town of Siauliai. In the late Soviet period it was destroyed, although it now has been restored. The entire hill is completely covered in crosses. Imagine that — it is only a hill, but, still, it is a fairly good-sized hill. And it is totally covered with crosses stuck into the earth. There is probably little more than a half meter — certainly no more than a meter — separating any two crosses.

According to Lithuanian custom, the Lithuanian Catholic not only erected a cross next to his dwelling to protect his home, but he also erected crosses at points where two roads meet. The reasons were simple. Perhaps a child was born, he erected a cross. A son returned from the war, he erected a cross. He got married, he erected a cross. The war ended, he erected a cross on another crossroads. This was the tradition of the Lithuanian Catholics.

A particular impetus for erecting a cross was the making of a serious vow. In that case, they would trek to the Hill of Crosses and erect a cross there. It was a place to which people came from all over the country when they needed something out of the ordinary. I was there before it was burned down during the Khrushchev era. First of all, it was simply an extraordinary sight. Picture it yourself — it was like a head with hairs sticking out of it, only the hairs were crosses and the head was a hill. I traveled all over Lithuania in my time and at every crossroads I have always made a point to stop and look at the crosses one sees erected there. They are amazing works of art.

I cannot remember who it was now, but one famous Western artist was confused when someone mentioned Lithuania. Then suddenly he remembered, "Oh, that's the only country that was actually doing anything of interest when all of Europe was dead." What he had in mind was the wooden sculpture I am talking about.

These sculptures depicting a scene of some sort also have inscriptions.

"Thank you for bringing my son home from the war."

"Thank you for sending the Germans away."

"Thank you for sending the Russians away."

"Thank you for sending the Red Army away."

"Thank you for sending the White Army away."

One inscription simply stunned me and I still remember it to this day. It read: "Lord, give me sense."

Do you see what I am saying? It is amazing. That is the level of ingenuousness that has intrigued me since my youth.

The *rupintoelis* sits and painfully ponders his endless number of cares. "So many cares! Oh, my, so many cares!"

This is the well I go to when examining Dostoevsky's characters. His people are extremely complex and contradictory — so much so that you cannot quite tell where they begin or where they end. But in them I find something extremely elementary. Something on the level of "Lord, give me sense." Something vulnerable. Something childlike. Something primitive. Because for all the complexity and intricacy of modern man, he is just as vulnerable and childlike as that person who appealed for sense in his relationship to the universe, to the death that awaits him, to an uncertain future.

This is why Katerina Ivanovna has all her little notes and pictures in *K. I. from "Crime."* I do not always know why I am doing things when I do them, although it usually becomes clear sometime later. But whatever the case, I know for certain that the little details in my shows come from my exposure to Lithuanian art. Katerina Ivanovna could just as easily have written "Lord, give me sense!" on one of those little notes she shows the spectators.

Indeed, in your shows there are a great many of these primitive or extremely simple elements. And I have noticed that your actors' eyes always seem to be following one specific main event. It is as if they are telling us with their eyes that, this right here is what is most important. Speech in your productions also tends to be simple and matter-of-fact.

That simplicity derives from my constant desire to reach the source, the place of origin where $1 + 1 = 2$ is a phenomenal discovery. I want to work on that level where you are stunned to take 1, add to it another 1 and come up with 2. Where that kind of discovery is almost impossible to imagine. To say nothing of the discovery of the wheel. That is completely out of the realm of possibility. Personally, I cannot imagine how the wheel was invented. That must have been something extremely complex.

The critics often say I am interested in people in extreme situations, moments of crisis, catastrophes. Why is that true? Because I believe those

Viktor Gvozditsky as the Underground Man in Ginkas's dramatization of Dostoevsky's *Notes from Underground;* Moscow, 1988. The sign hanging around Gvozditsky's neck reads "I do not exist." *Photo by Viktor Bazhenov.*

are the instants when a person reveals his true nature. Much unnecessary baggage that hinders our ability to understand others is discarded in those moments. I am interested in observing a man distinguishing between hot and cold. He suddenly realizes, "Oh, this here is hot! And this here is cold." What a difference! What a great discovery!

This is his skin at work, his physiology, his consciousness — when he realizes he is better off not touching this end and maybe it is not even a good idea to touch the other end either. But here in the middle, this is OK. That is the level I have always been interested in.

Modern man is so complex and confused that yes and no exist simultaneously for him. He is faced with an enormous number of choices. And so I, in working with Dostoevsky and trying to bring out all his complexity, am interested in discovering that place where everything is extremely simple. Where everything is as it was in childhood. Very primitive. As in the prayer of that Lithuanian woman: "Lord, give me sense."

The first time I ever formulated it for myself was when I found the script to Fellini's *La Strada*. I am talking about the published script and the stills, now, because the film itself was not available to me. I only had access to the photos and the printed script. Together, they simply stunned me. In fact, I would say the film is a bit weaker than the script on its own. The script is more psychological and simpler.

The heroes of this story are two primitives. Only each carries an opposite sign, so to speak.

One is an animal-like primitive, Zampano. This is a person who has one determining characteristic, one function in life. He has chains — he flexes his muscles — and he breaks the chains. That is it. That is his whole function in life. He travels to a new place, the public gathers, he flexes and breaks the chains. Then he goes to another place, flexes and breaks the chains. That is it. That is his everything. That is his level.

The one of the other sign is Gelsomina. She is specifically conceived as being slightly touched in the head because she is a child. She is not a child, of course, but psychologically she is childlike. She responds to everything literally. She sees everything as if for the first time. Whether it is a flower or music or a person or a road or a cloud — she perceives them each time for the first time. She sees this man who breaks chains. It is the first time she has seen him and she is amazed by her discovery.

She is told that she is to be married. She does not know what it means to be married. She was given in marriage. Basically she was sold to Zampano. What she does understand is that now she is the lady of the house. She fixes him food. She puts him down to sleep. She washes and irons. She immediately begins performing her functions. And he exploits that.

There is a great scene later on. He meets a prostitute in a tavern and brings her home. Gelsomina thinks her husband has brought home a guest. So Gelsomina receives her according to the custom and feeds her. But then they drive Gelsomina away and go off into his wagon where one assumes they go to bed together. Gelsomina remains alone, understanding nothing. Why is this guest in bed with her husband?

This is an absolutely fantastic, primitive, childlike level!

Later there is the incredible, culminating moment after all their travels around the countryside. She falls sick and disappears and he goes on with his life alone. All the while he continues to break his chains. But the day comes when he goes to break his chains and they do not break. He has grown old. He cannot break his chains. Here, he understands that *something has happened*. Nothing had ever happened in his life. Nothing at all. He broke his chains and that is all. What else can happen in life? But finally, something has happened. He cannot break his chains.

He is not able to understand what has happened. But then he hears the melody of a song Gelsomina used to sing. He runs to see who is singing it — he thinks it must be Gelsomina! He comes upon a load of linens hung out on a line. He pushes back sheet after sheet, probably expecting to see Gelsomina. But no, some other woman is standing there.

"Who taught you that song?" he asks.

"Oh, just some silly fool," she says. "But she is dead now."

And, now, this animal who never did anything in his life but break chains and satisfy his most basic physiological needs, slowly walks to the sea and sits down at the water's edge. We do not know exactly what happens — perhaps some water splashes up on his face from the surf or perhaps he has shed a tear. We only hear the sound of bicyclists passing by and ringing their bells. The bells ring, "Make way! Make way! Attention! Attention!"

In fact, we are witnessing the birth of a human being. Something human has arisen in this animal, this prehuman entity. End of film. Stunning. Unbelievable.

I must say that everything I am comes out of that film. I do everything differently, of course. I have done many shows that have nothing in common whatsoever with that film. And nonetheless, that is I.

When I read that script for the first time, I understood it as something near to my heart. I understood what I wanted to do. Ever since, no matter what I have done, I have sought to find those manifestations of the simple, vulnerable, first human — you could even say of primordial man. At what point does a human become a human? Where does the human element begin to manifest itself?

Despite all the complexity and confusion of modern man, there still remains the kernel from which he originates and which is his essence. Everything else is extremely complicated, but it is borrowed, it is not essential.

Look what far shore the journey of our conversation has brought us to!

I want to ask you about an image I have of you as a two-year old. It is based on stories you tell about the time when you were being sheltered from the Nazis. German officers often came to the house in which you were staying and you, a Jewish toddler, were often the one who opened the door for them. Every time you spoke, you were in danger of giving yourself away. Someone was standing over you trying to drill into your head that you *must not* continue to speak one way and that you *must* begin to speak another way. It was a matter of life and death. In that image, I see any number of the characters in your shows who also speak to me simply and forcefully of simple topics. It is perhaps as if I am somewhat stupid, or perhaps I am a child, and I am not quite able to understand without being prompted that this is a *matter of life and death.*

I would be willing to agree with you were it not for one thing. First of all, I naturally do not remember how I was spoken to. I have only been told the stories, and now I have evolved my own perception of it. But, more important, it was not a matter of someone drilling an idea into my head. I do not like that kind of obstinacy and that is bad if it exists in any of my shows.

The way I imagine it is this. Sofia Binkiene, the woman who was hiding me from the Nazis at the time, was an intelligent and beautiful woman. It so happened that she was also a woman of great heroism. She was speaking to a child who was merely two and a half years old. Here is what happened.

I would run to the door and say in Yiddish, "*Vos?*", which in German would be "*Was?*" That is, "What?" And she would say encouragingly, "You know what, Kama? *Vos* sounds just like *voz*" — which is the Russian word for *vezimas*, the Lithuanian word for wagon. "So why don't you just say *vezimas?*"

There is no coercion or pressure in that. It is just a gentle suggestion — "You see? This is death. Why not steer clear of it?"

If what you are suggesting really is a part of my productions, I would want it to be the way I expect it really was in fact. No drilling of anything into anyone's head. I would hope there is nothing intimidating in any of my shows. I would want the manner to be playful and gentle.

Sergei Makovetsky as Kovrin and Igor Yasulovich as the mysterious Black Monk in the dramatization of Chekhov's *The Black Monk;* Moscow, 1999. *Photo by Yelena Lapina.*

Let us apply this to my production of Chekhov's *The Black Monk*, for instance. In this show, the intonation characterizing the speech of Tanya might be that of a cheerful mother: "Oops, careful there, Kovrin. You don't want to fall, now. That is the edge of an abyss there, you know. It is quite a drop. Who knows what's out there? Maybe you'd better come away from the edge and play with the fluffy feathers over here. Dabble about in love and conversation. Why not come away from there? You'll be safer. And what's the difference in distance? A meter. No more. That is all. *Vos. Voz.* It is almost the same thing. You don't want to go over to the edge. Just stay over here, OK? OK?" I am certain that is how Sofia Binkiene spoke with me. And I would want it to resonate that way in my productions.

Basically, when I create my shows, I perceive them as gentle, tender, and ironic. I do not know how spectators perceive them, but that is how I perceive them. You see, in the example I have just given you from *The Black Monk*, the notion of playfulness is very prominent. It is the deception of a child. "What's the difference? *Vos? Voz. S. Z.* Just that one little change, that is all. And then everything will be fine."

As the author of the production, I recognize and know the abyss facing Kovrin. I am convinced that it presents a mortal danger. But that is another thing.

If I am Katerina Ivanovna in *K. I. from "Crime,"* I know what is on the other side of that door: my dead husband. But at the same time I think, "He isn't dead — he's just wandering around drunk somewhere. What's wrong with him? Where is he?" And still, I *know*. I can feel it in my gut. Death is out there. And then it is back to unbelieving again as she begins to berate the spectators: "Look here! See this little note here? Look at this. That scum, he stole my last penny. What a bum." As if he was still alive.

That playfulness, that bantering that covers up what is beneath, is closer to what I hear, to what I would want to be coming through in my shows and to what I want the spectator to be perceiving.

I am a bad actor, of course. Perhaps I misled you with a shabby performance.

But you do understand my distinction, don't you? That is crucial for me. Because if I am coming across the way you suggested, that is much too crude.

It is a whole different matter that it may be very painful for the spectator to take this in. When I tell you the story about *vos* and *voz*, you think, "My God, how awful! How terrible! Amazing what nonsense life and death hang on! The letter *S* or the letter *Z*."

You are horrified, although on the surface it is a humorous tale. Inside, however, you are appalled. Of course, if there was nothing appalling about it, the tale would be a mere whimsy. No big deal. But when you are confronted by what a minuscule hook life hangs on — *S* or *Z* — then you have the theater I make. That is right. That is what I try to do.

3

The Director as Alpha and Omega

You once quoted your teacher Georgy Tovstonogov as saying that a director is a demiurge. What does that mean for you if you, indeed, accept his definition?

I should clarify something. Tovstonogov did not actually say that. He hated big foreign words. His speech was always more simple, clear, convincing, and infectious. More important is that Tovstonogov — by example, by his way of life, his manner of creating theater, his manner of communicating with actors, designers, students, theater administrators, spectators, critics, Soviet theatrical bosses, and so forth — never left any doubt but that a director is the beginning and the end in theater.

The director is the alpha and omega. Nothing can arise in the theater without the touch of the director, and nothing can disappear in the theater without the director willing it. If the director thinks something must be, then it will be. By the same token, anything that must be done away with will only be done away with when the director says, "Get rid of it."

That was Tovstonogov's position. It is not something he enunciated. Basically, he did not teach us with words. He taught by example. His life seldom crossed paths with ours. He lived in a "divine, imperial space" both in his professional and private lives. He rode in a fine car — we rode on trams. We stood in lines to buy our food — he did not have the vaguest notion where his food came from. He lived in a state dacha. When Tovstonogov was still approaching the theater in his automobile, one could already feel the tension mounting from the expectation of his arrival. I saw that. I experienced it myself. The theater would go through entire stages of sensations as he drew closer, street by street, the tension reaching its culmination as he actually entered the building.

Tovstonogov did not teach us anything. It was up to us to learn from him, each according to his own abilities. He was a god. Or Joseph Stalin. Which was one and the same thing. There was no God by that time, and Joseph Stalin had only died relatively recently. We could still feel that. Tovstonogov, of course, had lived and worked in the Stalin era. He was a product of that era. He naturally hated Stalin and the Soviet Union; his father had been shot under Stalin. But Tovstonogov was a product of that environment. That became a part of us, at least those of us who were his real students, such as my wife Henrietta and me. It is akin to our genetic code.

As such, it is unthinkable for me to imagine that something might happen in one of my shows without my willing or, at least, allowing it. Willing something might mean forcing it to happen. But it might also mean that something occurs unexpectedly, and you allow it become a part of what you are doing.

That is the Tovstonogov school. That is his tradition. More precisely, that is the genetic code he implanted in us.

What I always say is this: If the actor performs badly it is the director's fault. He should have replaced him or camouflaged him in some way. If an actor performs well, the director can take credit for it even if he never once showed up at rehearsals because he was always out drinking and carousing. He can take credit because he didn't get in the way of a good actor at work.

We have entered a new millennium. And the kind of theater you are talking about — essentially, the Stanislavskian model of a big theatrical plant — is now quite outmoded. It cannot continue to exist without undergoing enormous changes. It already has experienced enormous

Kama Ginkas rehearses his dramatization of *The Lady with the Lapdog* with Yulia Svezhakova and Igor Gordin; Moscow, 2001. *Photo by Yelena Lapina.*

changes in recent decades. You, Tovstonogov's student, exist in a vastly different theatrical space than he did. What does that mean?

Perhaps that is one of the reasons why I do not have my own theater. I profess a different kind of theater. In the last ten, fifteen, twenty years, a theater of the kind that Tovstonogov ran has not been able to survive. In the last decade, the post-Soviet period, the big kind of theater, the theater as an organization, has simply become an anachronism.

Nevertheless, I always have been and to this day I remain the alpha and omega of my productions. It does not matter whether I am working in Moscow or abroad. Nothing, not a particle of dust, can fall in one of my shows without my knowing about it.

That may be a big plus, but it also can be a big minus because, still and all, one needs freedom in the creative act. Those who are taking part in this act must be aware of their own creativity and individuality and must not feel they are merely some element that has been plugged into a general scheme.

Let me tell a short story about the bad side of my controlling nature. When I was doing my first production, Viktor Rozov's *The Reunion*, in Riga, I went to the workshop where the set was being built. I wanted to see how things were coming. The old carpenters and artists there were stunned. No director had ever bothered to come work out their problems with them. Despite our age differences, we became quite friendly. By the time I made my tenth visit, however, I sensed their irritation. And soon they were seriously bucking me. I realized only later that they had begun to think I was coming to check up on them! Then they really started to hate me.

That is the down side of being in total control. It is almost as significant as the positive side.

You once were asked about working in a theatrical capital and your jesting response was something to the effect that "the theatrical capital is wherever I am." In another time and place I heard you say that you do not really sense your colleagues around you. I see in this a strong sign of isolation, which I suspect is connected to your position as the be-all and end-all of what you do.

I should say that my comment about "theatrical capitals" was made in reference to my frequently working in Helsinki, Finland. Many people might call that "the sticks" in a theatrical sense. That is when I joked that theatrical capitals are wherever I am and then I tried to explain what I meant.

The point is that theatrical capitals and backwaters are difficult to determine. Lithuania never used to be considered a theatrical capital. It had no status, just as Finland had no status. But, after Eimuntas Nekrosius appeared, you had the appearance of Rimas Tuminas and Oskaras Korsiunovas. Now, Lithuania is becoming one of the theatrical capitals of the world.

Wherever a new, fresh, talented theatrical idea arises, you immediately see others arising in response. How did Moscow become a theatrical capital? Stanislavsky appeared. Nemirovich-Danchenko appeared. And instantly Meyerhold appeared alongside them. Alongside him there was Vakhtangov. In fact, a whole crowd of people appeared. A truly talented person, a true theatrical phenomenon, gives rise to others. There is a word in zoology that fits the occasion — *viviparous;* that is, bringing forth living young. Maybe I am not using the word entirely properly, but my point is that talent encourages talent. It readies the soil around it where more can grow. That is what I meant by theatrical capitals being where I am.

As for whether I sense myself as part of a greater community, I do not remember the circumstances under which I might have said that. I would say I do not feel that way now.

The question you were asked was "Who do you think about? About teachers or colleagues?" and you replied "I do not think about anyone."

Well, that is true. I do not think about anyone. I only listen to myself. In the nineteenth or eighteenth century I might have said, "I listen to a voice from above." But I do not listen to a voice from above. I hear a voice inside of me.

As for my teachers — well, I am who I am because my teacher was Tovstonogov. That is a huge problem for me. It is the same thing as paternal genes. I want to be different. The times have changed. Even as Tovstonogov was teaching us — or, more precisely, when we were studying with Tovstonogov — there also existed the director Anatoly Efros whom I personally found more interesting. There was Peter Brook. There were the absurdists. There were millions of possible directions in which theater could develop. There was the theater of cruelty. There were street theaters. Happenings. I literally studied Meyerhold. He was very far from Tovstonogov and the Stanislavskian technique.

Still, I could not overcome the education Tovstonogov gave me. I struggled terribly. I only recently have stopped struggling, perhaps thanks to my age. This struggle was as pointless as trying to overcome my own anatomical structure. No matter what, my skeleton is what my father gave me. I cannot be taller. I cannot be more elegant, fatter, or whatever. My gestures are still what they are. I want to make a certain gesture, but the genetic code given to me by my father dictates otherwise.

I have strayed far from Tovstonogov. I have gone off into myself, into what I myself know, what has arisen inside me on its own, what I have seen and have absorbed. Still, no one knows better than I that my backbone — built by Tovstonogov — will not bend. We deceive ourselves when we think we can deviate from what we are.

So are your shows like Tovstonogov's or are they different?

I think they are very unlike anything he would have done. And yet I know they are extremely similar.

How are they similar? Because I would agree they are very different. Different in appearance, of course. But you are talking about internal similarities.

Tovstonogov *built* his productions. He built them with blocks of action. In professional slang the word is action. My wife Henrietta and I do the same thing. That is the backbone on which everything hangs. Once that is in place, you can deviate all you want but everything will hang on that backbone.

I think Anatoly Efros built his shows differently. Note that I say *built* again. He himself talked about "structuring things on a bent wire." I cannot explain what he meant by that. I would say bricks. You put one here, you put another there, you move one over here and you turn one over there. That is how I understand it. I sense it physically.

It only seems that a director's job is something ephemeral. In any case I sense very clearly that I am holding something very resilient in my hands. And that I stack things up, bend them, turn them around, and so on. That is action. That is the muscular system. Or the skeletal system, if you will.

No matter what the essence was of a Tovstonogov show — they were often very airy and atmospheric — I would say they were always a little fleshy. Regardless of what ailment or disorder they were illuminating, there was always something extremely healthy about them. That was specifically because of their construction. They had an extremely healthy constitution. Tovstonogov never messed around with hocus-pocus. If he exhibited any element of impressionism, it was always just a paint stroke on the surface. Down inside the structure was rigid.

My shows and [Henrietta] Yanovskaya's shows are extremely different from Tovstonogov's. They have always been shows with a subjective point of view. Tovstonogov considered it unnecessary, even wrong, for his own voice to be heard in a show. Of course, you always sensed his attitude toward a character or event, whether positive or negative, sympathetic or ironic. But Tovstonogov was never telling about himself. He was telling about certain objective phenomena while retaining his own personal attitude. In other words, he presented an objective story, an incident, a phenomenon, even a certain truth. He believed that the objective exists.

Neither Henrietta nor I believe that. That is not what we live by. I am more likely to be in dialogue with some phenomenon or event. That is: I and another person; I and a problem; where "I" am what is most important. In other words, my shows suggest: "that is how I think" — "that is my impression" — "that hurts me" — "I detest that" — "I find that silly."

Meanwhile, speaking strictly in terms of craft, it still is Tovstonogov's craft, not mine. Perhaps another teacher would have helped us better to express what we wanted. To a certain extent, his school — his method of construction — gets in the way when I have specific problems to solve. I want to knock down that structure; I want more subjectivity, more impressionism, more vagueness, less order, less logic. I would say I want less of the rational.

But there is no way to break free of it. Some spectators or even critics may think that Henrietta and I have done that. They might say, "Look how subjective their work is. How amorphous. How elusive. You cannot pin them down." Thank goodness, if that is true. That would mean we have achieved a certain artistic level.

But Henrietta and I know the truth. We build things the way Tovstonogov taught us to, even if it is not always the best method for the job. Perhaps we really wanted to say something else, but the Tovstonogov influence would not let us. Over the years we have evolved a series of methods that help us overcome that.

Critics have often called what I do naturalism. But it is a specific kind of theatrical naturalism. It is founded on the notion of play, of performance. Everything in it is entirely natural, and yet, at the same time, the naturalism is emphasized.

Can you give a concrete example?

My production of Sergei Kokovkin's *Five Corners* in 1981 was performed in a small space set up like a common room. At a key moment, a big mirror hanging on a very realistic wall fell and broke. It happened in a way that made it a real event in the life of the spectators.

In Russian folklore, a broken mirror bodes misfortune. That is not an intellectual concept; it is something of a physiological reaction. Even if you do not believe it, you will still react to it.

And there, in *Five Corners,* a real mirror fell off a real wall and shattered. For the first three or four seconds people shuddered in the hall. For those 170 spectators it was not an event of play or performance, it was a genuine event in their life. Their reaction was not that an actor's mirror broke, but rather "I have witnessed a mirror breaking." It was a personal thing. Five seconds later, they came to as they realized, "Oh, that's just plot development." There was often laughter at that point although there was nothing funny about the scene. That was a sign of their relief. But I had got them for that moment — with an event they accepted as completely real.

Do you understand what I mean? It was not something merely "realistic," it was real. It was something happening here and now.

When an actor chops up cabbage, as I had actors do in *We Play "Crime,"* it is real. You see the ax penetrating the head of cabbage and you shudder. You know it is not a person's head, but that combination of deception and nondeception has a very powerful effect.

That is what I mean by naturalism, by the real, by the literal. It is something that happens not with the characters, but with the spectators. Therefore, for them, for at least an instant or two, it truly does happen.

That is what you usually call physiology.

Our physiology reacts before our intellect or psychology. You stick your hand in fire by accident and before you know how to react, your hairs are singed and your skin is black. That is physiology. It responds earlier than anything else — earlier than intellect, psychology, or ideology.

Maybe I stick my hand in that fire because I want to prove something. I want to commit a heroic act. Well, my act may be heroic, but my skin still turns black. It has its own response. There is nothing ideological about that.

Another key notion in your vocabulary is resistance or defiance. Your mother said that you survived in spite of Hitler. You once said that you live "in defiance." In fact, even when someone says something effective or meaningful to you, your first response is often no . . .

That's true.

I say that because I suspect you were extremely fortunate to study under a director who was significantly different from you. That made you go against the grain.

That may be true, but . . .

You see, there's your *but* . . .

No, no, you are absolutely right. I am just thinking ahead already.

The fact is, no matter who I might have studied with, I would have discovered my "defiance." That apparently is my character. If I had studied with Anatoly Efros or with Peter Brook, I would have looked for something contrary, for something different.

The first person to notice that in me was a great teacher in school who fostered in us, and in me in particular, a deep love for Russian literature. She organized literary evenings and I staged them employing emcees and short skits. I gave them a certain complex form. I had participated in amateur theatricals since kindergarten. But toward the end of school, I began staging things as a director. They were not shows, but more like literary evenings. After I had done one or two of these evenings, my teacher said, "All I have to do is suggest something. Then Kama says no! and comes up with an idea of his own." She cultivated that quality of mine. As a genuinely gifted teacher, she saw that in my character.

As I understand you, one of your key notions is that an individual must differ from others. Every person, every nation, must have some specific, completely unique, identifying feature, must be different in some way. In fact, this person or this nation will go to any lengths to be different from everyone around. I suspect that is one of the key impulses of a creative personality.

Let me clarify. I do not think it is quite like that. Basically, that is not my idea. That is what I gleaned from my favorite writers on whose works I was brought up. In this case, I mean Dostoevsky.

Dostoevsky was not talking about a creative personality. Or, if he was, it was only in a general sense. Dostoevsky's Raskolnikov divides humanity into "quivering creatures" and "he who has the right." Let us set aside the criminal and the ironic elements — for Dostoevsky was very ironic about the individual who claimed rights for himself — and settle on the most basic, physiological level.

According to Raskolnikov — and I suspect this is generally true — any being who is not a quivering creature, say, a blade of grass, or some other low form of life, is invariably concerned about identifying himself in some way. That does not necessarily mean he will go to war or kill someone or build the tallest building in the world or swim the English Channel. He may be quite small, very simple, basically a nobody. But every person — if he is a person (that is what Dostoevsky writes in *Notes from Underground*, "if he is a person") — is concerned with identifying himself.

I am the one who . . . the one who swam the English Channel.

I am the one who in boxing class is second. Not first, but second!

I am the one who drinks vodka. I drink vodka.

I am the one who loves women. Maybe not more than others, but I'm the one who . . .

I am the one who is a Jew.

I am the one who is from Thus-and-Such Street.

I was always curious in childhood why kids from one street fought with the kids from another street. Our street versus their street. What could we possibly have been competing for? Nothing. It is just that I am from this street and you are from that one. Nothing more.

I root for team A; you root for team B. Do you really think B is better? Of course not. It is just that you are the one who roots for B. I am the one who . . .

That is the most naive, most touching, most human way of achieving immortality. Since there is no immortality, that is all that is left you.

Some achieve immortality by building pyramids, by writing *War and Peace,* by discovering penicillin, by swimming the English Channel, becoming the best high jumper. But, I cannot do that. I am the one who lives in the third house on such-and-such a street. I am that one. Or on the second floor. Or on the first floor. Or I live in the house on the corner.

I must be identified in some way. No matter what it is. I was. I am. Otherwise I do not exist. On one hand it is a very naive, even touching thing — not Dostoevsky at all. There is nothing criminal about it. Although the criminal may arise in it. Maybe it is something terrible. Maybe it gives rise to Ivan the Terrible or Tamerlane or Genghis Khan or Hitler. That depends upon the degree of ambition. But the nature of it is the same. And it is a part of nature.

I was recently asked what key notions of the twentieth century have been discredited in the eyes of history. One that actually began to be discredited in the nineteenth or even eighteenth century is equality. Of course equality in a civil sense is a tenet of democracy. But the notion that all people are equal is nonsense. Not all people are equal. Moreover, people do not *want* to be equal. Categorically. That is when you pick up the refrain of "I am the one who . . ."

This is why I say you must understand the notion of a creative personality in a broad sense. Because every person — again, if he is a person — is a creative being. I make shoes. I am a shoemaker and that is our shoemaker's guild. This is not just a social status. And it is not just a labor union. No. We are shoemakers. We are students. We are aristocrats. We are warriors. There is an element of creativity in that.

What is creativity? That is when, besides me, there is something else that expresses who I am. Something through which I can express myself. That is what a creative being is. I express myself by sewing clothes. That does not mean I am Versace. That is not the point at all. I am just a tailor. A bad tailor. But I am a tailor.

In almost all of your productions that I know, this exists both as a theme within the show and also as a method that is employed by you as one who is trying to express himself somehow differently from, let us say, Tovstonogov.

That is right.

This is a key notion for you as an artist.

Yes. I think so. I am becoming increasingly irritated by people saying that Kama Ginkas stages shows about death. That is not true. It is a truncated truth. It leads nowhere. It is vulgar. The topic that you and I are circling about right now is a greater truth and is much more characteristic of me. Of course, it leads to death, too.

In fact, what you are talking about is life.

And that is my point. Of course. The attempt to give oneself an identity, to leave some mark. The struggle for immortality in one form or another.

Naturally, if there is no death, then there is no problem. But since that problem does exist, well, maybe it is what makes a person a person. That is what forces us to acquire an identity and fill our allotted time with something of content. That content may be something extremely silly.

In my lifetime I drank a certain number of bottles of booze.

I had a given number of women.

I staged a certain number of theatrical productions. I am not talking about good shows; I am talking strictly about quantity.

I have more buttons than anyone. I collect buttons. So what? Who cares about buttons? But my house is filled with buttons. It is as pointless a way to fill up the time of life as counting bottles downed, women had, great productions staged, or great paintings created.

Take Cheops's great pyramid at Giza. That is the sign he left behind indicating that he existed. But if you collect buttons, that is what you do. It is the same thing. It is pointless. It is that attempt to fill space and time.

If there is no final end to what we do, then there is no need to do it and we do not exist.

This also pertains to Adam and Eve and their crime, the original sin. There is a taboo. A person to become a person must transgress it. And I will say it again, it does not have to be murder. In any case, Adam and Eve did not do anything at all. They merely copulated and set the human race into motion. But that was a taboo they violated.

A few years ago, someone told me that my main theme was freedom. I was amazed. I did not think I had ever staged anything about that. But then it occurred to me maybe it was true. Because what I am talking about is the problem of choice. Transgression is an expression of freedom. That individual who was issued the original taboo was faced with the question of freedom or nonfreedom. Man is not free and the measure of his nonfreedom has many different stages.

You think you are free but you are not. You are not if only for no other reason than there is an end — death — which has been measured out to you. You did not choose that end. It has already been determined that there will be an end to your existence. Maybe *determined* is not the best word — the end to your existence simply is. It exists. You cannot say, "OK, I'll die, or, OK, I won't die." That end, your death, is there anyway.

That is why it seems to me that human existence is bound up in the effort to achieve at least a certain amount of freedom. Within the limits of some space. That space might be your local village, or it might be your home. It might only be the expanse in which you can gesture, for example. To what extent can I wave my arms around?

My wife won't let me blow my nose in my coat sleeve. Why not!? I have the right! Damn it, I earned the money to buy this jacket! Well, OK, I didn't earn it — you did. So all right, I can't blow my nose in my jacket sleeve. But I can slam the door!

You see? This question exists on a level where you can create an entire philosophy. It is a crucial question, because how you identify yourself is how you demonstrate your freedom. Every person has limits to what extent he can identify himself. Maybe the most he can do is to leave behind the sign: I am the one who lies in a specific plot in a specific cemetery. That, of course, is taking into account the fact that somebody else buried him there.

The question arises about the characters in works of art. The most interesting are the strange, clumsy people you have been talking about — the guy who wants to blow his nose in his sleeve — because they are the closest of all to the elemental level of this struggle for freedom. In our lives we do not have the slightest interest in having anything to do with them. We do not want to have dinner with this guy who blows his nose in his sleeve. So there is a paradox: The most interesting, most affecting, most powerful characters in theater or in art are the very people we run away from in life. We see him standing on the street corner and we run in the other direction. Moreover, we run straight for the theater where on the stage we can watch him, or at least someone similar, and sympathize with him and weep over his sorry fate.

That's right. That character is able to be something that we cannot or will not allow ourselves to be. And we can take that one step further. In other words, let's not take the guy blowing his nose in his sleeve, but let's take, say, Macbeth. A criminal. A bloody thug.

Now, of course Macbeth is not me or the average spectator. Still, there is something awfully seductive in what he allows himself to do. In the theater, I can allow myself to observe him with a certain agitation. Later on he gets punished — justly so, thank goodness. Of course, once he is punished, he is not interesting anymore. But before he is punished, the agitation I experience grows as I watch him. I identify with him. I measure myself against him. I ask; could that be me? What if *I* were there?

The theater is a safe place. I can let myself go through that. In life, I am afraid. I cannot. I do not want to. Meet with this guy in a dark corner somewhere? Run into Macbeth in the woods? God forbid! That is obvious. But I'll come to the theater to watch him.

All those characters who intrigue us are fighting the battle of good and evil inside. That interests us because we can experience it with them. As soon as it is gone, there is nothing left to watch.

In your production of *K. I. from "Crime,"* Katerina Ivanovna is just the type of person we run away from in the street. But when people come to see her in your production, they pull money out of their pockets and give it to her children. True, Russians are softhearted people and they regularly give money to beggars on the street, too. But the difference is that in life we give money quickly and hurry on, so as not to be drawn into something we are afraid of. In the case of *K. I. from "Crime,"* spectators — who, not incidentally, have paid for a ticket to attend — give alms and then sit there waiting, wincing, and weeping to see what will happen next and how it all will end.

I suspect that theater exists to fill in those enormous gaps in experience that we cannot make a part of our lives. At the very least, we cannot die and be resurrected. But you can in the theater. Basically, that is every person's dream. It begins in childhood when you tell someone, "I'll die and come watch you cry over my dead body." Some of us even continue saying that in our old age.

In the theater you can watch Katerina Ivanovna go through everything she does and then you *die* in the end and *cry* — you are crying for yourself! You are crying for yourself with all the other spectators and you derive pleasure from that because you have just experienced that situation where everybody is crying for you.

On top of that, an actress comes out in the end for applause and bows! It is a kind of magic. A magic that the human cannot do without. It is one of the reasons why theater will never die. Why no other kind of art, no matter how refined, will ever replace it. Because of that extremely simple quality — "I will die and watch you cry." Nothing else can give us that; only theater can give us that.

That is why theater absolutely must be ingenuous, simple-hearted.

There is a word — *action* — that lies at the basis of . . .

My schooling . . .

Your schooling and everything you do. Everyone knows what *action* means, but I suspect most of us do not know what action means in the professional sense that you use it. Can you tell me what action means?

A dying Katerina Ivanovna (Oksana Mysina) looks at her oldest daughter Polya (Vera Romanova) in *K.I. from "Crime,"* a dramatization of segments of Dostoevsky's *Crime and Punishment;* Moscow, 1994. *Photo by Ken Reynolds.*

Stanislavsky explained it very clearly. I will try to explain it as I understand it, and as I apply it in a practical sense. The spectator who comes to the theater wants to observe something. Something must *occur* on stage. If nothing occurs on stage, there is nothing for the spectator to observe.

Let me take an example from life. A fly crawls on the window. I watch it. I find it interesting. If the fly is dead, there is nothing to watch. Maybe it is not even crawling. Maybe it is stationary, but it is cleaning its wings. I can be fascinated by the way it does that. Then it crawls on and tests this place and that. Then a car drove by and the window shook, so the fly took flight and alighted in another place. I start poking at it with a feather to frighten it and it flies off again.

You can watch that endlessly. It is interesting. Something is happening with the fly and something is happening *between* you and the fly. Or between the fly and other things — the fly and the window; the fly and the food. Or, let's say, the fly and its own wing.

Interaction. Interrelations. Actions cannot exist in isolation. They must be in interaction, an action directed at someone or something. And a response from that someone or something.

Like Katerina Ivanovna, I beat against the ceiling. The ceiling responds, doesn't it? In the sense that it does not give way. You see what I mean? Or maybe there is interaction between a person and his arm.

"Wait a second. My arm doesn't feel right today. What is going on here?" — I move it. I stretch it. I poke it. I massage it. I look at it. I frown at it. — "It's not doing what it should today. Am I sick? Is this rheumatism? Wait a minute. Wait a minute."

That is interaction with my own arm. As soon as interaction arises — action and response — we are intrigued. There is something to watch. That is the basis of theater.

Yes, but the author has already determined the action for you. Uncle Vanya grabs a pistol and shoots at the Professor.

Of course. If the author has no action, there is nothing for me to stage. But, the point is I have to make choices.

OK, the pistol is fired. That is what is written there. But what is important is what comes next — Why is it fired? How is it fired? In other words, what is the nature of the interaction or its impact? What is the reason for the action? Everything depends on that. When you see complex or unexpected actions, or actions that in some way remind you of yourself, that is interesting. When you have studied the author, you determine the motives for a given action, the logic behind it and the means to portray it. That is when you have a director at work.

Basically, action consists of several elements. I will probably distort Stanislavsky here, but this is how I would formulate it. First, what do I want of my partner? That is the goal or the task.

I am a fly. What do I want from that window? What do I want from my arm when it hurts? I want it to function normally. But for some reason it just will not today.

Then there are obstacles to my achieving my goal or engaging in my task. This is pure Stanislavsky. For some reason there are physical obstacles and my arm will not function. I am not talking about social or human problems yet. I am purposefully not taking on anything complex. Just the most elementary aspects.

Now, since there are obstacles, I take action in response to them. And this leads me to the next question: *How* do I take action? If we are still talking about my arm, I might shake it, massage it, take a pill. I might warm it or put it in a sling. These are various ways in which I attempt to take action in response to my specific obstacle.

Maybe you do not see an obstacle in this. Let us say your arm is bothering you, but you pay it no attention. But, you see, I cannot do that. I cannot even talk to you right now. I am trying to but — wait a second, there is something wrong here. This is really bothering me.

Perhaps, for me, an obstacle is that you keep nodding your head in affirmation. I know you understand nothing I am saying, but you keep on nodding your head. My character is such that I cannot function when my arm hurts, but you are the kind of person who nods his head and gets all excited when he thinks he understands everything.

These are two different people. Two different logics. Because the tasks are different. The obstacles are different. Where I see obstacles and what I do to overcome them is what determines my character.

How would Charlie Chaplin handle the obstacle of a sore arm? Imagine the enormous amount of fantastic gags he would come up with for his arm! That is an entire genre. It is a specific logic. Whole new meanings arise because there exists a specific task, a specific obstacle and a specific manner of overcoming that obstacle — that is, a specific action.

There is such variety in this that every director who stages the shooting scene in *Uncle Vanya* stages it differently.

This brings to mind a word I have never once heard you use: *improvisation*. I must admit that surprises me because I would say there is a lot of improvisation in your shows. Do you have any special attitude toward that concept?

I suspect I do not like that word. Maybe because in the last ten or twelve years that I have worked abroad, I have attended numerous workshops with people who are involved in improvisation.

It is nothing but fraud. I do not understand what it means. Improvisation. What improvisation? I have seen people of very high quality get all wrapped up in it. Maybe that is one of the reasons I do not like it. Maybe I just use some other word that I cannot seem to recall right now.

I am very fastidious in my work. From the very first day of preparations for a show I have my hands all over everything. I know the feel of every nail, including the first one that goes into the making of my set. Everything goes through my hands, everything is dirtied with the oil of my fingers, everything smells of me. That is how I work with my actors, too. Ask anyone who has ever worked with me.

I do that to achieve *freedom*. Freedom. I use my control to point out to the actor the various possibilities. I provoke them. I say, "Here is one possibility. Here is another possibility. Here is still another possibility." They are all possibilities of the same thing, but they are all expressed in some different way.

If some specific event takes place with an actor's partner — or with a spectator, in the case of *K. I. from "Crime,"* where the spectators are the actress's partners — then the actor has a choice of responses. These are things I have dictated, yes, but they are things that have been discovered — perhaps by chance — during rehearsal.

I try to build my productions on the basis of a strict inner structure. A very rigid inner path that the actor must go down. Almost all of the work in rehearsals is expended on discovering the best path for this specific role for this specific show in this specific genre for this specific actor or actors. My job is to keep the actor from becoming sidetracked. I do not want the actor loitering off to the side somewhere; I want him moving right down the proper path. Once the actor gets going, of course, the path itself will lead. And then at that point, my job is to stay out of the way. You see, the actor's nature takes over because everything I do takes into account the actor's nature.

At the same time, I also lay out or discover additional paths. When I rehearse, I am constantly involved in seeking out variants. The better the actor, the better I can work with him. More variants means more freedom. Perhaps a Western director might say "more opportunities to improvise." But the instant I just pronounced that word I sensed how much I do not like it.

What I want is for the actor to be free within the structure I provide him. That is what I consider the greatest pleasure. Improvisation implies to me that I can do whatever I want. I hate that. I do not understand that. What is the point of a director in such circumstances? A good actor can go out on his own and do a fine job of improvising.

I believe the greatest pleasure is to set up the framework of genre, of meaning and of the extent of playfulness you will employ, and then to go out and be startlingly free within that framework — when you have an enormous quantity of variations you can draw on, when you can play around in an area off-center from the main topic.

But, to do that, you must know your theme. You must know how to come back to the original path. I believe that is the epitome of acting. Not many actors can do it. It is crucial that the actor and the director be on the same wavelength. There may be wonderful actors who have never been able to do that because no director has ever challenged them to. There may be directors who are capable of it, but they too seldom work with actors capable of functioning in these complex circumstances.

My productions are complex in their theatrical language. They are not simple in their content or in the way the actor must exist within them. It is not always easy for an actor to work with me simply on a personal level. I put them into extreme circumstances. Moreover, I often have them communicating with the spectator in a nontraditional manner. My shows often lack the little things that help the actor — such as costumes and props. I have them in my shows, of course, but seldom in the usual way. And partners. An actor's partners are always a comfort to him. But in my shows their relationships are invariably set up in an unorthodox way. They are not lifelike, realistic relationships. In many of my shows, actors work without partners at all.

My actor must do everything I ask of him: function in the genre I have established, in the strange relationship with the spectators and with or without acting partners.

Music is another thing. We seldom think of music as a partner. We think of music as noise, not a partner. But music for me is always a partner. This jangling set of keys I have just picked up is a prop with which I open a door. But such seemingly insignificant objects can also become partners. They may end up becoming the most important partner of all. Take, for example, the newspaper clippings or the tiny photograph of Katerina Ivanovna's dead husband with which the actress repeatedly interacts in *K. I. from "Crime."* Many things can become living partners.

You must be free to pursue different variations. That is crucial. A role is dead as soon as an actor gets stuck on a single variant or a single intonation. That can happen to weak actors and it can happen to good ones too. They may get locked into sitting in the same spot every time. There are places in the show, of course, where they must be in a specific place at a specific time. That is the path I have been talking about, where the *mise en scène* or the device does not change. For example, the music cannot come in just anywhere, it must come in at one specific moment. And when the music hits a specific note, only then must the actress in *K. I. from "Crime"* lift her head and see the ladder that is descending from the ceiling. There is one specific instant when she must stand. That is all set in stone.

At the same time, there are countless variants to it all. Let us say the actress heard the music in a different way today. Every time I see her responding to the music the same way three or four times in a row, I will bring in new accents. You can imagine that when a show is performed for many years, a lot of variants get used up. They begin to atrophy. That is natural. So, over time, you must constantly shuffle around in your reservoir of possible variants. Where do you continue to mine? How do you look at things anew? I am not talking about one single aspect. I mean everything. I mean the whole show, the whole role. You need suddenly to be able to see everything from a different angle, in a way you have not seen it before. So that what you are doing can be renewed, so that freedom and air can arise.

That is essentially the answer I expected to hear.

You expected that, did you?

Yes, in the sense that I also hear in the word *improvisation* the echoes of the words "anything and everything is fair game." That has nothing to do with your style of theater.

I would say it has nothing to do with art.

I will not try to quote here, but someone once said that art is when we attempt to harmonize chaos. We trace the lines of a human silhouette and thereby partially capture it, this chaotic ever-changing thing that we call a human in general or in one specific instance. In fact, it is all very obscure.

Something is always changing, is always slipping out of our grasp. Not to the degree that the object of our attention will actually disappear physically. But the task is tenaciously to hang on long enough to capture that outline and give it harmony, a certain set of laws. That is why there are various styles in art. In certain eras, certain styles predominate. Say, the Gothic style. Or the Baroque. Then the eye grows accustomed to that and it no longer expresses anything of importance. Then another style arises. Constructivism, let's say. And so you come up against a chunk of chaos made of strange cubes and strange constructs, and that holds your attention.

I had a revelation some fifteen years ago when I was in Armenia, near Yerevan. It is a famous place that all architects know. There is a series of church buildings, including some spectacular ones underground. Also there is a small portico left over from the time of the ancient Greeks. It stunned me. It suddenly made everything clear. I understood exactly why it was made as it was. Behind the portico was a chaotic scene of trees and mountains. And there you have a triangle, a white triangle, and columns. It was a tiny cathedral. And that little white triangle, that small, three-sided space, served to create order and harmony amidst the chaos around it. Beyond it, everything was chaotic. Absolutely no order at all. Not in color, not in shape, not in texture. It was just a tangled mess. But this little portico represented peace, order, and organization. If everything was like that, it would soon lose its power to amaze. In that place in Armenia, that portico had such an impact for the very reason that it was surrounded by chaos.

The question becomes, how do you best organize things, summarize them? The point is not to overcome chaos, because you can never overcome it. The point is how best to frame chaos in a new way in order to discover the laws of harmony, even if it is just some small space.

That is why "everything is fair game" is antiart. In abstract art, where the artist squirts paint every which way, it only seems like it is random. It may be done spontaneously, but it is done by an artist who knows what he is doing. He knows the inner law. It only seems like it is the same as a monkey dipping his tail in paint and waving it back and forth. No! No! It may look the same, but it is not, in fact.

You probably know that you are close to the center of a fairly big controversy. Many contemporary writers are sick of the way directors mold plays to their own purpose. Some writers held up your production of Oleg Bogayev's *Room of Laughter* as an example of how not to stage a contemporary play.

I did not know that, but I can imagine it.

One thing puzzles me in this controversy about whether the age of the auteur director has come to an end or not. Playwrights have existed for something like twenty-five hundred years while the director, as we know him, has existed for only about one hundred years. I do not believe that the time of playwrights has come to an end, but if we are going to consider this problem on a purely mathematical basis, it would appear that the playwright is in greater danger of extinction than the director. It seems like a bogus controversy to me.

No, it is not a bogus controversy. Who is the boss in the theater? The director. What about the actors? The actors perform as the director directs them. This is hurtful, wrong, and unjust, these others think. They may ask, where did this director come from? Who is he? For twenty-four hundred years we did without him, so why do we have to kowtow to him now?

Think about it: Who do the spectators come to see? The director? No. They come to see their favorite actors. This is why actors — especially, the big, famous ones — are humiliated by the relationship they have with the director. They feel constrained.

Throughout the rest of the world, the notion of the auteur director, or the dictator director, is not nearly as strong as it is in Russia. I cannot say why. In the West, the director is basically the guy who stages a show in which actors must act. To one extent or another, it is a kind of commercial contract. Not all Russian directors are dictators, of course, but there is a tendency toward that here.

But this controversy is not bogus. It is a legitimate reflection of the state of our art. Actors feel like slaves. The author feels he is unnecessary. Nobody stages him. Even if someone does, they do whatever they want with his play. This is not a controversy; it is a rebellion. A natural rebellion. Against those who have seized power. This guy, the director, does not play anything himself, does not write anything himself, and what does he do? He enjoys success standing on their bodies! This guy is a usurper. The theater of the dictator is where everything is subordinated to the will of the director. And everything works toward what the director wants. Words, light, technology, the actor — they all work to express the style, the conception of the director.

It seems to me that this does not exist in the West. What we do see there, is the rise of a totalitarian director who does not enslave the actor, but who, essentially, does without the actor entirely. The most powerful show I have seen in many years was staged by Romeo Castellucci. I saw a brilliant show of his, *Julio Cesare,* in Avignon. He had no trained actors at all. This was not Shakespeare or Greek history but a combination of the two with some things added from nowhere at all. There are words, but not many and they do not mean much.

Antony or Brutus, I do not remember which now, comes out and speaks a monologue praising Caesar. A strange person of some kind sticks something in his mouth. Then, on a screen in back, we see the image of some strange, meaty image. That is when we realize that this person has inserted a medical instrument into his throat. We see the meat of his throat undulating. We watch this for two or three minutes while nothing else happens. Up above, a lighting instrument spins slowly, not in connection with anything, but simply following its own rhythm. From time to time it illuminates the spectators then leaves them in the dark again. All it does is establish a rhythm.

A person sits on a chair and then gets up from it and walks away. Then the metal chair itself up and leaves the stage. All this is very strange and very engrossing. You cannot make anything of it at first. But then you begin to get into the swing of it.

The man who had been broadcasting images of his vocal chords comes out and speaks his monologue of praise for Caesar. But he has a very strange voice. Then you realize that this person has had an operation on his vocal chords and the only way he can speak is through a voice box. He pronounces this monologue through this apparatus. As he tells how great Caesar was, his voice box suddenly turns off. But he has a great need for us to know that he is speaking the truth, so he approaches the footlights and continues whispering his monologue.

It is a chilling moment. Incredibly powerful. And you understand the whole point of what is going on. He is struggling to make you understand that he is sincere and right in what he says. You know he was speaking demagoguery. But there is no demagoguery, just his faint whisper.

They bring out a little old man who must be one hundred. He wears red clothes. They literally lead him out on stage because he can barely walk. He strips off his red clothes and remains there entirely nude. A corpse, but a living corpse. All shriveled up everywhere, his penis all shriveled up. He does nothing nor acts nothing because he cannot — he is too old. At this moment something is being discussed. And we understand that they are discussing whether to kill Caesar or not. This old man is Caesar. So, before anything happens, all your sympathies are with him. You are terrified for him. There is no conflict. Nobody is arguing over anything. They simply discuss who must be killed and why. Or why, perhaps, there is no point in killing him.

This is just a small, inexact example of what I saw. It is a fabulous theater that uses an old man's body, a man with damaged vocal chords, and a chair that walks. In one scene a horse is led out. Then it is replaced by a mechanical horse. The lighting and sound are always doing something. A stunning theater.

Now there is a dictator director for you. He has done away with the play and the actors. The whole production belongs entirely to the director.

I have never attended one of your rehearsals although I have a certain conception of the way you work. I see you and your actors communicating by doing and acting rather than by talking.

What happens in rehearsal is what should happen in the theater. Interaction. I do not deliver monologues. I act. I seek to have an impact on my actors. You see, that is something very different from telling a story and explaining something. I seek to instigate.

Admit it, when I tell you various stories, I do not merely narrate tales. I act upon you in many ways, through my tone of voice, my gestures, my facial expressions. I seek to make you *feel* what happened and to *feel* the logic, the mechanism of what happens in whatever story I may be narrating. You are not an actor, but I work with you as if you were. I try to make you recognize my logic within yourself.

That is what made me laugh earlier when you leaned forward and accused me, as if I were a dramatic character, of continually nodding my head yes even though I did not understand what you were saying. You reached inside me and pulled that physical response out of me. I could feel you working on me as a director and I could feel inside me the response you were after. You may have made me blush.

That's right! That's right! You see? That is the dialogue you are talking about. I would call it interaction or impact — my impact on the actor. I act so as to have an impact on him. I do that in any number of ways.

The main method is to find those words that will give me the key to the actor's imagination and nature. And, then, this is very important: to compel him to undertake that action which I believe is the proper one for the given situation. Of course you can just name the action you want and the actor will say, "Yes, yes, that's good." But then he will just sit there. What you have to do is to awaken in the actor the inner need to perform the action.

The ideal situation is when an actor interrupts me and says, "Kama! Wait a minute! Wait a minute! Don't say anything more! I understand! I get it!" He does not need words anymore. What came over him was the physical need to perform that action right now. To *do* it. And then he does it and you say, "No, that's not quite it. Now, try it again. Try it again."

He is right there next to what you are after and so you get him to

Actress Arina Nesterova and Kama Ginkas during rehearsals of *Pushkin. Duel. Death,* written by Ginkas on the basis of historical documents; Moscow, 1999. *Photo by Ken Reynolds.*

go at it again. And then he loses that electrifying impulse and says, "No, I don't think I got it."

That does not mean he did not understand me. It means he lost the internal need to perform the specific act I am after. So then he says, "All right, what about this way," and he tries something else. He says, "Is that it? Is that it?" And you say, "Closer! Closer!" And he says, "Yeah, yeah! I think I know what you mean. I think I can feel that."

My job is to awaken in the actor the need to perform the specific action I am after, within the system of logic I am employing and in the very manner that I want.

What happens as a result? We eventually arrive at an action that is similar to the one that has been haunting my imagination and that at the same time is natural to the talents and capabilities of this specific actor.

Moreover, what is most valuable of all is when this interaction awakens responses and impulses characteristic of this actor's personality alone. He comes up with nuances and details of the prescribed action that no one else could. That is when, suddenly, you see something other than what you had in mind, but it has come back to you in an enriched form thanks to the individuality of the actor.

That is the act in its truest form. And here I do not mean *act* as in *action,* but act as in the sexual act. I often draw this parallel in my descriptions of my work with actors — act as action and act as sexual act. There can be no satisfaction in the act or in the action if only one partner is participating. That is merely imitation. Satisfaction arises — and something is born — only when there is mutual interaction: When I suggest one thing and my partner responds with what I want, adding what he wants and what he is capable of in accordance with his nature. Then I, taking off from that, add my own and my partner responds again from his point of view. That is when things get going. In those cases, you never know what shore you may reach.

Basically, rehearsal is existing in anticipation of a new shore — one you know nothing about.

I began by saying that, as the director, I am the be-all and end-all. I know everything. Well that is a bunch of baloney, of course. If I really do know everything, that is very bad. Essentially, if I know everything, there is no reason for me to direct the show.

I begin rehearsing in order to sail to an uncharted shore. I love rehearsing. My first thoughts are always, "Where is this going to lead me?" Not every actor is capable of leading me to new territory. Without that, you think, "Well, that wasn't a bad job. Professional. We ended up more or less where we expected to." In those cases, you are satisfied if you at least went forward because it can also happen that you go backward. That is what happens when an actor is not able to do much of what you wanted. In those cases, you are just happy to get even a little way out to sea, more or less in the planned direction even though you came to a stop somewhere in mid-journey.

Then there are those cases when you are in luck, when you have an actor who is able to respond to your impulses. The greatest pleasure comes with that sweet anticipation of "where are we going?" Where are we going to be led this time? Take the author, for instance. Where is he going to lead you? When it is an author of genius — like Chekhov, like Pushkin, like Shakespeare — you *never* know where you are going to be led.

You once said, "I provoke actors in circumstances that are of interest to me." I take this to mean that since you already know that a specific circumstance is of interest to you, you can be somewhat certain that an actor working in those circumstances will head off more or less in the direction you want.

No, in fact it is just the opposite. I had forgotten that phrase of mine, but I am interested to hear you quote it — "I provoke in given circumstances." In fact, I provoke in the *hope* that my provocation will produce results. But I do not know what the result will be.

I provoke in given circumstances. In the circumstance of the specific characters of this work. Or, at least, what I think is the circumstance of these characters, something close to it. But even if I know my actor well, I do not know everything about him. And I certainly do not know him in these specific provocative circumstances. I often work with actors I know poorly or not at all. And so when I provoke such an actor, I draw back and wait. I am fascinated to see what he will do.

Let us take a concrete example: An actor must go not through ice but through fire. That is the situation of this specific character. If you are the actor, you might begin yelling and stamping your feet in terror. Or you may bull your neck and grit your teeth. Or you may howl with laughter and shout, "Ow-w-w, that hurts!" I do not know. And that is what is interesting. The richer you are as an actor, the more unexpected and paradoxical your response will be.

You see, I, as director, do not want to change my circumstances. I hope that you, as actor, will be able to do what I want. But you try what I ask and I think, "Hmm, that's not right." And so I change something. I do that to provoke you in a different way that might bring about what I want. That is how I try to achieve what I am after. If it brings uninteresting results or results that are diametrically opposed to what I am after, then I will go on changing things. But if they are not diametrically opposed, if they are just the product of the actor's individuality, if they are daring or paradoxical in some way — maybe they even seem totally impossible but I can see they are convincing and compelling — then I will set off down the road that the actor has discovered. That is what opens up the possibility of the actor and me arriving at some destination we had not dreamed of.

There is always searching going on. It happens first with the text — what can this text offer me? And even though I often write my own texts, I still only know as much as I know. So once I have written the text, the next step is to start probing its possibilities as director, provoking the actor to see what he might offer. This provocation takes place within the confines of several relationships — the circumstances of his character, the genre of the literary material, the actor's contact with me as director and his contact with his partners. Moreover, do not forget that each individual partner exerts his or her own influence on this equation.

When you have an actor who is a worthy partner, you have no idea what your collaboration is going to bring. And when you do arrive at something, you think, "Well, I'll be damned!" You had no idea it would come out like this.

Is that true of actors only?

No. Let us consider designers for a moment. What makes my frequent collaborator Sergei Barkhin so remarkable? Barkhin does not, will not and cannot — ever — do what I want. That is not because he resists me, it is because he cannot work any other way. He always views things from an incomprehensible point of view. Sometimes it has absolutely nothing to do with the author or my requests. His suggestions usually come out of the blue.

For example, Eduard Kochergin or David Borovsky are usually more or less on the same wavelength with me. They will take what I suggest and, after translating it into their own language, will add and build on in the same general direction I was moving in.

Barkhin will listen to what I say, but he will be thinking about something else entirely. Most likely, he responds to what I am saying as he might to music that creates for him a mood or excites in him some thought. But his own thoughts will be entirely different.

That is what happened when he designed the set for Henrietta Yanovskaya's production of *Ivanov*. Chekhov in rusty iron panels. You could not possibly come up with anything more anti-Chekhov. Or take his set for Henrietta's version of *The Heart of a Dog*. Henrietta explained what she was doing and Barkhin said, "I want to do Egypt." What does Egypt have to do with Bulgakov's *The Heart of a Dog*? It seems Barkhin had wanted to do Egypt for a long time. He loves Egypt. But what does Egypt have to do with anything?

Well, now it is up to the director. If the director has imagination, then the ideas come. The director says, "Hmm. I have been wanting to do *Aida*." That is anything but obvious in regards to Bulgakov's novella. There is only one word about *Aida* in there. But Henrietta says she wants to do *Aida* and that is when things begin running on parallel tracks. *Aida* and Egypt.

Barkhin and I did Dostoevsky's *The Idiot* in Helsinki. The standard texture of Dostoevsky is obvious — the murky, rotten physiology of St. Petersburg. That is Dostoevsky's own phrase, incidentally, "the physiology of St. Petersburg." Dostoevsky's architecture is always physiological; it is almost like a living being. It is always rather slimy, dirty, splattered. It has no color.

Barkhin proposed deep blue walls, a deep blue ceiling, and three-hundred white roses. What does this have to do with Dostoevsky? Can you imagine that? Dostoevsky and white roses. Amidst deep blue surroundings. Plus he added fireworks and sparklers. What does this have to do with anything?

But if you start thinking, you recall that the action in *The Idiot* takes place around Christmas. Dostoevsky does not make a point of that, but you know it is so. So the city is infused with the anticipation of Christmas. Next, one of the prominent events is Nastasya Filippovna's nameday, or Saint's Day. That means people will be bringing her flowers and gifts. Why can't the flowers be white roses? Then you think, maybe it is Rogozhin who brings them when he brings her the money that he promised. And since he is an expansive type, liable to do things to excess, he hires a sled, loads it down with white roses, takes the driver's seat himself, and delivers the flowers himself.

And there you have it, the connection with Barkhin's unusual idea.

The white roses turn the cold, Christmasy, beautiful blue space either into an affluent interior or a winter garden. Snow falling on the white roses creates a certain tension and interaction — white snow on white roses. And then there is the contrast of the white roses interacting with the blue space.

Moreover, I have always thought that large quantities of flowers evoke sensations of a funeral. And that ties into the finale after Rogozhin has killed Nastasya Filippovna.

Barkhin's suggestion corresponds to the novel's whole dramatic line. It may not be literal Dostoevsky. There is a distance there. It causes tension. You ask, "Where is the physiology?" Well, there is none. But there is something else. There are the gay Christmas games, carols, and singing of children. Their anticipation of Christmas.

You will recall that many have called Prince Myshkin a modern version of Jesus Christ, the appearance of Jesus Christ in Russia. He returns from somewhere — Switzerland, to be exact, although that is not what is important. What is important is Myshkin's arrival from somewhere else, his "second coming," as it were. That is what it is, after all, is it not?

Myshkin was here. He fell ill. Went somewhere. And then he came back. He was not accepted and there was an attempt to kill him. To an extent, Myshkin, in his second coming, is crucified. Dostoevsky provides extraordinary details. Myshkin arrives in wintery Russia wearing summery footwear. His sandals become a crucial image.

Next is the question of what moves the other characters. As it was in my production of *Macbeth*, it is the will to live, the fullness of life. The taste of life must be savored. Snow should crunch when you bite it. Icicles should snap when they break off and they should make you gasp and shout if they slip down your back. "Brrr, that's cold! But, brrr, it feels good! That's fun! That's winter! That's how it is in Russia!" The ability to savor life, to desire to live. There is in that something luring, something seductive. Life must be seductive. And suddenly I realized that in this show I wanted things to be achingly beautiful, even abnormally beautiful.

You know how it sometimes happens in winter that the sky is blue, the snow is bright white and the St. Petersburg architecture, decorated in frost, is, for once, not grimy and depressing. This happens very rarely, but it does happen. When the sky is blue, the snow is bright, it squeaks and crunches underfoot and you want to live! This is fabulous!

You want this to last. You want snow to crunch like this every time you bite it. Instead, it is all killed off. Nastasya Filippovna is killed. Myshkin essentially is destroyed. It is almost as though they kill themselves off in the suicidal fervor of life.

That is what happens when Barkhin suggests blue walls and white roses for *The Idiot*. A specific genre arises. Anti-Dostoevsky. This is something healthy. Blue is healthy. Snow is healthy. But the result is the same. Perhaps, it is even . . . well . . . stronger.

You have spoken about how the director provokes an actor. He provokes an audience. He even provokes an author. But here you are talking about a reverse act. Here it is a designer provoking the director.

True, but what I do as a director is to provoke consciously. The designer, in this case Sergei Barkhin, does not set himself that task. What actually is happening is that I set myself up to be provoked. I give in to a provocation.

One thing I always tell my actors — and, in fact, everyone who works in the theater in any capacity — is that they should always be prepared to be provoked. They should never fear provocation in the creative act. You need to be open to provocations. To suggestions. To someone doing something unexpected.

Many actors and theater people, to protect their egos and aspirations, close themselves up. In other words, they act in total contradiction to the creative process. You make some suggestion and they respond, "Mmm, yes. Perhaps. Yes. I think I'll try that."

Forget it. That response is dead in the water. It is pointless. Nothing can come of it.

You must be open to all suggestions, no matter how crazy they seem. Because what if you suddenly see some different approach? I mean, really, there is no way you can have a set made of rusty iron for a Chekhov production. Or have three hundred white roses for Dostoevsky. But you have to be open to that possibility. What if you *can* fit Dostoevsky in there? What would that give? What happens then?

Tovstonogov taught us not to be enslaved by our conception of the play. That director has become enslaved who says, "Here is my basic conception for this show and now I am going to set about building it. I am crazy about my conception." That is very dangerous. Many directors — including ones of talent — perish from that. They cave in on themselves. Because they dream up a great show and march off in a straight line to create what they see in their head.

But what about all those other fantastic possibilities that the actor brings to his work? I am not even talking about actual, concrete suggestions — I simply mean the nature and potential of his individual personality. Beyond that, unexpected suggestions may come from the designer or the composer. Or the specifics of the environment where you will perform may have an impact that sends you off in a slightly different direction. Maybe you are rehearsing in the winter rather than the summer and that has some concrete effect. The possibilities are endless. Let us say you expected to rehearse for three months but now you have to do it in six weeks. And so you have to change something. All these obstacles provoke you. That is, if you are open to them. They incite you to create a work of living art.

If you are programmed to some specific result, if you are the slave of your original conception, you will forego a fantastic number of fabulous possibilities that could have become part of your journey. You may arrive exactly where you had planned, but maybe that destination is the least interesting of all the possibilities you might have had.

Columbus sailed for India. Instead he discovered America. So what if he had made it to India? Big deal. Everybody knew about India anyway. But Columbus discovered a colossal continent. He made a genuine discovery. Because he sailed where his ship went.

4

Meyerhold, Stanislavsky, and Others

I, and not only I, have had occasion to write about your black humor. I tend to use the phrase knowing it expresses only one aspect of your humor. How would you define your sense of humor?

Black humor is characteristic of me, of course. Black humor is sarcastic. It is humor evoked by something inevitable. There is nothing left to do but laugh about whatever it is. Crying would be silly, laughable. There is the crux — it is laughable to cry. As such, all you can do is ridicule situations you have no power to change. That is one of the laws of our existence.

I would put it this way: Sarcasms are not only characteristic of me, they are everywhere in my work. That may be one of the reasons why I never gained a mass popularity. Sarcasm is a merciless humor. It is merciless to the character and, therefore, to the audience since we must assume that the spectator identifies with the character.

I never liked satire, for instance. Satire works on the basis of the writer putting himself above the person or phenomenon he is satirizing. The implication is that he knows a better way of doing things. He points an accusing finger at someone else. That is not characteristic of me at all.

The humor I strive for in my shows is that of a character laughing at himself. Of me laughing at myself. The point is that I could be in this predicament or I could behave just as stupidly. I am usually able to admit that when I stop to look at things objectively.

Another kind of humor in my shows arises from discrepancies. When we think of ourselves in the third person, we tend to see ourselves and our ambitions as very serious, important, and exalted. But from the point of view that exists far higher than we — a religious person might call that God, someone else might call it harmony — we and our ambitions appear small, silly, and awkward. We think we have done something terribly threatening when in fact what we have done is not even perceptible. We think we have slammed down our fist, but, in fact, there is no sound. We think we are stamping our feet, but we look more like a cockroach wiggling its feelers. That is the humor that interests me. As a rule, no matter who my shows tell about, I am talking about myself. On one hand, I respect myself. But on the other, I experience a bitter humor in regards to myself.

I do exhibit a kind, warm humor from time to time, although rarely. As a rule, that kind of humor arises in genre scenes. For example, a person in a bath keeps trying to pick up a bar of soap but it invariably slips out of his grasp. That is amusing and whimsical. You recognize yourself in that although there is no sarcasm in it at all. It is simple, good-hearted humor.

However, I can easily imagine how Meyerhold would have taken that scene and turned it into an exploration of a mania. The person grows increasingly intense as he repeatedly grabs for the soap in vain. He begins hitting things and hurts the knuckles on his hand. He begins kicking his feet, but his legs go out from under him. In the end he falls and dies.

I started out talking about Meyerhold, but I actually recognize myself in that vignette. Because with my character, my attitude, and my point of view, if I were to compose that sort of scene it probably would expand into something like that. I use small things to comment on larger topics.

On this topic, and in connection with Meyerhold, I often tell a story I once heard. It may have no basis in fact, but that is not important. There once was one of those silly Soviet amateur theater competitions. This one involved shows that had been put together by Soviet soldiers or military personnel. Among them the jury watched a short production of Chekhov's tale "Surgery," in which a deacon comes to a doctor to get his tooth pulled. The gist of it is how the doctor's attempts to pull the deacon's tooth are fraught with errors. He yanks and pulls, but no matter what he does the tooth will not come out. With each new failure, the doctor increasingly turns into an evil force, a devil, into Fate itself who tortures and torments the poor deacon. Chekhov wrote a humorous little story that was not bereft of sympathy and maybe a tad of tragedy. But it had none of the infernal qualities of the little show this jury witnessed. The doctor, in this interpretation, was transformed into an avenging angel or a devil of Fate who mocked and derided an unfortunate and innocent person.

The jury could not believe that some soldiers could have created this show unaided and they began asking questions. It turned out that the men who performed it had previously been employed as guards in a Siberian prison camp. They said, "There was a prisoner working as a bookkeeper at the camp by the name of Meringold. He helped us do it."

You can't help but wonder, can you? Maybe that prisoner Meringold was Meyerhold. Nobody will ever prove it. In fact, by some accounts, Meyerhold was shot almost immediately after being arrested — meaning he could never have spent any time in any prison camp as a bookkeeper. On the other hand, there is a value to this myth. It is like my production of *The Execution of the Decembrists,* where myth and truth stand side-by-side as equals.

Furthermore, this vignette illustrates how every joke, every gag, every situation, every scene, every author in the hands of a director can be transformed into something else. The determining factor is the outlook or perspective of the director.

I am curious to what extent Meyerhold has had an effect on you. I can imagine a scenario whereby his impact might not extend beyond a few pointed tales.

No, no. My awareness of myself as a person of the theater came to me in the period extending from the end of the 1950s to the beginning of the 1960s. At the end of the 1950s I found in the library a book of

Meyerhold that had not been removed from circulation. You must picture me as a young person from Lithuania who did not consider himself Soviet — that is, I was inclined toward the West, toward radicalism, toward the avant-garde, toward antirealism and toward nonpsychological theater. All of that means that I was inclined *away* from Stanislavsky. I was interested in everything that was forbidden and inaccessible. Of course, I read Meyerhold. As I also read Gordon Craig.

I would say that Meyerhold empowers directors with rights. He is an enemy of dogmatism. He affirms diversity. At the least, he points the way to the non-European theater, that is, to a theater that is not concerned with imitating life. Japanese theater. Chinese, African, Persian theater. Puppet theater. Meyerhold absorbed all of this and he absorbed styles of painting and music. He did not limit himself to life and the tradition of European theater of the nineteenth century. He fed on different origins of inspiration and discovered that you can draw on influences which have nothing in common with what you are doing. Not only *can* you do that, but it is one of the great methods of enriching what you are doing and achieving surprising results.

In the Soviet era everything was terribly serious, theater included. But, the element of playing the fool was very strong in Meyerhold. That was very attractive and it encouraged in me a sense of freedom and independence. One of his phrases has become one of my own, something I repeat constantly: "Pranks that are characteristic of theater." Primarily, that means the unexpected is characteristic of theater, for pranks do not necessarily mean something funny. It means provocations. In my theater, these elements are often not very funny or are not funny at all, but they are theatrical pranks.

In *We Play "Crime"* the dead pawnbroker and her sister came out on stage with axes sunk in their heads and they danced a waltz. Sometimes the spectators laughed, sometimes they did not. But that was a "prank characteristic of theater."

The genre in which I function has been called one of provocation. Were I to translate that into Meyerholdese, it would come out "pranks that are characteristic of theater." I think that is one of the primary aspects of my theater. For all my ability to be serious and tiresome — something I do not like in myself, something I struggle with greatly,

Razumikhin (Oleg Kosovnenko) looks on as Raskolnikov (Marcus Grott) plays at hanging himself in *We Play "Crime"*, a dramatization of Dostoevsky's *Crime and Punishment;* Moscow, 1991. *Photo by Igor Kravchenko.*

and something I cannot overcome — my chief method of work is to seek out pranks that are characteristic of theater.

I want to find ambivalence. I want to find a playful approach, an approach that is based in playfulness.

Take for example *We Play "Crime."* That is not my title. That, naturally, is stolen from Dürrenmatt's *We Play Strindberg.* And I am sure that even if Dürrenmatt did not know it himself — maybe it came to him by way of Brecht or someone else — he stole it from Meyerhold. That is, that notion cannot exist without Meyerhold. To some extent, everything for Meyerhold was play; it may be bloody or intellectual or romantic, but it was play.

Meyerhold saw elements of theater in everything. He saw elements of theater in *life*. In fact, they are very easy to discern. Shakespeare's formula of "all the world's a stage" has become old and tired and does not really say much to us anymore. But look at that through the prism of Meyerhold and it comes to life again. All you have to do is find the slightest logicality in things — for example, in the way that you are nodding your head again. Look at that not as at a random action, but give it a certain rhythm and regularity, or give it a certain emphasis, or bring it up into the foreground and you will see that, in fact, it is an element of play.

Soviet theater was considered the theater of Stanislavsky although nothing could have been farther from the truth. It is just that it was considered so. You cannot blame Stanislavsky for Soviet theater. He was a thousand times more brilliant than what they turned him into.

But, Meyerhold was interested in movement and the visual aspects of theater. And he attracted me because the visual side has always been of great importance to me. In my younger years I was fascinated by the static and bas-relief theater that Meyerhold worked with during his Symbolist years in the early twentieth century. I was fascinated by the common, everyday object that turns into a symbol or metaphor. Later on, I struggled with this aspect because I came to abhor it in myself and in others. I came to distrust metaphors. But there was a time when this interested me.

Work with space. That is Meyerhold. Because Stanislavsky's realistic theater, the theater of everyday life was not concerned with space. It was interested in finding a lifelike milieu. A person within a lifelike milieu. But Meyerhold was not after a lifelike milieu, he sought a theatrical space. True, sometimes that space might take on the aspect of a living space, but Meyerhold was after variety.

I cannot help but bring up the fact that we are presently sitting in the white room where several of your best productions have been performed. *K. I. from "Crime," Pushkin. Duel. Death,* and, figuratively speaking, since it was in a different white room, *We Play "Crime."* In *We Play "Crime"* Viktor Gvozditsky performed on the outside of the room, looking in through the window. In *K. I. from "Crime"* the action takes place partly in the neighboring foyer, partly here inside this room. In *Pushkin. Duel. Death,* there are unseen people sitting in the next room who manipulate the table that seems to rise as if by magic before the spectators in this room.

That's right. I would say that my main feature, or even my main illness, is my visual memory. This was especially true when I was younger. It was so highly developed then as to be pathological. I do not remember names. I do not remember telephones. I do not remember titles. I forget words all the time. Maybe that is because I was born into two languages or maybe that is just the way I am.

But thanks to the fact that I was interested in painting, sculpture, and architecture, and because I myself drew, the photographs that I saw of Meyerhold's productions became fixed in my mind. They are a part of me. I cannot remember which show the photos are from. But his visual language, his lines, his form all exist within me. I never think about it in advance, but I often know when I am creating some scene that it is coming to me out of my memory of Meyerhold. From *The Inspector General* or some other show. It is never a literal quote. I do not steal. I do not really even remember. But those images are in me. They are a part of me. I know that well.

But let me come back to what I was saying about the element of play. Meyerhold was not as openly provocative as I am. His provocations were somewhat different.

There is a phrase that all directors use nowadays, even the very worst. I suspect it originated with Meyerhold. I cannot prove that, but I suspect it is true. Directors come to their actors and say, "How are we going to amaze our audience?" Basically a phrase like that irritates me. I do not really think like that. But Meyerhold did. He knew that if he did something in green in his last show, then in his next show he would reject color altogether. He would completely avoid everything to do with painting and color and he would do something entirely different. Each successive stage of his career contradicted the previous one.

What I mean is that he was not so much provoking the spectator right now during the course of the performance, but more in terms of the way he developed his relationship with his audience over time. He constantly thought up new surprises for them.

So this may not be a direct correspondence, but I would say it is a place where my path crosses that of Meyerhold. It is where many of my impulses come from.

The Black Monk (Igor Yasulovich, above) appears in a vision to Kovrin (Sergei Makovetsky) in the dramatization of Chekhov's *The Black Monk;* Moscow, 1999. *Photo by Ken Reynolds.*

A well-known contemporary of yours, Yury Lyubimov, also draws a great deal on Meyerhold. And yet Yury Lyubimov and Kama Ginkas have almost nothing in common.

I would even say that, to a certain extent, we are antagonistic. Not in a personal sense, naturally, but in our art.

How does that happen then? You talk of the influence Meyerhold has had on you, and it is clear Meyerhold had a great influence on Lyubimov. Obviously differences arise because you and Lyubimov are different people with different talents. But I suppose an even greater factor was that Meyerhold was such a protean talent.

Exactly. He was a Proteus. An enormous amount of different theatrical movements can arise from Meyerhold. They have, in fact, arisen and they will continue to do so. No doubt about it.

I would say that Lyubimov is, if not a continuer, then a follower of Meyerhold in a new era. There is not a direct line from Meyerhold to Lyubimov. He is not a follower of the actual Meyerhold, but of Meyerhold as filtered through Brecht. Lyubimov, picking up that reflection, relates to us his own version of Meyerhold. Between the two is the transcription of Brecht who helped carry Meyerhold through the rugged mountains of the 1930s, 1940s, and 1950s in the Soviet Union, a time and place where Meyerhold's legacy simply disappeared. His manner of art was completely out of step with that time and era, one that was savage, false, and inhuman. Brecht translated Meyerhold into the language of that time, the late 1930s to the 1950s. So Lyubimov received Meyerhold in Brecht's transcription. Not in the original, but in transcription. He was easier to handle that way.

In my opinion, incidentally, Lyubimov is much more interesting than Brecht. When you come down to it, Lyubimov is grounded in the style of the variety theater. He is something of a showman. Take away the negative connotations of that word and leave behind merely the genre. All of his productions consist of small, individual numbers. Musical, physical, and, to a lesser extent, narrative numbers. That is also a Meyerholdian trait, by the way. Meyerhold also worked with what we call "attractions." Eisenstein later developed that notion and used it in cinema — the montage of attractions — but it came from Meyerhold.

Brecht did not have that. He has a story he is telling, an epic narrative. It is no coincidence that for a long time Lyubimov did not stage traditional plays at all. Because plays have their own laws. Instead, he molded and fashioned shows out of all kinds of different sources with varying themes, rhythms, and emotions.

Now, I would say I am an antishowman. If I do not have a dramatic line — I am not talking about literature, I am talking about dramatic structure and development — I do not know what to do. Lyubimov does not work with dramatic movement; his shows consist of discrete segments.

I saw his reconstruction of *The Good Person of Setzuan* in 1999. I had read a lot about the original and had seen a lot of pictures, but I was quite surprised to see that, indeed, the show consisted primarily of various numbers.

I gather you did not like it.

I can imagine it was an amazing show when it opened in 1964.

I must say it was a stunning production. There was a great deal of play on various themes that developed in different ways. It made a very strong impression by working through allegories, tales, and minute changes in the plot line which served as links between segments. At that time, it was a very strong show. That show earned its fame. It was an artistic and political event of the first rank.

I would like to quote from *True and False*, David Mamet's book on acting. It is a clear, straightforward polemic with Stanislavsky that is as easy to take issue with as it is to agree with it. In one place he writes, "The only reason to rehearse is to learn to perform the play. It is not to 'explore the meaning of the play' — the play, for the actor, has no meaning beyond its performance." He follows that up by stating that rehearsal "is not to 'investigate the life of the character.' There is no character. There are just lines on the page."*

---

*David Mamet, *True or False* (London: Faber and Faber, 1998), 52.

This, it seems to me, is diametrically opposed to Russian theater in general, and to your theater in specific.

Well, Mamet may be an actor, too, but it is obvious a playwright wrote those sentences. That is the sore spot of an author who wrote words that are never spoken as he wrote them. Not because the actors are falsifying him, but because he wrote a specific intonation into his play. A bad writer will do this. You can always hear in their characters the specific intonation the author is trying to give them. But the surest way to a lousy production is to perform in the intonation the author wants. That is guaranteed failure.

Mamet's utterance reveals the painful complexes of an author who is never satisfied with the intonations his text is given. When he says "play the text," he means, "I have given you the intonation, now just reproduce it."

When he says there is no character, that is a comment on the level of his plays. This is, of course, a case of arrogance on my part because I do not know all of his plays and I am taking it upon myself to pass judgment. But the works of his that I do know are "well-made plays." Neatly built texts in which there are no characters, no living people. There are lines and punchlines that must be spoken as written and then you wait for the audience to laugh or fall silent. He wants the spectator to heed the text.

That, in his opinion, is the key strength of his plays. In my opinion, the key strength of a play, his included, lies in the extent to which the author taps into a living person. Mamet is a talented writer. As such, from time to time, he scratches the surface of humans, of lifelike situations, captures the living language in which people speak. When he does, his characters are, to a proper extent, alive. They are not as alive as Shakespeare's characters, or Chekhov's. But they are alive enough for the American public, which does not like stylizations, to see in them a reflection of themselves. They are written for a public that wishes to see its own reflection.

I suspect that one of the reasons Mamet writes so categorically is that he wishes to peel back the mystical cloud that surrounds the Stanislavsky system and its stranglehold on acting all over the world.

That I understand. I can see he wants to eliminate the coating of fraud, magic, and mysticism surrounding Stanislavsky.

But Stanislavsky has nothing to do with that. Stanislavsky was a sincere, searching person, one who took things to their logical conclusion. He was interested in everything. He was into spiritualism and bundles of energy. He went through various phases. He did not arrive at a school. School is when $2 + 2 = 4$. When you understand that $2 + 2 = 4$ and you can take 4 and add another 2 and both you and I will arrive at 6. That is school, that is a system. It is a mass of building blocks, the details, the elements out of which you can build something. Not everybody can build with them. You also need talent. You need an internal structure that will help you give birth to something living, rather than something dead. However, a gifted person working in the theater can use these tools and help himself. That goes without question. There is no mysticism in that.

Inspiration, on the other hand, is something greater. Inspiration is not something you can grab with your hands. You can, knowing yourself, do everything in your power to prepare yourself in such a manner that the flash of inspiration will come. It is a very individual thing. Stanislavsky writes about a group of general, objective tasks that are capable of inducing individual inspiration and are able to help you comprehend your own individual instrument.

To what extent do you work with a system or laws in your productions?

A great many ideas arise intuitively. And that is what you want. God forbid you should construct a show rationally. Later, however, you begin to discern the laws at work. You realize that everything follows a natural order. If it does not, then you have made a mistake. Things can show up in what you are doing by coincidence. But in the end they must take their place in the natural order of things.

In *Five Corners* I stumbled by accident upon a piece of music that later became a part of the show's fabric. Well-wishers advised me that the music was out-of-date and that I should find something else. I refused. Ultimately, I could not have created that show without that music.

I had something else entirely in mind when the actress Oksana

Mysina and I went to work on my production of *K. I. from "Crime."* But now this show could not possibly be any different. Oksana's nature became the nature of Katerina Ivanovna. You could find a better actress. But she could not perform the show. It would be an entirely different show. And in my opinion, it would be much worse.

If I understand you correctly, it sounds like you work in such a way as to discover the laws and natural order of whatever it is you are staging and then you try to work around them.

That is a dangerous assumption. For more than twenty years I have specifically attempted not to create laws or build around them.

I did not mean that you build a show according to those laws, whatever they are, but that you attempt to feel them out, to discover them, to reveal them. Perhaps doing so blindly.

Yes. Reveal them blindly. If there is no order there, there is no show. Even bad shows are structured on the basis of bad or primitive laws. The great shows are structured on profound, almost indiscernible laws. It may take, for example, one hundred years to discern the laws of Chekhov's drama.

Consider Anatoly Efros. In my opinion, he was the greatest director of the postwar period. Before the war there were Meyerhold, Stanislavsky, Nemirovich-Danchenko, and the like, so I will not try to go that far back. But in the postwar period, I believe that Efros was one of the two or three greatest directors in the world. This is a director who is essentially unknown outside the former Soviet Union. That is so purely because of the Iron Curtain. The theater that Efros gave birth to was unlike anything anyone has done, including Peter Brook, Giorgio Strehler, or any of his other great contemporaries.

All of Efros's productions were marked by their own unique internal structure, but I have never seen a single critical or scholarly article that can describe to me the natural order of Efros's shows. And that is something that has always been of vital interest to me — to peer into Efros's method. I have always wanted to know how he did what he did! I do not understand how he did it. But I know damn well that he knew exactly what he was up to!

You could sense the structure of an Efros show. You knew an Efros show instantly without being told who had done it. His shows never resembled any other, whether superficially or internally. That inner Efros structure — the way the show was molded, the way it developed — was unlike anything I have ever seen by any other director in world theater. But how did he do it?! I do not know.

I can explain Yury Lyubimov rather easily. Tovstonogov is more difficult, but I can explain him, too. I know him from the inside out. I can explain much in the shows of Peter Brook that I have seen — say from the era of *King Lear*.

But Efros I cannot explain. Although, doubt me not — the laws of his method were iron-clad. In fact, when Efros tried breaking free of those laws he was completely helpless. An example is his production of Maxim Gorky's *The Lower Depths* at the Taganka Theater. This was his attempt to align himself with the style of Lyubimov's theater. Another example was Svetlana Aleksiyevich's *War Does Not Have a Woman's Face*. It was a total waste. Because, in fact, these laws are like an artist's genetic code. It is a given from nature. Efros tried to break out of his nature — a nature of genius — but he could not do it! He wanted to be simpler in these shows, but he could not do it.

The kinds of shows you are talking about — Efros's, your own, or others like them — are most clearly perceived through feelings or, as you put it in regards to yourself, through physiology. What I find is that when I turn off my head, when I forget about trying to understand intellectually, the show reveals itself to me with amazing clarity. All of its nuances, all of its details, all of its implications are absolutely clear. But then when you walk out on the street afterwards an interesting thing happens. You still feel everything with the same fullness and intensity, but if you try to talk about why that is, words often fail you.

The alternate example is when you have seen a bad show or even a good show and you come out and you are able to put all the pieces in place. For example, at the culmination point the director turned on loud, rhythmic music and your heart began beating faster. You were aware of how and why he was manipulating you at the instant that it was happening but nothing changes, grows, or stays with you after that other than the simple end result.

This is why I asked about fumbling around in the dark to discover the laws or the natural order of your shows. Because when you as director discover something by intuition rather than by a schematic, we as spectators are apt to perceive it intuitively ourselves.

What you are saying is that you are searching blindly with me; that you are stumbling down the same path I stumbled down when I was creating the show. In other words, you are not marching down a well-worn, neatly trimmed path, but are seeking out the path together with me.

Maybe that is so. I do not know. However, even if I cannot put my finger on what Efros did, I am able to lay out on the table every single detail of my own shows. And I hate that. I really hate that. That is why I have spoken about trying to overcome that all-encompassing awareness that Tovstonogov instilled in me. I would also like to overcome my own Jewish rationalism that sits so deeply within me. You might even say I have spent my whole life trying to do that. Sometimes I am able to. But, for all my attempts to work on an intuitive level, I know perfectly well where my ideas come from and how I put them together. I repeat, I may not know that as I am doing it, but it always comes to me later on.

I must say that in recent times the more sophisticated theatrical public — including critics — has begun to notice certain trademark elements in my work. I mean that specifically in terms of my craft, not in terms of my themes or ideas, which are often interpreted in a very primitive way. An example of the latter is when they say I make shows about death. That is a bunch of baloney. But the observations about my craft are another thing altogether. I myself have noticed a certain repetitiousness, although I quietly keep that to myself. I have often wondered how I might make some changes. And yet I keep on doing what I do.

But an artist has his own signature, his own style. You have talked about an artist's backbone that cannot be overcome. A personal style, too, is something that cannot be violated without dire consequences. I see up to a hundred and fifty shows a year and I see many directors, good and bad, quote themselves or echo themselves. These echoes may be more or less effective or pleasant. Some directors simply repeat themselves. I am not cheerleading here, but I must say that I have never noticed you repeating yourself. What I have observed is your development of a singular, natural style or vision.

I would like to think that, too. In fact, I do think that. I may find something in my work on a show that the spectator will not even notice. I begin to work around that kernel and develop it into something new. But I also may just use something I have discovered in the past and have used many times since. This is what catches the attention of that sophisticated spectator I mentioned. And he is right. That is called skillful use of my craft.

So, I do not deny that I have a few recurring trademark elements. I can even reveal one of them to you. To my recollection only one person has pointed this out. But it has never been brought up again.

You have noted that I begin everything with a negation. That means that, as a rule, I begin everything with a provocation. All of my shows begin with a specific, provocative action. This has been true ever since I staged a show called *Pushkin and Natalie* in 1979. That is, for over twenty years. Every show since then has begun like that. Each individual provocation may be more or less insolent, more or less daring, more obvious or almost not discernible at all. It may be something as simple as: "Are you all seated? Then stand up!" "Are we going to watch? No, we're going to listen." "You came to laugh? You're going to cry." "You came to watch depressing Dostoevsky? No, we're going to entertain you."

Evidently I will never escape this approach again. It has almost become a cliché. Someone who does not like me will call it just that, a cliché. And I would be in no position to contradict that.

You differ from Stanislavsky in many ways and I would like to pin those differences down.

Stanislavsky will be with us forever. There obviously is no doubting that. And yet, one hundred years after he created the Moscow Art Theater and began to evolve his extraordinarily influential acting system, it seems the time has come to draw some conclusions about him. I would maintain that theater has moved beyond him in many ways.

I cannot talk about that. I have not read him for a very long time. I have no right to take issue with him or to defend him. And I am not going to read him.

That is already one answer to my question.

Yes, that is true. On the other hand, I know that my profession, what I do, is based on Stanislavsky. It is based on Stanislavsky as his ideas were understood and applied by Tovstonogov who then passed them on to me. Of course, I received Tovstonogov's teachings in my own way, too. I molded them to fit me. But I know that the basis is Stanislavsky, with additions, corrections, and the intrusion of temporal factors that pose new tasks. Changes are inevitably introduced as I understand him in my own way, as I work with new playwrights, new actors, new knowledge that perhaps was as yet inaccessible to Stanislavsky.

I cannot take issue with that monstrous mountain that is called Stanislavsky because it has been ages since I was interested in him. I simply am not interested in how they teach him in schools or how his ideas are applied by directors in theaters. Earlier, maybe twenty years ago, I was painfully aware of the criminally — and I mean criminally — stupid and literal way that Stanislavsky was interpreted. His ideas were taught as were the sayings of Mao Tse Tung or Stalin.

Stanislavsky was a genius. But dogma inevitably followed him. The same thing happened with Christianity. First was the idea and then followed the dogma. It is impossible to make contact with the living Stanislavsky. An enormous amount of fictional, harmful structures have been built up around him. But I cannot take issue with that. To do so, I would have to study the dogmatists, learn their logic, and know what they are doing. I have had no contact with such people for a long time and I have no desire to do so now.

Theater is conflict. Action arises from conflict, antagonism. That was known before Stanislavsky. He included it in his system. As a rule, conflict is understood on the level of verbal strife, as an argument: You say one thing, I say another. But that is a frightfully primitive level of understanding. You can never stage Chekhov on that level. You cannot stage Shakespeare on that level. You cannot stage Molière on that level of conflict. You cannot even stage a decent contemporary writer on that level. In fact, verbal conflict arises when the actors assimilate the text as an element in the art of debate. That is something else altogether.

One of the basic elements of Stanislavsky, as understood by Tovstonogov and taught to me, is that an action expressed in words is not a true action. Under no circumstances can an action be expressed directly in the words. That would be a tautology. That is one of the most basic tenets of theater that Tovstonogov passed on to us through his own understanding of Stanislavsky.

I wonder if any discussion of what we call the Stanislavsky system is bound to fail? Stanislavsky was what he was and, as such, he will continue to have an impact on theater people no matter what. As for the notion of a system — that is, a theatrical system by which one can live and function to achieve good theater — I rather suspect that leads us nowhere. The notion of a system and living theater are probably incompatible.

Well, I cannot agree with that either. On one hand, yes. There must be freedom. But that is not enough. The genius of Stanislavsky's system is that he, as a person who worked with actors, knew the basic elements of nature.

A doctor, for instance, must know the basics of anatomy to heal the human body. He knows that red corpuscles have one function, that the lymph glands do something else, that the nervous system does still another thing. The doctor must know that. The Chinese know that to heal a certain part of the body you must stick a needle into this part of the body. That is a system. Acupuncture does not cancel out other kinds of medicine. But all of the various medicinal systems are based on the similar knowledge that a human consists of bones, nerves, meat, muscles, blood, etc.

Now, commanding that knowledge, you can act one way, say, as an acupuncturist, or you can act another way, say, as a surgeon. And, of course, each of these doctors may have different goals. Moreover, some system of medical healing may be based on the notion that the psyche must be healthy before the body can be healed. Another medicinal system may not take that aspect into account at all. It may assume that a person consists of nothing but bones and meat. This system posits that, since the human soul cannot be located practically, it is unimportant in the healing process. Another system knows that the soul exists and so for it, it is crucial, when the doctor is performing some physical maneuver, to say "Lord have mercy" three times. Upon hearing these words, the soul relaxes and the body becomes susceptible to healing. There are those who believe that and insist it is true.

Nevertheless, even in that system, there is also the physical side. The material side — in other words, what Stanislavsky was talking about — is definitely there. That is why his system is, indeed, a thing of genius and it is applicable at least most of the time if not all of the time. Maybe we do not know how to apply it or we do not apply it at all, but that is a different story.

There used to be a Soviet phrase that I cannot remember verbatim anymore. Something to the effect that "Communism will be victorious because it is true." I would say this about the Stanislavsky system: It is true. You do not have to know it inside and out, but intuitively you will still find yourself working in and around it. Stanislavsky bared the natural laws of theater. We may work with those laws without being conscious of that; he consciously revealed them and worked with them.

Certain tasks fall outside the purview of Stanislavsky's system. Chinese theater, for example, has no need of them. The goal there is entirely different. Stanislavsky is applicable to the psychological theater, or at least a kind of theater that is more or less grounded in psychology.

The theater I make is essentially a psychological theater that includes limited elements of a nonpsychological theater. There are other approaches of psychological theater that allow for the invasion of larger doses of nonpsychological theater and I find this kind of theater extremely interesting. I believe that Stanislavsky is still applicable in these cases.

Even clownery, if it is done on a high level, can fit into the Stanislavsky system. Take Charlie Chaplin. He did not know any system and had no interest in anything of the sort. He would only have been hindered by psychological analysis.

But imagine this: Here comes a clown. He steps on the elongated toe of his own shoe then trips and falls. He looks around to see what made him trip. The ground under his feet is as flat as it can be. He runs his hand over it to make sure there are no obstacles; there are none. He begins walking again and again trips and falls. Again he starts looking around to see what made him fall. He takes a broom and sweeps the area clean. But as soon as he starts walking again, he falls again. Now he sits down and falls into thought, trying to figure out what is going on. He looks his shoes over. His left one is in good shape. His right one is in good shape. The ground is as smooth as it can be.

I have just described to you a typical bit of clownery. But if you think about it, the Stanislavsky system can be applied flawlessly to such a scene. At its basis is the same logic that Stanislavsky worked out. All the parts fit. Belief in the circumstances. That is, my task is to walk across the arena. That is right out of Stanislavsky.

Obstacle. I trip and fall. I have to overcome the obstacle. I must understand why I am falling. Maybe there is too much sand in my shoe. I take it off and bang it a few times.

Of course, there is an additional element here that sets the dramatic actor apart from the clown. That is the clown's childish enthusiasm for play and his artlessness. The clown becomes carried away in a manner that Hamlet probably never could. The clown becomes obsessed with the ground he is walking on or with the shoes in which he is standing. So there is an additional nuance here above and beyond what the dramatic actor exhibits.

But it is only an additional nuance. After all, every genre has its own nuances, whether it is melodrama, vaudeville, tragedy, or drama. Each of those genres has its own degree of verisimilitude and its own conditions for performance. For each, there are various degrees of how far into the material I, as actor, actually go and how much I actually believe in the circumstances.

Chaplin was totally immersed. He cannot for the life of him figure out why he cannot walk past that spot without tripping! It is as flat as can be! Chaplin is capable of pushing this situation to a level of tragedy, so that we, too, will experience his frustration. And at the same time it is pure clownery.

What I am trying to say is that Stanislavsky's system is eternal.

I recently heard you comment on the "pleasant or agreeable" shows that have become so popular of late. You suggested that in another ten years or so these shows would again lose their attraction for the public. But right now they, indeed, are very prevalent. Does this make you feel that you are, again, going against the grain? That you exist in defiance of what is going on around you? Or do you not care about it?

No. That defiance that you mention is not a part of me because I choose it. It is my character. There are people who automatically agree with anything that is said to them. It is not necessarily because they actually agree, but because it is more pleasant for them to be in accordance. Or because they have a great respect for another's opinions. On the other hand, there are people for whom it is easier to exist in a state of — well, I will not say *conflict,* but I will say *defiance.* Only then are these people — and I am one of them — able to find the truth of things. We may be defiant not so much because we do not agree, but because we do not want everything to be so smooth and easy. We want the truth to prick the skin. We want to feel its texture. We do not want it to dissolve in vanilla ice cream.

I do not know why this is true of me. I suspect it has its roots in history and geography, in the complexity of the life I have lived. But it is probably more than that, too. Simply put, that is my character.

On the other hand, what seems to attract modern man the most are the simple things. Getting up in the morning. Taking a bath. Going to work. Good weather? Bad weather. He takes his umbrella. His feet usually get wet in the rain so he takes a different route, one less apt to soak his feet. Details, details, details. All of which are recognizable and verifiable. There is a pleasing comfort in this.

From this point of view people do not differ in their world views or in their biographies, be they tragic or fortunate, but in the way they sit or the way they wear their coat. One person speaks loudly, another quietly, a third has something of a stutter. This is all very human and it appeals to us. It is what gives rise to pleasant, agreeable theater.

As a rule, this is a frame of mind that arises following cataclysmic events. Meyerhold saw himself as a monster in the 1930s. He remained a revolutionary artist who dealt with topics of extreme, revolutionary conditions. Meanwhile, by the 1930s — true or not — it seemed to most people that the cataclysm was over. The revolution and the civil war were events of the past. Famine had ended. Political struggles had ended. Now life had taken over. People were interested in what it was like to ride a tramcar or whether you could go down to the store and buy herring. They were interested in the difference between textures on sofa upholstery.

Life had entered a natural flow, or so it seemed. The simple things attracted: falling in love, meeting friends. What was interesting was what people shared, what made them kind and good.

Nikolai Karamzin, the eighteenth-century sentimentalist, was very popular in his age but he essentially does not exist for us as a writer. That is because he reflected the needs of the day, the need to sense the aroma of the moment. It seems to me that the artist will not last who cannot express deep-seated paradoxes and contradictions even if he captures the flavor of the day. Pasternak defined the nature of his day, but he did so within a cosmic context.

It would seem that Chekhov was an impressionist. But why do you think he did not like the way his plays were performed? Because they played his characters as if they did nothing but drink tea and wear their suits. That is where the "pleasant, agreeable" Chekhov comes from. But he himself did not like that. He did not see himself in that light. We know he was not like that. If he had been, his works would not have survived. Chekhov was the most tragic, the most disturbing, the most avant-garde writer of them all.

For the time being, I — and people like me — will appear as monsters. We will look very old-fashioned. Meyerhold looked old-fashioned. Terribly so. Spectators did not need what he was doing. Even those talented, intelligent spectators who truly loved theater. These spectators could not understand what Meyerhold was struggling so hard for. That just did not interest them then. That is not what they wanted; it was not what they lived by.

And yet, Meyerhold remains Meyerhold while we somehow do not remember all those other wonderful, talented, busy directors who worked around him.

5

The Pathology of
the Actor

The essence of the pathology of the actor is that his nature contains a paradox.

The actor constantly wishes to exist publicly. An actor cannot exist without a public persona. Without a public you have no actor. This quality usually becomes evident in childhood — the child is always goofing off and attracting attention and the teacher does not know what to do with him. I was like that. What do you do with a kid like that? The teacher seems to realize that the child is not bad. Perhaps he is even a capable or smart student. But as soon as the teacher comes in and the pupils are in attendance, this child will leap at the slightest excuse to show off. It is not important what he does; all he cares about is demonstrating the fact that he exists, that he is different from everyone else.

A craving for public attention is a characteristic of the actor's nature. I would even call it the pathological craving for attention, because it is unnatural for a normal person. A normal person strives to remain hidden and out of the spotlight. That is why we are "brought up" as young people; it is why we are taught how to conceal our emotions, our fears, our joys, our love, our hatreds, our furies or happinesses, our tendernesses. We have all been formed and disciplined. That is done to cloak what we have in us, to disguise our animal nature, our complexes, our stupidities, our ugliness, our lack of education, etc.

Is an actor, then, a criminal of sorts, a transgressor? By that I mean is he someone who violates the rules?

Yes and no. He has an unnatural craving. It is an anomaly, this craving for public attention. But in everything else he is a normal person.

On one hand he is a person. On the other, he is liable at any moment to jump up and start clowning around, attracting attention. Then he might suddenly withdraw, thinking he was mistaken in his timing — perhaps this is not the place for that kind of behavior. Everybody looks at him as if he were a total fool. Or, consider another situation: People have gathered to party and have fun and suddenly one person leaps up and starts yelling, "We can't go on living like this! There is war in Chechnya!" Everybody is embarrassed. They know there is a war going on. But this is not the place for political demonstrations.

As a rule, an actor lives like that constantly. He has a desire to undress publicly, to strip down naked before people. At the same time he is not sure about himself at all; maybe his or her sexual attributes are not so attractive. Or, he thought his voice sounded quite attractive as he told a witty joke, but it turns out that everyone thinks he has an unpleasant, squeaky voice.

This is the conflict that exists within the actor. That is what it is all about. In essence, the actor constantly wants to walk around naked. In fact, he does. And that makes him extremely vulnerable.

When a normal person walks by we know nothing about him. Maybe he has crooked legs, but he has covered that up with a nice suit. Nobody sees whether he is very witty or quite stupid, for he interacts with people using all the accepted clichés. Sure, you can tell he is not a great wit or is not terribly intelligent, but it is all within the boundaries of the norm. Nobody will call him a moron because he does not reveal enough of himself to evoke such a response. The actor does. Therefore he is defenseless. And this combination of his defenselessness and his constant need to jump into the fire creates what I would call a tragicomic situation. That is the actor's pathology.

The actor bears in his soul an enormous number of wounds. These wounds are inflicted on him by everyone. Take the audience. When the actor was rehearsing, there was one line that was intended to arouse laughter. During the performance the actor speaks his line but the audience does not laugh. Do you realize what an effect that has?

Let us say the play stipulates that a young beauty is supposed to make her entrance. During the preceding scene, as it was always done in old-fashioned plays, all the other characters were talking about her beauty: "Oh, what a beauty! Oh, what a beauty!" Out comes the actress, not very young and, by the standards of most in the auditorium, not pretty at all. No matter how much she paints her eyes or how low her décolletage, there is no way to make her a beauty. It is impossible for the actress not to feel this discrepancy. Then, of course, it is up to her to do something about it.

Let us say an actress bursts out on stage and flings herself against the wall, wails in agony — she is playing Medea to the hilt. Everybody in the auditorium is expected to weep and wail with her. But she hears, as do many in the audience, that no one is weeping. Nor are they even paying much attention. They are just sitting coldly, waiting for her hysterics to end. Finally, some members of the audience become restless while others might even mutter, "My God, she's loud!"

If it is a Russian troupe traveling in the West, you might hear a reaction like: "Oh, Lord. That Russian acting! Shrieks and tears and emotions! Can't they control themselves any better? My, but aren't they savages?"

The actor senses it instantly when the spectators are repulsed by what they see. That is traumatic for the actor. He or she, when resolving to become an actor, dreamed of the day when his or her portrait would be on the covers of magazines. In fact, the actor is lucky to be named in a list when some little newspaper writes that a show's episodes and mass scenes were played well. There is your big moment.

I well remember wanting to become an actor. I used to dream of what it would be like to see my name on a poster or in a newspaper. I thought that must really be extraordinary. When I was still studying to be an actor, before I dropped out in the third year, I performed in our student productions. As a result, my name occasionally cropped up in print and that was a big event for me.

When I entered the institute to study directing, I asked one of my teachers, "What do you feel when you see your name in print?" I was older then, of course, and I asked the question with a healthy dose of irony. But still, my curiosity was sincere. Naturally, my teacher made fun of me and quoted a line from Chekhov, from *The Seagull*. Nina asks Trigorin what he feels when he sees his name in print and he says, "When they criticize you, it's unpleasant and you forget about it right away. When they praise you, it's quite agreeable."

My point is that everybody has this inclination. It even affected Chekhov. He did not just dream that up. That is something he took from inside himself. This craving is especially strong in actors.

Wounds are inflicted on actors constantly. Many are inflicted by the director. You can start with the most basic one — the director passing an actor over for a role the actor knows he can play. Then there is the case of the actor getting a role which he perceives as an insult. He knows he is Hamlet and King Lear wrapped in one. So what if he is young? All he must do to play Lear is glue on a beard. As for Hamlet, all he needs are the black tights because he has that heavy brow and the pale complexion. People have been telling him that for his whole life — every time he would put on a black sweater, all his friends would say, "You're the spitting image of Hamlet!" When he was fourteen, he even used to walk up and down the tree-lined boulevard reciting under his breath, "To be or not to be." And tears would come to his eyes. "What a pity!" he now thinks, "that no one was there to see it! Damn, I used to do that well!" True, every time he tried doing it aloud, it never came out quite right.

So, this poor actor never gets cast as Hamlet. And when he does get a role, it is always something insulting. He must stand there holding a halberd, or play insects or rabbits in matinees for kids. Even then he is not chosen to play the main rabbit; he is just one in the litter, the fourth one down the line.

This is horrible! But it gets worse yet. Because even when the actor is finally cast in the role of the fourth rabbit, he becomes quite agitated and he thinks, "This time, I'll show them!" He is all aflutter as he goes over in his mind how he will come in and say his only line. But then it turns out that he is going to be playing the part in turns with another actor and the director always has the other actor do the rehearsing. Still, our intrepid actor knows how he is going to do it when he gets the chance. And, finally, the day comes when he gets to speak his line.

But the director was busy doing something else at that very moment and he never even heard him.

The actor is crushed. He immediately sensed that the director was paying no attention to him. He begins thinking that the director has merely taken pity on him by casting him as the second-string actor of the fourth rabbit.

Or, maybe the scene played out differently, which is no better, believe me. Picture this: The director grumbles, "You've only got three words. Can't you do it any better than that? I explained the whole thing and you heard what I said. You've been sitting here for a week while I was telling the other actor how to do it."

That is something an insensitive director might say.

Another scenario is that of the gentle, cultured director who spends a great deal of time courting and flattering his actor, explaining what everything means and how it is supposed to be done. He thoroughly clarifies the context for the fourth rabbit's three words and, finally, the actor gets his chance to say his line. But he sees there is no optimism on the director's face. This director is a great educator, so he is patient and he says, "That's all right. That's all right. Let's do it again." That is all very kind of him, but the actor knows the director is unhappy with what he has done. He knows that.

But, do you know what? It gets worse still. Imagine the following scenario. The actor knows he is Hamlet. He is King Lear. But they just gave him these three measly words. And he said his three words and the director said, "Wonderful!" The actor is in ecstasy! He dances out onto the street, thinking, "What a spectacular day!" He does not even notice the city is shrouded in fog. He is in a great mood. And he loves everybody because everybody is good. What is the cause of this bliss? Somebody said "good job" when he said three measly words as the fourth rabbit.

Now, this actor is no idiot. He understands perfectly well the bogus reason for his ecstasy. So, by the time evening rolls around, his mood has been ruined entirely. He realizes to what depths he has sunk. What is there for him to be happy about?! This director is an imbecile. Everybody says so. The actor knows he's an imbecile, too. He's seen proof. They won't give this director anything to stage except kids' matinees. And when they do, they give him the worst play available. And the worst actors. And he's right there in the middle of them! The worst of them all.

Do you begin to feel what the actor feels? I made that story up, but I did not make up a thing. That is the psychology of the actor; that is his logic.

It is a situation that stimulates the imagination and the impulse to fantasize, for better and for worse. It gives rise to the actor's belief in his greatness. He heard the director say he spoke his three rabbit words well. In his mind, that means the next step is playing Hamlet.

Now, the more talented an actor is, the more strange and complex is his nature. And for this talented and uncommon actor, even a modicum of success is based on an enormous number of coincidences. First of all, the director must have a feel for this actor's peculiarities. Next, there must be a play that is right for him. Next, the backroom politics of the theater must be in his favor — there must be someone who understands this young actor should get the big part instead of the theater's experienced leading man who always gets the good roles. Of course, a director always prefers working with experienced actors. So, there must be a confluence of an enormous number of factors.

Actors are always accusing directors of being bossy ingrates throwing their weight around. There is probably something to that. But, believe me, that is not the determining factor in a director's behavior. Some directors may indulge. It is the same with money. Some people use their money to good purposes, others to bad. By the same token, some directors may abuse power. But it does not have to be like that.

That is not so uncommon in Russian theater. Russian directors permit themselves to insult their actors.

They do. That is true. That is one of the methods of influencing an actor in Russian theater.

But when I raise the topic of the pathology of the actor, I am talking about paradoxes. I do not refer merely to an actor's vulnerability as a pathology, but to the actor's nature on the whole. Vulnerability is only one aspect of that pathology. The actor's pathology is so paradoxical that you sometimes cannot understand why an actor feels pain. You did nothing to hurt him. But he feels pain.

Let me tell you, for example, of an incident that occurred when I was rehearsing *Hedda Gabler* with Sergei Yursky. He was an actor I had worshipped from the time I lived in Leningrad. He was one of my favorite actors and one of my favorite people. He was absolutely like no one else, especially at that time. He was completely unique in every sense of the word. He was not only a talented actor, but also a man of great intellectual powers with a deep understanding of poetry and prose. He was extremely personable. He had a great sense of humor. He was energetic. He was a man of impeccable honesty. I was very proud of the fact that we were acquaintances — if not friends — even back in the Leningrad days when he was already a great actor and I was still a nobody.

When I had the opportunity to cast him in one of my Moscow shows, I did so. I asked him to play Tessman in *Hedda Gabler* and he rehearsed brilliantly. As with any actor, he had his problems and I had my problems with him. In other words, everything was just as it should have been. But at times he was simply brilliant in rehearsals. And there was one instance when he was working so beautifully, so subtly, that I leaped up and shouted, "Brilliant! Stunning! Genius!" I was so excited by how great it was that I just could not contain myself.

Yursky stopped the rehearsal. He said, "Kama, you should be ashamed of yourself!"

I was amazed. Yursky is no poser. He is not one to do something like that for effect. I realized he very sincerely had been wounded by something. But I could not figure out what. It was only later, when carefully going back over that moment, that I understood what had happened. My outburst had made him feel like a trained monkey. It was as though I were a trainer saying to his monkey, "Good boy! Good boy!" Do you see what I mean? I thought I was praising him. It was as if, for an instant, I had ceased to be a director and had become a simple spectator. But my outburst had the opposite effect from what I would have expected. It insulted him.

There you have one of the actor's complexes. In the professional actor, human complexes become intertwined with professional complexes. This is because in the director-actor dichotomy the director is a male and the actor is a female. But, on a personal level, the male actor is often inclined to balk at that, he wants to assert that he is *not* a female. In the case of Yursky, it was as though he was objecting, "Why are you sprinkling me with cheap compliments?" But, in fact, he needs those compliments. There is an internal contradiction here.

I suspect that for the Western reader we need to start from the beginning. Otherwise, what I am saying may not be clear. The Western person considers himself — and may, in fact, be — a free, independent person. When the boss praises him, he thinks nothing of it. He assumes the praise is because he has done something well. He does not take it as a comment on his personal self. It does not concern his individuality; it concerns his work. In this lies a colossal difference between the Russian or Soviet person and the Western person. And to understand that, we must back up and take a social and historical digression.

Human relationships in the East, including the Far East and the Near East, are more hierarchical. This concerns the Eastern notion of power; that is, the tsar's power originating at the top and trickling down to everyone else. The same is true of the Orthodox Church. These are hierarchies and they are founded on the personality of the one holding power.

The East encompasses countries with a slave mentality. Relationships here are structured on those of master and slave. They are not just the relationships of people occupying different rungs on the social ladder. Russia was a country of slaves and we have remained so. Both genetically and by upbringing, we have the psychology of slaves.

Europe originated as a collection of feudal states. The king lorded over his vassals, counts, barons, etc. Beneath them were less significant noblemen and beneath them all were the peasants. These peasants belonged to the count or the baron or whatever. They were his property. But now comes a fascinating nuance. The interrelationship of responsibilities was very complex. It was not so simple as the peasant being obligated to the baron, the baron to the count, and the count to the king. No. The king was as obligated to the baron as the baron was to the king. Their responsibilities were different, but both were obligated to one another. The baron was bound to come with his warriors and peasants to defend the king. But the king was also bound to defend the baron's land if someone attacked it. What is bad for the baron is bad for the king. They have mutual responsibilities before each other.

In a similar fashion, the peasant must pay a tithe to his baron. He must serve in the baron's army to defend his lands or those of the kingdom. But if one baron strikes the peasant of another, the master of the offended peasant is bound to defend him. Those were the basic structures on which Europe developed.

In Russia it was different. Russia was a genuine slave state. There were no rights, no mutual responsibilities. It was a despotic autocracy. The nobleman did not take a set tribute from his peasant; he took whatever he wanted whenever he wanted it. Perhaps he took everything. There was no reason for the peasant to work.

How do you think the bourgeoisie arose in the West? Because the peasant understood that the more he produced, the more would be left to him. There was an advantage to his working hard.

The West is more rationally constructed. Dostoevsky, of course, vilified that rationalism, but that is another topic. The West is a milieu in which a rational mode of thinking was developed. A man sits down and asks himself, what is advantageous to me? He knows that he may be someone's peasant, but he is not a slave. He may be a servant, but he is not a slave. He is a free person.

That has never been the case in Russia.

Consider the Decembrist revolt in 1825. In Soviet times the interpretation was that the Decembrists had struggled for the freedom of the serfs. But that is not true; the Decembrists did not struggle for the freedom of the serfs. They merely struggled for freedom.

Do you understand the difference? The Decembrists were not free in relation to the serf just as the serf was not free in relation to them. They were not free in relation to the tsar just as he was not free in relation to them. There was an all-pervasive lack of freedom. That, in part, was one of the questions I wanted to raise in my production *The Execution of the Decembrists.*

In my production, the tsar *does not want* to hang the Decembrists.

He does not want to. He cannot bring himself to do it. But his hands are tied, he is dependent. The question is, on whom or on what is he dependent? Well, he is dependent on everything around him. It is a case of mutual dependency. Mutual slavery. The man at the top of the heap is just another slave. He is a different kind of slave, of course. He has palaces and power. But he is still a slave.

So, you see what a long, historical road we have taken. But there is no other way to explain the Russian, the Soviet person who is constantly struggling for his freedom. He conducts that struggle everywhere, at all times and in the most inappropriate circumstances.

Years ago I had an acquaintance, a woman from Germany. As a journalist, she had a car. I, naturally, did not. One time when I got into her car, she put on her seat belt but I did not put mine on. She said, "Buckle up." I said, "Why?" She complained, "Savages! You'll kill yourself! You Russians are barbarians!" Now, I don't even remember whether I buckled up or not. Maybe I did and maybe I did not.

Just a few months after that incident, I made my first trip to Finland. The first time I got into a car I did not bother to buckle up because I did not have the habit. The actor who was giving me a ride asked me to buckle up and I did. I did it as a sign of respect to him. That is what they do in Finland, so that is what I did. I spent a month there in Helsinki and I spent a lot of time in cars. Naturally, I always buckled my seat belt. At one point, I came back for a three- or four-day break in Moscow. I flagged down a car to give me a ride, as is common in Moscow, and the first thing I did when I got in was to buckle my seat belt. But the driver said proudly, "You don't have to do that." I said, "What do you mean?" He said, "In *my* car you don't have to do that!"

Do you hear the subtext in that phrase: "In *my* car you don't have to do that!"?

You see, this driver perceived the domain of his automobile as existing outside the influence of the authorities. He perceived his car as an autonomous fiefdom, one that is not subject to anyone else's laws, no matter who they are.

Bound up in this is the typical relationship of the Russian toward representatives of authority. The police are not a force that might protect him or serve him. The Russian has no need of a policeman. What is a policeman to him? You Americans are the ones who have need of policemen. Do you need policemen in America?

Yes.

Of course you do. Everybody needs policemen. They serve and protect. In Russia, we have no need of policemen. We do just fine without them. A policeman in Russia is merely an authority figure who uses us. We almost never gain anything from a policeman's work. He does not protect us. He cannot catch criminals and murderers. He does not do any of that. He just uses us for his own purposes.

That is why the driver of the car that picked me up perceived seatbelt regulations as something he could ignore — because those regulations were written by the authorities whom he does not consider himself bound to obey. He may have to reckon with them at times, but in his own car he is a free man. In his car, he is a rebel, a revolutionary. He is a freedom fighter. That is what my driver was when he indicated I did not have to buckle my seat belt. You see, this is the only place he can fight for his freedom. It is an act of defiance against the powers that be. It does not matter that he may die in a car crash as a result.

The Russian is constantly struggling for his freedom.

Many of the Russian's strange qualities — his swagger, his fecklessness, his recklessness, his drunkenness, his pointless aggression — are all various manners of his struggling for freedom.

With that understood, we can return to a discussion of Russian and Western actors. When I was staging my first show in Finland — *The Theater of the Watchman Nikita,* based on Chekhov's novella *Ward No. 6* — I had good, mediocre, and bad actors. One or two in the group were entirely worthless.

Now, I am always nervous before beginning a show, but this time was special because it was my first production abroad. It was the first time I had worked in unusual conditions with actors who spoke another language. My nervousness manifested itself in a way that was unusual for me. I restrained myself, seldom allowing myself to raise my voice. I worked on, keeping my temper under wraps. However, as the opener approached, I could not contain myself any longer. One actor in the cast was particularly weak and he was performing a crucial part. A couple of times I lost control and permitted myself to yell. I yelled in Russian, of course, and I suspect my translator translated me delicately, but there could have been no mistaking about what and at whom I was shouting.

This actor might have been a bad actor, but he was no fool. He was not in the least offended. Not at all. He listened to me attentively and then went on doing the very thing I had been trying to get him to avoid. After a while, he began doing it a little better and, in the end, he did it as well as he was able.

As a rule, when an actor plays badly, I do not get angry. That is absolutely pointless. But when he fails to carry out elementary directions, that is another thing. There are two basic reasons why an actor might not carry out instructions: one, he might be nervous, or two, he might just be a bad actor. As the saying goes, pants keep a bad actor from walking. Pants do not bother him in his off-hours, but as soon as he sets foot on the stage, he cannot walk normally.

But my yelling at the Finnish actor had not the slightest effect on him. It did not irritate him, insult him, or freeze him up. It was as though I was shouting into a vacuum. I was amazed. Later I figured it out. He did not perceive me as his boss, as a superior on whom his future depended. His attitude was this: I was the director. That is, the person who directs the play. He is an actor who plays in the play. If I resort to yelling, his feeling is that I was either badly brought up or I just have that flaw in my character. Or maybe I am not entirely healthy.

But the main thing was that he recognized my sovereign right to behave as I wish. My behavior was not something connected with him. The actor may have thought my behavior was strange, and he may have thought my face was not very attractive when I behaved like that — when I shouted and spittle flew and I waved my arms and stomped my feet — but none of that had anything to do with him. I would actually say my behavior aroused in him a certain sympathy for me. It was as if he were thinking, "Well, unfortunately, this man is incapable of behaving any other way."

It simply could not have occurred to this actor to be personally offended by my behavior. How could I insult him? He was independent and I was independent. Two individuals who came together as a result of their jobs. The director was doing what he could and the actor was doing everything he was capable of.

This attitude is diametrically opposed to that which exists between a director and an actor in Russia. In Russia, an actor's entire fate depends upon his boss. I do not only mean his financial well-being. I mean his fate as a creative artist — his career — even his sense of well-being on a personal level. The director is the boss. A good director, of course, is not going to abuse his position of power. Frankly, I do not believe I have ever abused it. It is another matter that the tone of my discourse in Russia differs from that which I use in rehearsals in the West. I know that. But I do not think I abuse this power. I am sure talented directors do not.

Figuratively, the Soviet actor says, "I refuse to put on that seat belt!" And I say to him, "But you'll be crushed to death!" But, still, he says, "No!"

I tell him that on a certain cue he must sit down. He immediately objects: "Why should I sit down?" I explain to him that it will look better that way, and that this action will help him play this scene better. Maybe this action is also crucial to my interpretation of the play, although I will not go into that with him. Still, the actor bucks me. "Why should I do that?!" he wants to know.

You see, he suspects me of using him as a trained monkey.

The actor's condition is always one of opposition — the actor versus the director; the actor versus the audience. His fate depends on them!

When I was still studying to become a director, I had my first practical professional experience at the Lesya Ukrainka Theater in Kiev. As it turned out, the show I was sent to stage never came to fruition. But, in fact, I was not just sent there to direct a show; I had been sent there to "rescue" the theater. My teacher Tovstonogov actually sent me there to revive one of the best Soviet provincial theaters that had fallen on bad times.

Obviously, the word *rescue* must be written in quotes. Naturally, no one anywhere in that theater gave me the opportunity to rescue anything and, indeed, I rescued nothing. I was just a kid, really. And I looked even younger than I was. I had a beard, but it was not coming in very well. I was up against famous, old-time actors loaded down with awards, honors, and titles. The types of roles they usually played were Soviet generals or benevolent Communist Party leaders, so they had been inundated with laurels. Many of these actors were very good; some of them were even great.

You should have seen how they greeted me when passing me in a corridor. They would greet me with all the pomp that they would any distinguished superior. I repeat, I was still a student, very young. I slept on a chair in one of the dressing rooms. But I knew perfectly well why they were so respectful to me — it was because I was The Director. I was nobody yet. I officially had not yet been given the job of chief director, and I had not yet even graduated from the institute. I was a nobody. But they knew I was the person on whom their future might depend. That is, they knew they had to behave in a very specific way with me.

It was a terrible sensation, believe me. To this day, I remain skeptical of compliments from actors and of their expressions of gratitude. That is, I tend to believe them, but at the same time I know the impulse behind their kind words. Maybe their deferential behavior comes from subconscious impulses. But the fact remains that they are dependent. They are dependent on me, ingrate that I am. It is terrible. It is a very unpleasant sensation. A director cannot enter into a normal relationship with actors.

Despite what I have said about how Westerners differ from Russians, actors still are actors. I was amazed when I worked in Helsinki with Asko Sarkola, one of the top Scandinavian actors. He had played all kinds of different roles, including Hamlet, and was an excellent comic actor. For fifteen years he had been the managing director of the theater in which he worked. He was in the prime of his life, in his forties. He was very popular. And, while he probably could not be considered especially handsome, he enjoyed great success with women. In other words, he had everything you would expect of a genuinely big actor.

Nevertheless.

We rehearse. Asko is an excellent actor. He picks things up

immediately and does them. When an actor picks things up and does them right away, you naturally begin suggesting new ideas. Asko was able to incorporate them into his acting, too. That is the moment when you realize you can do much more than you originally had thought. So I suggested another new idea, but this one was more difficult to perform. I made my comments and he tried again, but it still did not work. I explained it to him, but still we could not get anywhere. I explained it again and I began to notice he was growing angry. That was followed by a tantrum the likes of which I would expect to see only in a provincial Soviet theater. I worked in a lot of provincial Soviet theaters and I know what I am talking about. He objected that I did not tell him what I wanted. Well, of course, I did tell him what I wanted. Then he protested, "Why are you constantly changing what you want of me? First you want one thing and then you want another." That was just the kind of primitive self-defense I was used to hearing from actors in a Russian provincial theater.

Why do you think he became so defensive? He is a star. He is the theater's managing director. He is surrounded by his actors. He did not want to be criticized in front of his employees.

In the West a good actor is considered someone who does what you want right away — not the actor who does it fully, deeply, and well, but the one who does it immediately. The director gives his direction, the actor performs the task. You do not waste any time on him. He is an expensive actor. He is paid well for the fact that he works quickly. The bad actor is the one that you waste a lot of time on. So he is cheaper.

The Russian perception is different. We do not really care if you do it quickly. If you do, that is fine. But that is not the goal. What is important is if, in time, you can do better and then do still better than that. In the Russian theater you want an actor who, performing well, can take you off in directions you did not expect to go. That makes you change your conception and that is good, because the part is becoming more interesting. The actor knows that.

By Western standards, a good actor does what you want the first time you suggest it. The mediocre actor does it the second time. The bad one does it the third time. And here is Asko and he was not able to do what I asked even on the third try. This was a blow to his authority.

What is this? This is the pathology of the actor.

There is a videotape of you and Asko Sarkola discussing the text for *Life Is Beautiful* before rehearsals began. You are arguing to cut some lines and he is arguing to leave them in. My impression is that the discussion really was not about the text, but about power and image. I suspect it was important for Asko to let you know he is an intelligent person, that he knew the text well, that he understood Chekhov, and that he would not just be your puppet in this upcoming production.

Yes. That is interesting. He, indeed, is an intelligent person. A talented person. He has a feel for things. As an actor he is capable of playing a character who is better and better educated than he.

You read that scene right. His action was prompted by his desire to prove he had the right to his own opinion. He engaged in that discussion knowing full well that he would end up playing what I wanted him to.

The fact of the matter is that, as director, my job is not to cut the wood but to direct others so that they cut the wood. In Russia, you have constant problems with that. The director-actor relationship is not a professional one; it is a personal one because it is very difficult for a Russian to admit that someone else is in control. The Western attitude is simpler. One person commands, others obey. It is not a personal relationship. Nevertheless, Asko, in the incident you describe, was intent on making sure that I knew that he, too, had an opinion on this matter.

There are some interesting interview clips in a Finnish television show about the preparations for *Life Is Beautiful*. Some of Asko's responses are very revealing. He said something to the effect of, "Kama is a good director, but he does not understand that an actor must preserve himself. And the actor must maintain distance, otherwise he cannot preserve himself." I have worked my whole life with actors and I must admit that I do not understand what he means by having to "preserve himself." But it is obvious that it is something very important to him.

My method, the Russian method, is that I invade the space of the actor and the person himself. Asko, being a very accomplished actor, did not allow me to do that. His task was to defend himself.

There you have a paradox, of course, because Asko simultaneously made himself vulnerable to you even as he defended himself. I say that because he clearly did open up to you. He performed brilliantly for you in several shows.

Yes. He did open up. That is the nature of the actor: to open up. What we had to find was a balance.

In the school of Russian acting, that balance is almost completely lacking. That is why Russian theater and Russian actors are so revered. Western audiences sense that the Russian actor does not shield himself. Sometimes it becomes too much for them and they complain of excess — "Oh, those Russians are always shouting and crying." But that is a matter of taste, of the director, the actor and the spectator. Nonetheless, the West loves Russian actors and Russian theater. Russian actors do not safeguard their personal independence. They give themselves up — to me, the director, to their audience. Western audiences are impressed by the way the Russian actor is willing to bleed. They, the members of the audience, would not do that. Their actors, for the most part, do not do that. But these Russians, they will. And that amazes Western spectators.

They do not think about it that explicitly, of course. It comes to them as a vague sensation. But, still, it has a concrete effect on them because they clearly sense the difference between something being done no-holds-barred and something being done within accepted bounds.

Western actors are more secure in all ways — socially and personally. And, as I have just described, the Western theater tradition differs from that of Russia. The Western method is more heavily based in technique. It has less spontaneity, less personal involvement.

I do not know American theater all that well, but, as I understand it, the best American theater is based on the Russian school. The basic attitude there is that you should do it as the Russians do. That is why the great American actors — true, I mean film actors here and not theater actors — almost do not differ from Russian actors in that they leave themselves wide open to spontaneous behavior. They strip themselves of shields and protective devices.

Marlon Brando, in a biography by Peter Manso, appears as an extremely difficult person, rude, unpredictable, the whole works. The only place Brando was able to find some semblance of order in his life was in his work. And, if Manso is to be believed as I suspect generally he is, Brando, at his best, was merciless to himself and to others when on the stage or before the camera. Much of what you have said about the Russian actor could be applied to Brando.

Perhaps. Jack Nicholson, for instance, I know absolutely nothing about. But I am certain that he is, by nature, a Russian-style actor. But, I want to return to our discussion of the actor — vulnerability, that is, openness and defenselessness which lead to vulnerability.

I have told a few rather simplistic stories about actors. But, in fact, the actor is extremely defenseless and naked. The better the actor is, the more defenseless and naked he is. All you need to throw an actor off is to look at him askance. Let us say he walks into the room and he thinks the director gave him a strange look. Or maybe another actor glanced at him in a way he did not expect. Or let us say the actor tells a joke. Everyone laughs, but he has the feeling they did not quite laugh as he wanted them to. Either they laughed too politely or they did not laugh quite enough.

Actors go through terrible things. Let us say an actor has become accustomed to his fellow actors and to his director. He walks out on the rehearsal stage where the prototype of the future set is in place. Now, out come the lighting man, the sound man, and the props man. The props man leaves, but the lighting and sound men stay — they have to push the buttons to keep the rehearsal moving. The rehearsal begins. The lighting man waits until he has to turn a spotlight; the sound man sits and waits to push a knob. These are the actor's first spectators.

The actor, if he is experienced, is aware of this consciously. If he is inexperienced, he still senses it intuitively. Now, as the actor performs, the sound man leans back in his chair and rustles the pages in a book he is reading to see how many are left.

That's it. Catastrophe. The actor is destroyed. Believe me, that is enough to keep an actor from ever performing this scene as he should.

Put yourself in the actor's place. The actor is sure this is an important scene. He has been doing it well. The director has been happy with him. He believes a rapport has arisen with the other actors. And now, the very first time someone from the outside has entered the rehearsal process, the actor was unable to grab his attention. This spectator was not interested in what the actor was doing.

This is a terrifying moment. Very terrifying.

Imagine it. The actor comes out on stage, walks over to the other side and already, the sound man is blankly staring off into the distance or falling asleep.

This is a moment of truth. The sound man does not know anything about this show yet. It is not like later when he will know everything inside and out, and he can be forgiven for not paying attention. At this moment he knows nothing and yet the actor still was not able to arouse his interest.

And that is the truth. If the sound man pays no attention, that means the actor and the director and everyone else who created this scene, were insufficiently stimulating. That is why, at this crucial moment, I always keep an eye on the sound man and the lighting man, as well as the props man who is standing by waiting to hand an actor something. I want to know if we have earned their attention.

It is a tormenting moment. The actor is terribly defenseless. That is why he is forced to be defensive. That is the source of many of his strange, awkward behavioral traits. The actor will often behave illogically. It is often said of actors that they are spoiled and obstinate. You mention Brando. I know nothing about him. But, knowing what I do about other actors, I can imagine that is true.

Where does this difficult personality come from? First of all, a genuinely talented actor is a very sensitive emotional instrument. He is able to crank up to full emotional speed in a split second. That means he can be set off by something extremely insignificant. It may be enough that, while the actor is working, someone in the room picked something up to read. He did not even do anything. Moreover, when he picked up his reading material, he did it very quietly, very carefully, so as not to bother anyone. Nobody even heard him. It is not his job to watch every second of the rehearsal, so he is not shirking his responsibilities. But the result of his action may be that the actor will instantly begin yelling at his partner. Or he might break off in mid-scene and explode at the director: "I don't know what you want from me here! I don't know what to do! I don't know how to play it!" Or he might shout, "I can't work in these pants!"

Pants. What do pants have to do with it? He has been rehearsing in these pants all week long without any problems at all. Anyway, these are not the pants he will wear when the show opens. It is just a rehearsal costume. New pants will be made for him before opening night. But there you are, right in the middle of a huge scandal, all blown out of proportion. The actor is furious with the props man, with the other actors, with his pants, and with the director.

He might even lash out at the lighting man who picked up the book, but the chances are less likely he will do that. It is all because he is so defenseless. Because he was destroyed in that instant when the lighting man picked up his book. He was destroyed utterly.

I want to insert a phrase of yours that I picked up from an interview you gave in the past: "The inadmissible openness of the deranged; that is what the actor should have."

Well, I made that comment not about all actors in general. When I said that, I had in mind *K. I. from "Crime"* and, to a lesser extent, *The Black Monk*. It does not apply to my other shows. That is true of Katerina Ivanovna in *K. I. from "Crime."* That role requires of the actress an unnatural openness. I say unnatural because I moved her out from behind the safety of the fourth wall. In my shows *The Execution of the Decembrists* and, in part, *Pushkin. Duel. Death,* there is a certain measure of audience participation, but only a certain measure. In *K. I. from "Crime,"* the spectators are the actress's partners. And the show is designed to evoke a sense of horror in the spectator when his own personal space has been invaded. I want the spectator in that show to recoil as we do when we are approached on the street by someone who is mentally disturbed.

Katerina Ivanovna (Oksana Mysina) engages a spectator in *K. I. from "Crime,"* a dramatization of segments of Dostoevsky's *Crime and Punishment;* Moscow, 1994. *Photo by Ken Reynolds.*

Therefore, do not confuse my comment with a description of actors in general. There are plenty of roles in my shows that are not "inadmissibly open." And I use various closed styles that do not fall under that description. For example, in Ibsen or Chekhov. Chekhov's characters are sufficiently closed. They are ironic. But that is something else.

Of course a good actor differs from a bad one in that he is capable of opening up instantaneously, in a way that, shall we say, is inadmissible in polite society or everyday life.

It is necessary here to bring up another kind of actor. This is the actor who never opens up. This is the one who is always playing the fool, putting up masks, hiding behind different voices that are not his own. We call them character actors or eccentric actors. They play different people and never, but never, take down their defenses. They will never perform as themselves. If they happen to get a part in which they must play someone similar to themselves, they will do it terribly. They are not capable of it.

All of this clowning is this kind of actor's method for refusing to make himself vulnerable. You will never get him to open up even a little. Try to get him to say something in his natural voice — you cannot; he will not do it. Instead, he will start cutting up and goofing off. He will paint his face with makeup and dream up a wild costume. And he will be fabulous. He will lisp or make up a guttural voice. He will start limping.

What is that? That is the opposite side of the coin. This actor is terrified of letting down his defenses. And when he throws up his defenses, he is brilliant! Craving public attention and fearing it simultaneously, he will begin to parody his own inadequacies. If he is overweight, he will parody his figure. He will include that in his act as if, by doing so, he is concealing it. Charlie Chaplin, being small and thin as the wind, trips and falls, trips and falls, trips and falls, as if he has no more substance than a rag or a piece of paper. He jumps up and spins his cane as if to say, "Look how clever I am!" and then he falls again and again gets back up. Of course, Chaplin's genius consisted of the fact that he also had the ability of suddenly opening up.

That, in my opinion, is the mark of the great contemporary actors: the ability to cut up like a born fool, playing on that device of self-defense, and then, suddenly — boom! — the complete stripping of defenses. Chaplin, of course, would split himself wide open. He would show you that there is nothing else left to show. That ability to walk the tightrope, that is the ultimate in acting.

I often create parts with this in mind. *K. I. from "Crime"* is representative of this. The character bounces back and forth between self-defensive clowning and complete vulnerability. And the actress must do that too. She might jump up and down like a monkey, suddenly lie down on the floor, or start harassing a spectator. But none of that is worth a thing if the actress does not immediately turn around and rip herself open to a degree that should actually alarm the spectator — because we know that only a child or one who is mentally unbalanced is capable of behaving like that.

If the actress opens up only to a degree, then it is all for naught. I cannot say whether I did this consciously or not when we rehearsed. You do a lot unconsciously in rehearsals. Which is to say, you simply do what comes naturally.

I have talked about the Russian-Soviet school that preaches the opening up of the actor. And we have talked about the Western approach, where Asko Sarkola says that he must defend himself against the director invading his psychological space. When Sarkola says he must defend himself from me, I do not know what he means. He may mean he does not want me reaching his personal core. I do not mean in the sense of interfering in his personal affairs. I never do that. I often know certain things about my actors, but I never touch that. That is wrong.

In bad examples of the Russian tradition, you do find directors abusing their knowledge of actors' lives. Such as, "Now, remember what it was like when your husband left you." Or, "Remember how you felt when your mother died." That is horrible, completely wrong. In fact, that approach will not provide any useful response. It is cheap speculation.

What the director needs to do, even if he does know some biographical facts about an actor, is to work in circles around what he is trying to achieve. The point is not to get the actor telling stories from his past, but to engage his associative memory in the back of his consciousness. What you want is an echo, a rhyme of some sort. You want the actor's emotional memory to awaken. I do not mean his memory in the sense of his remembering specific incidents, I mean his emotional baggage, his ability to plug into his feelings. In fact, he may consciously remember nothing at all, but you get him to tap into it in the back of his consciousness. That, and nothing else, is the goal.

My task as a director is constantly to make the actor aware of himself in the given circumstances, within the given logic. I have several methods of achieving this. I often attempt to provoke the actor by confusing things on purpose. When speaking of the character, I allow myself to begin talking about the actor. And he may become confused about what I am talking about. I am not talking about events from the actor's life. I mean it literally on the level of the here and now; what is going on between us at that moment.

One of the simplest examples — and a humorous one — is something I often do with you as I speak. I will be telling you about some scene or plot or device and you start laughing because you realize I am using you at that moment as a character in my tale. Or you start nodding your head, thinking I am talking about you until you realize I am making up a story about somebody else. When that happens, you are transported into that fictional situation. It becomes *you*. Not someone or something else, but *you*. You become aware of yourself at that moment. These devices may be extremely elementary. But what the actor needs most are the simplest of devices.

I want to backtrack for a moment. Of what consists the director's work with an actor? Stanislavsky has several stages: preparing the role, working on character, selecting a costume, etc. I do not spend much time on that.

Primary is this: How do you free the actor of blocks? How does the actor's nature open and reveal itself? The actor wants to open up, but he remains blocked. He remains blocked because he is afraid of the director. He remains blocked because the part is large and complex and he is not used to such parts. He remains blocked because he does not know the actors he is working with. Or, perhaps, one of the other actors is very witty and very talented and he fears he is not as talented. Perhaps he perceives the other actor as a rival. There are millions of possibilities. These are just the first that come to mind. The actor may be blocked because he has trouble remembering lines. Maybe he does not pronounce the letter *R* very well and there are a lot of them in his lines.

I am convinced that every person is interesting. And I am convinced that every person is capable of playing a whole scene or at least part of a scene very well. If you can remove the blocks and provoke the actor to exist comfortably in the given circumstance, he may be extremely interesting, extremely unexpected. Profound, funny, and so on. However, he will not be able to repeat that. Being able to reproduce it time and again is the mark of a true actor.

If we boil it down, the actor's craft can be said to consist of two things. The first is to open up. To be able to open oneself up despite the natural blocks that hinder him every time for different reasons. To be able to be distracted from whatever it is that causes blocks. That is where the work of the director comes in — to distract the actor from those impulses that block him. At the heart of the Stanislavsky system is the art of finding something else to distract the actor, thereby allowing him to forget that there is an audience watching him, that a director is watching him, that a partner is watching him, that the lighting man, sound man, and props man are all watching him. That is the basic thrust of the Stanislavsky system. That is where the genius of his discovery comes in.

The second is to believe in the circumstances of what is transpiring. To become caught up in these circumstances. To make them your own. To believe in the circumstances and the logic of the action. The logic of the character. My logic is one thing, yours is another. Every person and every character has his own logic and it is my job as director to reveal that. I must set up the parameters so that the actor is able to feel the limits of that specific character. Then, I can put him into any situation and he will still exist within the logic of the character.

I have named two key elements of the actor's craft: (1) the ability to open up, to believe in the given circumstances, and to become caught up in them, and (2) to accept the logic of the character. Basically, beyond that it is a matter of talent.

These two key elements of the actor's craft can — to a greater or lesser extent — be learned through training. A good director who knows how to impart this knowledge can more or less get anyone to open up. It is harder to get just anyone to accept the logic of another, but that is also possible to do.

Third, and this is something the director has no control over, is the actor's ability to be infectious. Basically, this is talent. This is the actor's individuality. He may not be an infectious personality when you see him walking down the street, but when he walks out on stage he magically manifests charisma. When he opens up, when he engages that "public isolation" of which I have been speaking, something happens inside him. He may actually be a tightwad, an incorrigible womanizer, not very intelligent, and on and on. But when he walks onstage, he is stunning. And the fact that he is a tightwad becomes part of his charm — he is extraordinarily expressive and we recognize in him something of the truth. That behavior which offstage is loathsome womanizing, on stage comes across as something wonderfully attractive, elegant, and sexy. That is the measure of talent. Although, of course, you still need those other elements we have been discussing.

Some people have charisma, some do not.

Take a woman with extraordinary sex appeal, the kind that just knocks you out. But she walks onstage and there is nothing there. It all disappears. She is not even pretty. You cannot explain what happened. She takes one step off the stage, and once again she is a gorgeous woman. I understand less about this in regards to men, but the same force is at work here with them. And then there is the opposite side of the coin — the actress who is not very attractive seems to disappear in a crowd and does not dress very well. She walks out on the stage, and you are knocked flat on your back.

What happens is that this actress's nature is revealed onstage. When she appears she is surrounded by a sexual aura. The men in the audience respond to that the way bees respond to honey. It is natural. It does not matter what she is playing or saying. It does not matter what language she is speaking or whether you understand what she is saying. Because I, as a man, respond to her through my senses and my instincts. She has revealed her nature and she is "infectious."

You ask what I do with actors. I must open up the actor's nature. Remove the blocks. Each time the blocks are caused by something new. I must calculate what is in the actor's way today. It is impossible to do it once and be done with it. In the course of this single rehearsal, a dozen or more reasons for blocks may arise. Often it is because of me, the

Anna (Yulia Svezhakova) passes Gurov (Igor Gordin) who is flanked by two resort bathers (Alexei Dubrovsky and Alexander Taranzhin) in the dramatization of *The Lady with the Lapdog*; Moscow, 2001. *Photo by Yelena Lapina.*

director. For I am the primary force acting upon the actor. I do something incorrectly. I head off in a wrong direction. I erroneously provoke the actor. I use the wrong word or a wrong intonation. I am too loud or I am too quiet. Too early or too late. In fact, I may have said exactly what needed to be said, but I did it at the wrong time and, therefore, it had no impact on the actor.

That is what we call rehearsal.

As I listen to you speak, I almost see the image of you as something of a kind magician during rehearsals. And yet when I look at you, the notion of Kama Ginkas as a kind magician does not fit. Or does it?

I will tell you: Both images are true.

Henrietta is like a hen sitting on her eggs. She warms them on one side then moves them around and warms them from another.

As you know, I am considered merciless, unrelenting, and implacable. But if I was only that I would never accomplish anything. It is impossible to achieve anything only by hammering. There is a physical law of equal and opposite reactions — as hard as you shove in one direction, you will be shoved back just as hard. So, what I do is act upon an actor and then quickly move on to something else and come back at him from another angle.

I am not the same person in the workplace that I am in life. As a person I tend to be closed, impatient, and have bad manners. It might appear that I am also like that when I am rehearsing — more like that, anyway, than a kind magician. You see, magicians work magic, they do good. I do not do good. I do my job. And that is always evident. I am engrossed in my work. I am busy. Even when I am joking or playing the fool or flirting with an actress and making her blush because it seems I have crossed some barrier — even then the actor knows I am working. As does everyone else around, myself included. I am busy with some task. I am laboring at some difficult chore. And depending upon the role, the play, the author, the way the actor is working and the way I am working, my approach may be imbued with more or less humor, charm, or flirtation. Often enough I will allow myself otherwise impermissible liberties with an actress during rehearsal. I will say more about that in a minute.

But this is not "having a good time." There are directors that actors love to work with because they are so nice and pleasant and kind and their rehearsals are comfortable and pleasant. If there is pleasure in rehearsing with me — and some actors do find pleasure in my rehearsals — it is something else. It is not fun, happy pleasure. No. It is the kind of pleasure that arises when — lo and behold! — suddenly you veer off in some unexpected direction. We are groping in the dark and we can feel we have hold of something, even if we do not know what it is yet. Maybe the actors do not have hold of it yet, but they sense that I, as director, know it is there.

The actor always has the sensation — I know this is true — that I know what I am doing. I cannot say that, in truth, I know literally where we are headed at every moment of the journey. I often do not want to know. But I have premonitions of what lies ahead. I am in a state of expectation, waiting for that moment when it will come. When an important thought will come, an intonation, a necessary image, a manner of playing a certain scene. When it does come, I will pass it on to the actor, and he will use it to give birth to something new.

Rehearsals are a time of mutual expectation. It is not a case of you sitting there waiting for something to happen. But a case of you being in constant motion, groping for something, taking action to provoke some response, heading off down various paths. Exploring the role, the actor, yourself, the environment. Forging blindly ahead, trying whatever can be tried, discovering something for an instant, then losing it and going on ahead again. That is the pleasure of my rehearsals.

A magician is one who does nothing for himself but does good for others. Like a fairy, he turns a saucer into a carriage. How beautiful! He turns a hunchback into a handsome prince. By the same token, the magician-director turns a hunchback actor into a handsome leading man. I do not do that in rehearsal. The hunchback actor knows that, maybe, ultimately, after the process of rehearsing with me over time, his part will emerge as that of a prince. But that is only something to look forward to, something to hope for in the future. That is not what concerns me today as we are rehearsing.

Moreover, the actor knows I cannot remake him into a prince. He must help. Unfortunately, there are actors in the Russian tradition who sit and wait for the director to do everything for them. But they wait in vain. Nothing can come of that. We can only do it together.

Kama Ginkas rehearses Alexander Pushkin's *The Golden Cockerel* with Alexander Livanov (top) and Arina Nesterova (left); 1998. *Photo by Ken Reynolds.*

The other extreme is the actor who pontificates on how "we" will create a role together: "Well, I have thought it through and I have decided how I will play this role. This is the way I am going to do this scene . . . " Nothing of the sort. You are not going to do the scene that way. If you have some inclinations to perform in a certain way, by all means, go ahead and do it. But it is not the place of the actor to plan everything out. Just as I will never tell an actor, "I have decided that you will play it this way or that." I have my perceptions of how I want it played, but that is another question.

What I am saying is that together we move toward each other. Together, we move toward the role. We grope and take chances. Sometimes we beat our heads against the wall or against each other. And that can hurt. The Russian tradition has something that is lacking in the Western tradition — that is, making the actor hurt. And that is done consciously. There have been specialists in that, directors who have had great success.

Roza Sirota was one. She was a teacher and assistant director who was famous for her success in preparing actors. She was not able, in the final analysis, to construct an entire role or an entire production. But she was brilliant at paving the way and preparing the ground for a director — usually Georgy Tovstonogov — to come in and do the job. She warmed the actor up, so to speak. In fact, that is a reputable component of the Russian tradition — the director or assistant who prepares the way for the producing director who may not have the patience or ability to do dirty work with actors.

This is what Sirota did for Tovstonogov. She is credited with being the person who discovered the great actor Innokenty Smoktunovsky. She is the one who worked with him individually for nine months on the role that was to make him a legend — Prince Myshkin in Tovstonogov's 1957 production of Dostoevsky's novel, *The Idiot*. They may have worked some in groups, but my understanding is that she worked primarily with Smoktunovsky alone. She is the one who opened him up. She did not create the role of Myshkin for him, but she did everything imaginable so that the actor whose name was Innokenty Smoktunovsky was able to perform Myshkin.

I did not see how she did that. I met her later when they were reviving that show in 1966. Subsequently, we crossed paths often. She was rehearsing something at the Moscow Art Theater at the same time I was working there. I cannot say we were friends, because she was much older than I, but I always respected her and she seemed to relate to me well.

She had no qualms about hurting actors. She could harangue them to the point of destroying them. Knock them down so that they would have trouble getting back up. At the same time, her actors knew no one loved them as she did. They knew she would make a fuss over them, she would mother them. That is something I have seen with my own eyes. It is not an isolated example. It is part of the Russian tradition.

I can say that I, too, on occasion, employ this method. It is like giving an injection. You poke and create a moment of pain. Naturally, every director has his own methods and territories.

I remember seeing Sirota become carried away sadistically. It was as though she were possessed. This was not the painful poke I might use. She might launch an attack that lasted for an entire rehearsal or even for a series of rehearsals. I do not work like that. Just as it is my method to toss the spectator back and forth between hot and cold, it is my method to expose the actor to extremes. I never want him to think that anything has settled and hardened.

I mentioned that I allow myself "inadmissible" behavior with actresses. Of course, I never allow myself to cross boundaries of decorum. But I do like to have a woman in the group. When there are no women present, I immediately recall Chekhov's comment about his novella *Ward No. 6:* "How tedious," he said, "to write a tale lacking women." Maybe it is not tedious, but it is harder work. Something is missing. When a woman is present, or two or three, I begin imitating a relationship with her. I allow myself to say things that people generally do not say in public. I might say something like, "Why, you are so beautiful today, I am completely incapable of rehearsing today." And then we will continue rehearsing until I stop again and stare at her for a moment before again continuing. I am making this incident up, but it is the type of thing I might do.

If I see that the actress responds to this, I might well continue to do it throughout the entire rehearsal period, constantly changing and developing it. We have, then, the semblance of a complex relationship between us. I may also switch my "affections" from one actress to another, involving them in intrigues and creating confusion and rivalries.

This is a game, of course. As are all relations among the sexes. And this is a useful game. Perhaps the actresses cannot tell whether I am joking or not. So when the actress arrives for rehearsal, her feminine intuition is piqued. And, of course, the nature of all actors — male or female — is a feminine one. There is hardly a show that can be created without this bit of sexual excitation.

This is one method of opening an actress up. (It works the same basic way with men, only in different circumstances.) I catch the actress when she both is and is not in character. She is rehearsing right now; is existing within the circumstances of the play. But I will confuse her — I will try to make her wonder if my behavior is something that applies outside our working relationship. That way, she does not have to think deeply about some situation in which she must be prudent. She is already in it on her own.

The situation I have set up is not complex at all. Directors often make the mistake of loading actors down with complex logic and explanations. They take *Hamlet* or Dostoevsky and start piling it on. The actor is astonished at the director's intellectual gymnastics, but basically dies as an actor. He dies. The younger and more inexperienced the director, the more he is apt to make that mistake.

In fact, what you need to do is just open up the tiniest little crack. And then the steam will pour out on its own. When the little crack begins to clog up again, you must carefully act to open it. The fact is that all of the energies acting upon a rehearsal — that of the text, the actor, and the director — are constantly being clogged up. They are like thrombosis or infarctions in the role. My job is constantly to strip away the clots.

I have what we might call the slalom system. In my school, the school of Georgy Tovstonogov, the role is built logically. We have talked about the task in building a role. Let us put it simply: The actor wants something. Naturally, there is an obstacle to his desire. That obstacle is a flagged pole, as in a slalom. For the actor to keep moving, he must shift or swerve. Whatever he does, his speed and trajectory change. In other words, his task is constantly changing. He cannot go through the obstacle, but he can go around it. After all, his ultimate goal is to be down there at the bottom of the hill. So he makes twists and turns to keep on his feet. Now, other obstacles arise. Perhaps another actor or some other circumstance has changed, forcing him to respond in some way. But by this time he has already come closer to his goal.

Another problem here, one that is very difficult to explain, is bound up purely in the technique of acting. Flagpoles or obstacles often are not obvious, and the action you take to avoid them must not be direct; you need sensitivity and subtlety.

Let us say I keep explaining something to my actor over and over, but I just cannot drive my point home. So I change the circumstances. It is, as it were, as if I find I have run out of coffee so I offer you some tea. That is, I do not abandon what I am doing entirely, but I come at it from a different angle.

It may be enough to tell an actor, "Right now, pick up your cup and sip your tea." He thinks, "Why should I sip tea precisely at this moment?" But I do not need to tell him why. I probably do not even know myself. It is not an action crucial to the development of the plot.

Here is what is happening: This particular actor in this particular situation is wound up too tightly and needs help loosening up. So I myself pause to have a sip of tea. And then I slowly and calmly, set the cup back down. Very carefully, very deliberately, right there in the center of the saucer. Now, before I remove my hand from the cup, I lean forward and say to him in a firm, steady voice: "John, if you refuse to understand what I am telling you, I will refuse to meet with you ever again. I have been explaining the same thing to you for two hours straight. And you cannot get it through your head. You understand me? All right, Let's move on, now." And I sit back properly and continue.

You see, a moment like this allows us to clear away the tension. It allows us to plug into a new attitude. When I calmly set down the cup of tea, I allowed myself to concentrate, to fill myself with the necessary emotions, to collect in my head the proper words I need to have an effect on John. Not to yell at him or stomp my feet. But to calm myself and hold everything, all my energy, under control. To be as calm as my hand resting on the cup as I make my point.

There I have just invented a hypothetical problem spot in a rehearsal.

I did not know what I was going to say when I reached out for the teacup. But I sensed I could change something in the immediate situation. I felt if I began setting my cup down slowly and calmly, I would begin to fill with energy.

That is how you do it. Slowly calming yourself and gathering energy. When you deliberately and painstakingly engage in any minute, concrete action, it allows you to concentrate all your forces. And once you have done that, once you have prepared yourself, you are ready to say what needs saying with all the proper force. This is the way I work.

It often happens that spectators or critics think, "Oh, what an expressive moment when Kama had his actor hesitate and set that cup down." But this was not done to create an expressive moment. It was done to help an actor make the transition from one state to another. That is one of the flagged poles that I might use from the slalom system.

Let us say I slam down my fist and start shouting, "Stop! Stop! I can't take this anymore!" That is another kind of flagpole. It is assistance for the actor. Then, calmly, I say, "Now, go over there and sit down. Get a hold of yourself and start again." This is a flagpole. Or I say, "Now, take a deep breath." That is another flagpole.

A flagpole might be my shouting a bit, after which I quietly tell. the actor, "Now, say this word quietly." That is another kind of flagpole, to help the actor physically sense the act of suddenly quieting down.

So are you erecting obstacles for your actors or removing them?

Do not confuse obstacles with what I am calling the flagpoles of a slalom system. This is very important.

There is no theater without obstacles. Without conflict. Without action. There must always be obstacles, otherwise there is nothing for the actor to do or play. Obstacles might come from another actor, from some prop, they might be inside the actor himself.

For example, the actor says to himself: "I am talented. I am a talented person. I am going to rehearse well." That is, down deep, he really does not believe it, so he keeps telling himself that in order to convince himself it is true.

"She loves me." This is creating an inner obstacle, one against which you work. Right here you are holding the letter in which she wrote that she is leaving you. But you do not accept that. You say, "No! She loves me! She won't leave me. She loves me!" As you say that, you are crumpling up the letter and setting it down on the table, because it has no interest for you. That is similar to an actor finding an obstacle in a prop.

Perhaps you confused obstacles and flagpoles because my examples of slalom flagpoles were too exaggerated. In fact, they might well be very subtle. They might not involve obstacles at all.

It might be a sound. Music. It might be a pause. I might tell an actor he needs to pause at some given moment. After that pause, I tell the actor to go on speaking. I do not do this to create an effect. I do it to help the actor make a transition between states.

Then there are devices which differ from flagpoles or obstacles. These allow the director to express something specific, an idea, for instance. There are devices, for example, which designate a specific character. Whenever he speaks, he invariably accompanies that with some physical action.

But there are also devices, which I use often, that are intended as assistance for the actor. Let us say that whenever you speak with an actor, you pay him no attention. You are busy looking at something else, rustling papers and moving things around on the table in front of you.

Rather than explain certain attributes of the character to the actor — let us say, arrogance — I show them to him in my own interactions with him. In this case the actor senses immediately what interests me and what does not. It is a device that aids the actor in doing what he must do.

Marcus Grott, the Swedish actor who played Raskolnikov for me in productions in Helsinki and Moscow, did not have any particular problems with blocks. But as I was working with him at one point on *Crime and Punishment,* it was necessary for me to help him focus his attention. Basically, that is how you break down blocks: You get the actor to focus his attention. In any case, I told Marcus, "Take your tongue and carefully run it along the front of your teeth. Check to make sure there is no food caught in the cracks." When he did that, he immediately began speaking in just the way I wanted him to.

You would think that what was needed was to explain to him the idea behind the necessary intonation. Well, I had tried explaining it to him, but that had only made the task harder. Because then he began playing what he thought I wanted. He began giving weighty significance to the words. He piled on much that was superfluous. Sometimes you do not want any of that. You just want a phrase or a single word to have a ring to it. And so you get your actor to say it after carefully running his tongue over his teeth.

Why did I suggest that to him specifically? I do not know.

Sometimes I might tell an actor, "Keep talking, but while you're doing that, focus on the fact that you are hunting in your pocket for your handkerchief or a coin."

The spectator will not even be aware that the actor is groping for something in his pocket. It has nothing to do with such an image as "At This Moment the Actor Is Searching for Money." Not at all.

There are millions of such devices. You do not think of them in advance. They come to you naturally as you work and you find you have need of them. They arise from experience and intuition. These are not the flagpoles I was talking about. The flagpoles are built-in markers that help the actor move from one place or one state to another. Right now I am talking about devices that help the actor perform some action in the manner that I want him to perform it.

An actor may be in a semi-exalted state, a frame of mind when he does not sense the reality of his own body sufficiently. But you need him to have a concrete feel for his physical reality.

I guess you could say that something I do in this case has become one of my own personal clichés. Take Oksana Mysina in *K. I. from "Crime,"* for example. She performs in oversize shoes. All the critics write about the fact that the actress is performing in a man's shoes and that this has something to do with the image of the character. True, to an extent, it does eventually become a part of the character's image. But that is not why I originally put the actress in a pair of man's shoes. I did that to get her away from playing the fragile, delicate, otherworldly being which she was rehearsing at first. That is not what I wanted. I was after a woman with a horselike quality, I wanted to tap into Oksana's earthy quality. Since I had selected her to play this role, it was her personality that I needed to reveal. I had to bring her down to earth. I did not want her to be characterized by her long, slender, dainty fingers that play the violin — I needed fingers weathered from doing the wash.

Where do you think I came up with the idea of having her smoke a crude, filterless cigarette, the kind workers are apt to smoke? I needed a device — that is, the cigarette — that would help her play a specific scene. I taught her how to hold the cigarette, how to let it dangle in her mouth as she spoke. Do not forget, she has a very dramatic monologue in that scene where I gave her the cigarette. The last thing in the world I wanted was to have her play the words literally.

You can explain that to an actor in detail, and he will nod his head as though he understands everything you are saying. But he still will not do what you are asking him to do. The words themselves draw him in another direction. They are written in a way that, no matter what he does, the actor will pronounce them in a pitiful voice. But that is precisely what you do not want, so you say, "OK, pick up a hammer. And take a nail. And hammer that nail into the floor." Maybe it is a bent nail and the actor cannot get it to go in. And you keep him busy with that task as he is pronouncing a text about a child whom he loves and pities.

You see? The action in which the actor is involved takes over the performance of this scene. It sends the actor off in another direction; it does not allow him to speak the words literally. If that device of the hammer and nail fails to work, then you find something else and try it.

I gave Oksana a cigarette to smoke. I have her bite off the end and spit it out. That is all part of the device. Someone may say this is a shade of character. And, of course, again, I admit that eventually it does become that, too. But this device that worked for this character in this instance cannot be used for anyone else in any other situation. I perceive this character as a kind of homeless person, a nosy neighbor from a communal apartment. I never had the idea of, "Let's play her with a filterless cigarette in her mouth." That specific notion arose for the very reason that we were not getting anywhere with this scene during rehearsals.

For me a good actor is one who can express opposites in the same instant, can proclaim yes to the two-hundredth degree in one instant, and in the next can turn around and proclaim no to the three-hundredth degree. He develops along different lines at the same time.

Sure, he develops along what Stanislavsky called the through-line, but simultaneously, inside of the through-line, he develops in other directions as well. As a result, the diagram he draws is very contradictory, very unstable, very jagged. That is the amplitude I am talking about. I always tell my actors that everything must be in flux. The cardiogram, so to speak, must be filled with peaks and valleys.

Perhaps all of my shows hover around the notion that the ridiculous and the catastrophic stand shoulder to shoulder. Death and the exultation of life. Perfidy and heroism. About how dubious and clichéd many of our beliefs are: "Never say never."

You once told me how you never explain to an actor what it is you are attempting to do with your production. You said, "If I were to do that, the actor would listen to me attentively, nodding his head, and he might even say, 'Hm! What an intelligent idea!' But when it comes time for him to go out and play that, there is nothing left for him to play. All has been said and done."

Of course.

Is that not the opposite of the Stanislavsky system, by which everyone sits around a table for a long time discussing the play, what it means and what needs to be done to play it?

No, you are off base now. When I staged *The Seagull* or, say, *Macbeth*, in Finland, we spent a good deal of time analyzing the plays. What I do not explain is something else. I do not explain my overall conception. I do not tell the actors, "We are going to perform a show about the tragic aspect of power. About how bloody it is." The actor hears that and he nods seriously and says, "Hm. Yes, that is very timely right now. That is something we need to do a show about these days." And it produces absolutely no results of any use.

Or you say, "We are going to perform *Romeo and Juliet* and tell the story about how love conquers all even though the two main characters perish." The actor hears that and thinks, "Hm. Yes. It has been a while since I had an affair. Yes, I would like to do a show about that."

That is what I never talk to the actor about — my conception of what the show will be about. I always have a good sense of what my conception is before I begin rehearsing. But it may change in the course of rehearsals because I do not stage shows to express some conception or idea. I am not interested in slogans.

"Thou shalt not steal."

"Anti-Semites are bad."

Those are not reasons to stage a show. They may be among the forces driving me forward. But what you do is try to sprinkle as much debris in there as you can. Then the conception becomes more flexible, more subtle, and not quite so literal. It might even become something else.

You must know what you want, but must not hang onto it for dear life. If you do that, you would be better off sitting down and writing an essay. Or, better yet, just hang out a banner with a slogan on it.

Here is what is more important. Let us say an actor is carried away with some specific idea. For example: "Down with Soviet power." But that is not something an actor can perform. An actor must perform specific, concrete tasks. He is a father. He has a child. His child is skipping school and getting bad grades. He has to help his child do his lessons. He has no money, or maybe he has lots of money. He has a lover. And on and on and on. How can you play "down with Soviet power?" You need specific tasks you can perform. Maybe in the end, once you have played all those other things, the sum of your performance will evoke the notion of "down with Soviet power." But you cannot set yourself the task of staging or performing anything like that. I do not believe that is possible.

Stanislavsky worked on analyzing the play and I do too. But I do not do it in a literal, scholastic way. What I like most is to be moving forward, sensing where I am going but not actually knowing where I will end up. I have a place in my head where I want to end up, but I do not know for certain that I will go there. Maybe there is another place that is better yet.

Do you keep a close eye on your actors as they play a show that is up and running?

Experience has taught me that once the dress rehearsals begin, I start getting in the way. The problem is that I do not allow my actors the necessary freedom to run through the show properly.

There is a phrase I use to describe this. It originally was uttered by Henrietta in Krasnoyarsk when she was doing her first shows there. She had an assistant sitting nearby during a dress rehearsal, writing down what she wanted to tell the actors later. When she went back over those notes, she found a phrase that obviously had nothing to do with any concrete aspect of the show. It was just an inner observation which she had uttered out loud and which her assistant dutifully had recorded. The phrase was this: "A time comes when the actor must get inside the role and the director must get out of the show."

It is a brilliant phrase, one that any director will recognize as a revelation. It is true, literally. The time comes when you must let the actor go to work. The actor needs to take his role and run with it. But that is an unbearable process for a director to witness. It is excruciating because you see that everything is wrong. You want to stop the actors at every step of the way.

People less nervous than I, like Henrietta, merely utter clever phrases that get written down after them. More nervous people do as I do — which brings me to a story about my rehearsals of *The Toastmaster* at the Moscow Art Theater.

This was in 1986. We were working on the main stage. There were fifty-two actors on stage and backstage there was an enormous number of support personnel. I sat alone in the hall. Maybe my designer David Borovsky was there, but probably not. So picture this: The dress rehearsal begins and I get up and leave the hall. I walk down the corridor and out onto the street and begin wandering around Moscow. And there they are, fifty-two actors playing their hearts out to an absolutely empty hall. I gave them five or six run-throughs like that. Naturally, I would not go out for three-hour walks. I would leave for ten or fifteen minutes. Then I would come back. That is enough, in fact, for a professional. You see everything you need to see. Then I could give them my commentary.

By the same token, once the show is up and running, you need not watch the entire show to know how well it is going. It is enough to enter the hall once for a minute and then again later for a minute or two. Everything is clear. You more or less know the finite number of variations that the actors may give at any time. Today one actor went down this road when he should have gone down another. I am able to see by the way he is playing this episode that he swerved off course at an earlier crossroads. That meant he missed something else that was important in between the two.

It is similar to Chinese medicine — you do not have to go inside the body to know where the problems are. The doctor presses one point on your body and all of the reactions that follow tell him what he needs to know. The key is knowing where the pressure needs to be applied. You touch the hand and you see there are problems with the liver. Do not be fooled, there is nothing phony about this at all.

It is the same in the theater. A production is a living organism. Actors, of course, are offended. They say, "But you didn't see the show!" I did, though. I saw everything I needed to see.

Similarly, you can learn all you need to know about how a show is running by listening to the sound transmission backstage. You only need to hear a few phrases. And when you come out for the curtain calls at the end of the show, you can hear whether the applause is polite, confused, delighted, or stunned. You can feel it. So you know how the show ran today even if you did not see it in its entirety.

Alexander Tairov once wrote that the actor, like the text, is material to be molded. I rather suspect that actors do not like that idea. What is your attitude?

Indeed, actors are very sensitive about that. But, yes, they are material to be molded. I do not have much in common with Tairov, but he is right here. It is simply a professional approach.

I consider the director the author of the production. So, let us take a look. What kinds of material does the author work with?

First, there is the actor. He uses the actor to express himself and to express what he wishes to say.

Next, he may or may not use a playwright. He may use a written text, he may not.

Next, he uses space. He may use a designer or he may not.

Next, there is music that he may or may not use.

But without the material of the actor, the director does not exist. It is as simple as that. Without the actor, the director becomes someone dreaming up abstract projects.

Of course the actor is material to be molded.

As such, the tension that arises between the actor and the director derives from the fact that the actor senses his lack of freedom. The actor knows he is being molded like clay. That is why you have great actors striving to interpret their own roles. Olivier, for instance, created his performance of Othello. As a rule, he would hire a director who was nothing more than competent and he would create his own role himself. He did not want to be someone else's material. Perhaps what he did not consider was that, even in doing this, he, as an actor, still remained material for himself as director.

Of course an actor is material.

And that gives rise to conflict and wounded egos, to a sense of humiliation. Some actors admit that openly. Sergei Yursky says, "We are nothing but paint! They are the artists. We are the paint. They take us as they would paint and use us as they will."

It is very hurtful to feel that way about yourself. After all, the actor wants to perceive of himself as an independent artist. And, of course, he is an artist. And he is also independent. This is a very vague area. And the director must be very careful not to offend an actor.

Musicians perform or render other people's notes. And the actor is willing to perform or render Shakespeare. He does not consider that humiliating. But he does not want to be putty or paint in the hands even of a Peter Brook.

It is another matter that there a lot more major actors than major directors. Maybe there are only three or four Peter Brooks to go around, so good actors find themselves being used as paint by lesser directors. But that still does not change the nature of the relationship. Yes. The actor is material to be molded.

Having said that, I must add that the actor is not dead material. He is not a piece of paper that you trace, cut out, and paste where you want. I am not entirely sure how to say this. The actor is a material that responds to contact with the director.

But you know what? I am going to go back on my categorical definition of the actor as material. No, the actor is not merely material. The word *material* does not express the true nature of this complex relationship. Instead, I am going to fall back on something I have already said.

The actor is a being of the female sex.

The actor-female is a being who, after intercourse with the director-male, produces something independent of them both. The actor-female gives birth. And it is worthless to attempt to determine which of the two is more important. Each has his or her own function. Their functions, physiologically, are different. And those two functions coming together bring about a third entity.

That is the best description of the relationship between the director and the actor.

When a director uses the material of even a good actor, he will not achieve satisfaction unless he engages in give and take as the male does with the female during the sexual act. Without that, it is little more than masturbation. If the director-male only uses his actor-female for his own selfish reasons, he will not achieve real satisfaction. Only mutual gratification, only the conjoining in a fantastic act where both partners are equally committed, will lead to the creation of something else that neither of them could have imagined on their own. Such ideal theatrical intercourse occurs extremely rarely.

A recurring theme in your speech is that of the family. First of all, in Moscow you work almost exclusively in a theater run by your wife Henrietta Yanovskaya. Second, whenever you speak of your productions of *Crime and Punishment*, you eventually come around to the topic of a father-son relationship. Third is your vision of the director-actor relationship as that of a pair of lovers, or a mother and father who give birth to a child. Finally, you often say you know your actors better than their own mothers do. I do not imagine you are the only director who frequently resorts to the vocabulary of the family in his speech, but I do suspect your relationship to these terms is more developed than for most. For starters, what do you have in mind when you say you know an actor better than his mother?

That probably does not have all that much to do with my sense of family in the theatrical sense. But I will say this. My job is to reveal the actor's nature. That is what I do. That is my profession. Perhaps it is even my talent. If I am unable to reveal an actor's nature, that means I have failed.

You see, an actor, like any other person, only reveals as much of himself as necessary in regular, daily life. Let us say he reveals only as much as is advantageous to him. A wife only reveals herself to her husband from that angle which is most profitable to her. Some things she will never reveal to her husband or father or mother. That may be because they are unnecessary or even harmful. And then there are aspects of herself that even she is not aware of. She does not know all her own qualities. That happens quite frequently.

As such, if my work with an actor is progressing well — if I am revealing the actor's nature — I become privy to certain aspects of his character that even those closest to him do not know.

I have discussed how the actor is easily hurt. He responds in one way or another to those around him who may be capable of exposing or unmaking him. I have in mind the director, other actors, the lighting man, or whomever. At home the actor has more defenses, he has less to fear. At home he might never behave with anyone as he does when he harangues the costume girl at the theater. He probably does not behave with his father as he does with his director. He probably does not behave with his brother or friend as he does with his acting partners. Perhaps at home he never gets involved in all the intrigues and politicking that keep him so busy at the theater. At home, he is a completely different person. It is very possible.

When the actor is at the theater, he exists in a very particular environment. It is one that exists nowhere else in his life.

I actually do not want to say that I know the actor better than his mother. That would not be entirely right either. But there are times when what I know about the actor is more substantive than what his loved ones know. You see, I am involved in getting to know him *substantively*. My purpose is not to know him as he would like to be or as he has learned to be through education, but as he is in fact. Because I employ his essence.

That, of course, is the nature of my work specifically. Another director may work in another way. I do not concoct characters or roles in my head. I attempt to discover what is interesting in the actor and apply that in my work. I look for his essence, for what is most fundamental in the actor's nature. It may not always be very positive. It might even be negative if perceived from the point of view of everyday family or social life. That is unimportant to me, however. That is why I sometimes say I know the actor better than his mother or, at least, that I know a side of him others do not even suspect exists.

But I do not think that is what you mean when you talk about my use of the word *family* in my speech. Family is something else, even aside from the paternal-filial relationship of Porfiry Petrovich and Raskolnikov in *Crime and Punishment*. Because, after all, those are simply my own personal associations.

An actor belongs to a different tribe. Theater people as a whole are a tribe unto themselves, but this applies especially to actors. A director may or may not belong to their tribe.

Let us say we are Jews. Amongst ourselves we experience the whole gamut of human emotions, good, bad, and indifferent. But in a certain sense we are all alike because we are Jews. And we have a certain understanding of each other because of that. In certain social situations, Jews will stick together and understand each other. It may be something as simple as others rejecting us, therefore forcing us to band together.

The very same thing occurs in the tribe of actors. Actors are defenseless and naked. They are different from all of those who are clothed. Including the director. The director undresses only partially and, even then, only for a select few.

Actors are a family. Of course they are. And since we are at home among family in the theater, we often do not stand on ceremony. People do not wear tuxes at home. They wear bathrobes or nothing at all. You are at home, right? Who cares?

Aside from that aspect is a certain love and tenderness that is different from that which workers in an office may have for each other. And there is competition. There are power struggles. Who is the boss in this house?

One of the things one often hears actors say about themselves is that they are children. It is as if that explains everything and excuses everything in one fell swoop. As if they are saying, "I can do whatever I want because I am a child."

The fact of the matter is that the spectator and the director demand that an actor be childlike. What does that mean? It means being open, being ingenuous. An adult does not have the simplicity and spontaneity to exclaim, "Oh, what a pretty flower!" Or, "Oh, look at that woman that just went by!" Or, "Oh, look at that man that just went by!"

An actor requires the spontaneity that is not characteristic of a usual adult. To say nothing of mobility, imagination, and love of playacting. Actors play, after all. Adults seldom play, at least in the same sense. They play at war, at politics, at love. They gamble. Of course, there is an element of play in adult life; otherwise people would not need theater. But for the common adult, it is all maintained within certain boundaries. It would seem silly to us for adults to play as children do — to play mommy and daddy and here is our baby. That would strike us as insane, as it does in *Who's Afraid of Virginia Woolf?*

Actors do that, however. They hunger for play. The less interesting they find life, the more they are carried away by playing, by other people's passions, other people's lives and words. They are required to be like that. That is their nature. It is their gift. They remain children even as they grow old.

Listening to you speak, one might infer that you do not really like actors.

It is like family relationships. You never really know. At a certain point you do not know anymore whether you love your wife or not or whether you love your child or not. Often you hate them. It often happens that you hate your own child. Only just watch what happens if anybody tries to take him away from you. Do you see what I mean?

Your question is a fair one.

They say love is blind.

One thing I can say is that puppy love in the theater does no one any good. It might be fine in real life, but those situations in the theater when everyone loves everyone and is happy with everything — they invariably end badly. There is nothing more terrible.

6

We Play Literature:
Chekhov, Pushkin, Dostoevsky, Shakespeare, and Others

Paustovsky, Mayakovsky, Dürrenmatt

As your career advanced, you essentially moved away from staging traditional plays and began writing your own texts for performance: dramatizations and pieces based on documents —

Let me interrupt and correct you.

You mention literature. In recent times some very serious critics have written weighty works on this topic. I say this with a certain amazement because I have always related to critics with a great deal of irony. Naturally, I have always known there are good critics. Fortunately, these very few good critics have begun writing about me and doing it well. They have noted that my work is closely bound up with the high-quality literature of the classics, usually from the Russian tradition.

These critics have recognized — it is not hard to do — that I have a Dostoevsky period, a Chekhov period, and a Pushkin period. Most of them surmise that there is a Shakespeare period. This is true. I am rooted in culture, especially Russian culture. And I am steeped in literature, especially Russian literature. I imagine there are unique, brilliant artists who arise on their own, as if in the middle of nowhere. They may not even have an education — they are self-sufficient geniuses. One can only envy them. I am a shrub of culture. I was raised in the greenhouse of culture where exotic, colorful plants of different kinds are cultivated in conditions of controlled light, climate, and watering. I drew sustenance from the same soil that I shared with other cultivated cultural specimens growing around me. Perhaps you could say this began in school, although it probably goes back even farther.

My father was a rather tiresome type. And I was a bad student. I goofed off a lot. Father not only hit me a lot — well, let us say he used his hands — but he sometimes even lectured me. He loved to find formulas and then impart them to us. I always thought they were very funny, very artificial. He used to say, "You must not merely study, you must examine things to their core." He believed in examining things to their core. And so there came a time when he decided it was time for us — my brother, my little sister, and me — to examine literature to the core.

At this time in the Soviet Union, a new collected works of Chekhov had gone on sale. It was a green eleven-volume edition. I still have it at home. It is all marked up now, although I did that later. That collection was my father's, the one he bought because it was something he wanted his children to study in depth.

We would be out in the countryside, wanting to run around, go swimming, or play soccer, but father would sit us all down, open up one of the stories, and read it. It was horribly boring. Sometimes he would read someone else, but I do not remember what now. What I remember is Chekhov.

We had the collected works of Leo Tolstoy, a really cheap edition. You just go and try to read *War and Peace* when you are thirteen or fourteen years old! It is nonsense, impossible. You read one page and you quit. And if you do not, then you hit on the French text that makes no sense.

So, a certain level of introduction to literature took place on the home level although the main place where that happened was in school. I had the great fortune in the eighth grade of having a new class teacher. Her name was Roza Glintershchik and she was a genuinely brilliant teacher. She loved Russian literature and the Russian language. And she loved teaching. Curiously enough, although she did not speak

Lithuanian, she taught at our Lithuanian school. And she instantly induced all us school kids to fall in love with Russian literature. Can you imagine her making us fall in love with Mayakovsky? Naturally, this was not the official Soviet Mayakovsky — although she loved him too. But she introduced us to the Mayakovsky who wrote prior to the Revolution, something none of us suspected at all at that time. This was in 1955 and 1956.

So you have this class full of kids who are essentially anti-Soviet, even anti-Russian, in their sentiments, certainly anti-Mayakovsky. But there we were, falling in love with Mayakovsky.

Then she made us fall in love with several writers of the Soviet era who were outside of the mainstream — Konstantin Paustovsky; Alexander Grin, a romantic writer who had just resurfaced at that time; the émigré writer Ivan Bunin. We could only read certain of his stories because most of what he wrote was still banned.

Little by little, with her help, we began to understand something about poetry and literature. We learned they are not just ideological tools, but that they are linguistic flesh and meat. That they contain meaning, music, and emotion.

On top of that, Mrs. Glintershchik organized a literary circle for which we put on "evenings." These were not so much theater productions as they were literary shows. The scripts were written partly by her and partly by me. Actually, she would write them and I would redo them. I, essentially, was taking on the role of the director.

It was around this time that I staged something about Mayakovsky. This was long before Yury Lyubimov did his famous show. There was no Taganka Theater yet at this point. In my show I had three Mayakovskys — Mayakovsky the Futurist, Mayakovsky the official Soviet poet, and Mayakovsky the lyrical and tragic hero.

Can we consider this your first production?

No, my first production came even earlier. This was a show based on Paustovsky's story "Snow." It was very avant-garde. I think about it now and I am amazed. The school stage was hung with lots of thin sticks of various lengths. At an interval of every twenty or thirty centimeters, these sticks, all painted white, hung from the ceiling. The visual effect was that of snow falling. It was a sad, atmospheric tale. As the actors walked about, they would bump the sticks and they would sway. Some would sway more, some less. The point was to find the rhythm of falling snow. The story had no plot, it created a melancholy mood.

I would call that my first production.

Or maybe it was something we did based on excerpts from *War and Peace*. Naturally, Tolstoy himself was the master of ceremonies and he pronounced the author's text. These were literary evenings for school kids, after all. We hooligans would get together and act these things out. And people would watch and listen.

The Mayakovsky thing was a full-fledged production. Down amidst the audience — not on the stage — I had this big metal construction welded together, a structure of cells that resembled a beehive. They welded this thing together right there in the school auditorium. The people in this hypothetical city wore black pants, black shirts and hats. Their faces were wrapped in masks made of bandages. This was my city. It was quite avant-garde, there was nothing realistic at all as the actors crawled all over the metal construction. At the time it was considered quite frightening.

Naturally, you were all over the place, taking charge.

I drew the model. I oversaw the making of the set. I staged it all. The first Mayakovsky to appear was the Futurist. And then there was some pantomime imitating the life of a city. It was awful.

But that is not all. When the tragic moment arrived and the lyrical Mayakovsky suffered a bad love, when he was left alone and the official critics turned their backs on him, a young girl jumped out of the audience and began speaking in her own words. This is the same kind of thing I am still doing today! The timing and manner in which she appeared were rehearsed ahead of time, but the exact words were not. She said something to the effect of: "Is it really possible that something will happen to Mayakovsky?! Can that be possible?! Is there nothing we can do?! I sense something is going to happen!" This was followed by the suicidal gunshot.

In other words, everything you know about me already existed in that sketch about Mayakovsky. Some of my most basic theatrical ideas were already taking shape then. They were founded on the basis of literature, not plays.

I am lying a bit when I say that, of course. I staged these things when I was still in school, but, later, when I began studying to be an actor, I staged plays. In 1962 or 1963, when I was studying to become a director in Leningrad, I would return to Vilnius for vacations and Mrs. Glintershchik would get me to stage things with her students.

But you see where the basis for my attraction to literature lies.

I very much fell in love with Tsvetayeva, with Mandelshtam, with early Mayakovsky, with Pasternak. Akhmatova for me was more difficult. She was too uncomplicated. For me, a young person, that simplicity was too difficult. It seemed excessively feminine and, as I thought then, sentimental. In fact, of course, it was no such thing. But for a caustic young man like me, it was easier to get into literature that was more ragged and temperamental, like Tsvetayeva, for example. Mandelshtam, Mayakovsky, and Pasternak, of course. You can feel his language on your teeth, you can chew it.

When I went to Leningrad to study, Henrietta introduced me to Joseph Brodsky and his poetry. This was another of the literary phases in my life. I am certain that much in me is determined by the poetry that I love. I have been strongly affected by certain rhyme images — I do not mean the rhymes themselves, I mean the images that arise from them, that echo and interact with one another.

I never loved being literal. Poetry is often considered something "beautiful." No. That is not what I liked. Poetry is an indirect route to achieving awareness of essences. Poetry showed me that the indirect route is much quicker and much more profound than a literal approach to things. There are a great many things you cannot grasp with your hands, but if you make an indirect, poetic gesture around them, so to speak, you can sense them approximately.

When I first began studying in Leningrad, someone told me to read Dostoevsky's *Notes from Underground*. I knew some Dostoevsky, things like *Crime and Punishment* and *The Idiot*. I had seen the film of *The Idiot*. They were OK — a bit heavy and gloomy, but very serious. I had studied in a Lithuanian school, so his language seemed dense and old-fashioned to me. People talked a lot in his books. But I figured he was probably a great writer.

I loved Tolstoy. He made for slow reading, but I liked him. Mrs. Glintershchik had revealed him to me. What attracted me in him was his ability to convey aspects of the subconscious before Proust and Joyce came around to that. By then, of course, I knew Proust and Joyce. And it was quite a discovery to learn that Leo Tolstoy had been doing similar things much earlier. Take, for example, his unexpected rhythmic rendering of the old Prince Bolkonsky's death rattle. The Prince utters three sounds that only his daughter can decipher as meaning "my soul, my soul is in pain." His gibberish sounds like something from Velimir Khlebnikov! They were not words, just phonetic combinations through which Tolstoy attempted to describe the approach of death. This was amazing that one of the classics, a book you assume to be deathly boring, already contains whole layers of what the avant-garde did later. And I knew the avant-garde inside and out.

So I read *Notes from Underground*. And I was stunned. Essentially, it changed my life. I believe I became a different person when I read *Notes from Underground*.

What was the year?

I believe this was 1962.

During my first year at the institute, one of my independent projects was to stage a work by Dürrenmatt, *Conversation at Night with a Despised Character*. It is a tale about how an executioner comes to kill a writer. The writer hates him because he is a representative of power. He spits in his face and humiliates him, but for some reason, the executioner puts up with it all. Probably because he is not human; he is a killing machine. However, it turns out that even a machine is capable of being surprised and having feelings.

This machine is amazed that people do not know how to die. In the old days, people died splendidly. They died with meaning. As a result, his work was filled with meaning, too. He used to execute bandits and murderers in the public square, and so he was fulfilling an important state function. He executed people in the belief that his work was important and necessary. Then came the revolutionaries who hated the authorities and hated him. They struggled against him and he against them. But they were equals and, therefore, his work still had meaning. He represented a coherent set of beliefs.

But, nowadays, people die silently, they die drearily. Nobody struggles. He cannot understand this. And he is unable to kill anymore. His wonderful work, for which he used to don a red cape and appear on the public square, now must be conducted surreptitiously under the cover of night. He must sneak up to the fourth floor and climb in windows. This is hard, because he is getting old. And he must strangle his victim with his own hands. But the victim does not struggle. The executioner no longer understands what he is doing and he is upset. He cannot understand what has happened in the world.

In response, the writer howls, "What happened?! An executioner is stalking the earth!" But the executioner does not accept that argument. No matter what the writer tries, he is unable to humiliate his killer. The executioner tells the writer to open his window and shout. He says, "You'll feel better that way." And the writer yells, "The executioner is killing me! Look at the state of the world you all live in!"

Nobody answers.

The executioner cannot understand why nobody responds. Every night he goes out and kills and nobody pays any attention.

Quite a work to stage in the Soviet Union in the 1960s.

There you have it. I staged that in 1962 in my first year of the institute.

What did it look like visually?

This is a radio play. Which is wonderful, and is one more answer to your original question. It was not a traditional play. It has stage directions like "footsteps are heard" or "a plate falls." When a voice is heard we hear the question, "Who is that?" Or, "Do you see me or not?" Or, "I know who you are! You are the executioner who has come to kill me!" Nobody answers.

I staged a radio play. I loved it. I seated two people on a bench. Nobody walked around or moved in space. Someone would bang a cup against a plate or one of them would make stomping sounds with their feet. They would both begin talking at the same time or one would ask, "Who are you?" and the only response would be the other stomping his feet on the floor. The writer would shout, "Will you answer or not?!" but the other would only stomp his feet in response. The interrelations between the two actors were real, but physically, they did nothing at all. This created a distance between the actors who, despite doing absolutely nothing, performed according to all the laws of the psychological theater.

I really liked that. If you wish, you could call it my first attempt to do what I did much later when staging the prose of Chekhov's *The Black Monk*. Or, when in *Pushkin. Duel. Death* and *Pushkin and Natalie* the actors perform letters.

As for Dürrenmatt, I staged his play not merely as a series of dialogues — I also brought out the sense of physical alienation in it. The actors existed in a completely lifelike manner. I structured all of the nuances of their interaction. But, physically, their actions were not appropriate for the situation in which they existed. This was an extremely important discovery for me, and I have continuously gone back to it throughout my entire life. The crux of it is this: To create action that does not correspond to what is being said or what is being done. Sometimes the actors may speak about an action but not perform it. For example, a character may say, "I spit in your face," but my actor does nothing of the sort. Dürrenmatt helped me, because, in writing for the radio, he often wrote about things you cannot see. The strange quality of his play taught me a lot.

Dürrenmatt was my first directorial success. When Tovstonogov saw it, he expressed the first few words of praise I had heard. I think they were probably more powerful than any other I have heard since. He said, "That is 80 percent art." A student production and it already had art in it. Eighty percent. In Tovstonogov's opinion.

After I graduated, my period of unemployment began. It was broken up on occasion by rare opportunities to stage something. Sometimes I went two or three years without anything. I was filled with theatrical ideas, but I had nowhere to apply them. And so I began to write what I would be able to stage only in another twenty or thirty years.

The first thing I wrote was a dramatization of *Notes from Underground*. Actually, I wrote this play when I was still a second or third-year student. You saw this show, didn't you?

Yes, I did.

I finally produced that work in 1988 almost word for word as I had written it more than twenty years earlier. So, you see, it all began back then. The end of the eighties was not a time when I "finally began to do something."

CHEKHOV AND PUSHKIN

My first attempt at staging documentary materials was in 1968. It was a play called *My Mocking Happiness,* based on the correspondence of Anton Chekhov with various people. Written by Leonid Malyugin, a writer who was quite popular at that time among intellectuals, it was a very bad play constructed on the basis of badly edited letters. Basically he wrote a piece of sentimental slop, a portrait of Chekhov as if he had been an exemplary Soviet citizen. He went to live in the country and then traveled to Sakhalin Island to find out how strong-spirited people live. He was the kind of person who did not accept the tsarist regime, but he fell in love with the famous actress Olga Knipper, became involved with a good theater, the Moscow Art Theater, met "the stormy petrel" Maxim Gorky and, then, finally saw the light. Still, he was a lonely man and he died when he got sick. It was a banal version of the loves and works of Anton Chekhov. I was not at all interested in that. I did not give a damn about Chekhov's first love or his second love. I rewrote the whole thing. All I left untouched were the characters' dialogues and the basic plot based on historical facts.

I went back to a prerevolutionary edition of Chekhov's letters in five volumes and reread them all. That was when I realized that all the quotes in the play were inaccurate. They often broke off right when the most interesting thing was about to be said; something that would transform what Chekhov had been saying up to then into something else. I left the basic structure of the play intact, but filled it out with quotes from Chekhov's actual letters and threw out everything Malyugin had inserted on his own.

It was then that I first realized the tragedy of Chekhov's nature. I discovered the paradoxes that existed inside him and the breach between others' perceptions of him and his own perception of himself. This breach existed even with people who loved him. I discovered the paradoxes that affect any person in Russia who dedicates himself to art. Perhaps that stands true not only for Russians, but it is especially true of Russians.

Essentially, Chekhov wholly renounced himself, declining to have a personal life. And I began to understand that that "old man" who died at the age of forty-four was no old man at all. I was used to judging him by his photographs, which make him look like an old man. In fact, he was a passionate man. As all in the Chekhov family, he was an alcoholic by inheritance. That is, he was not an actual alcoholic because he did not allow himself to become one. But his brother Alexander was an alcoholic, and his brother Mikhail died of alcoholism and tuberculosis. That was hereditary. Anton was in the same position, but he did not allow it to control him.

He was a tall, handsome man with a great sense of humor. He was charming, a great ladies' man. He adored women. And, yet, he avoided them, too. Chekhov rarely talked about himself, but if you know how to read him, you will see that he loved plump women with tough characters. He was not interested in elegant women, no.

He had a famous affair with a well-known provincial actress whom he described, in part, in the character of Arkadina. This woman often created public scenes. She was capable, at a society gathering, of falling down before Chekhov on her knees and declaring, "Oh, great writer of the Russian land! How I love you!" He hated the theater and theater life with all its vulgar scenes. And yet, this affair lasted several years. Because, even as he hated this crude, vulgar behavior, he was drawn to it.

Our impression of Chekhov is that he was a very proper person. But he was actually capable of being very explosive. Admirers would travel to visit Chekhov at his home in Melikhovo. Teachers, usually associated with liberal populist groups, would come and ask him how to educate children or how to improve the life of poor Russians. He hated all those populists and social progressives! He saw their superficiality, how badly educated they were. Yes, they were devoted to their cause, but he saw how vain they were about their virtue. Chekhov was unwell, he wanted to write. But these people would sit there for hours, talking and asking him questions. One time, he began smashing plates and yelling at his sister, who was in charge of the house. Couldn't she possibly find a way to protect him from these intrusions?

When I did *My Mocking Happiness*, I took my actors to the Chekhov museum at Melikhovo. One thing that amazed me among the exhibits was a big beret. The tour guides told me that Chekhov had terrible migraine headaches. He would literally yell from the pain. The beret was a method for easing the discomfort. They would put out a basin and fill it with hot or cold water, I do not remember which now. He would put his feet in the basin and, instead of pressing a towel to his forehead, would put on that extremely tight beret which would squeeze his head. And he would sit like that for hours.

Imagine Anton Chekhov sitting there with his feet in that basin of water and his head in that beret. That is a completely different person from what we know. This is not the man we see in the crisp white shirt with his hair combed perfectly.

As always, I am going off on tangents. But this was one of the first of my shows that you could call documentary in nature.

Somewhere around 1969 I wrote the dramatization for Chekhov's *Ward No. 6*. I called it *The Theater of the Watchman Nikita* and wrote it culling appropriate phrases from various stories which I thought suited the characters. I also incorporated segments of prose narrative that were not originally intended to be performed. Naturally, I could not stage *The Theater of the Watchman Nikita* at that time because *Ward No. 6* was too controversial a work for the Soviet authorities. *Notes from Underground* could not be staged for the same reason. I wrote them and then they lay unused in my desk drawer.

In Krasnoyarsk, I wrote a dramatization of Ray Bradbury's *Fahrenheit 451*. After Krasnoyarsk came my big period of unemployment, a time that was very hurtful. This was when I wrote *Pushkin and Natalie,* a one-actor play based on letters. This was a singular work that, essentially, marks the birth of a new Ginkas, the one who continues to work today. Obviously, some things change, but the core is the same.

By this I mean the idea of performing letters or, more to the point, nonconversational texts. *Pushkin and Natalie,* which I wrote in 1976 and 1977, consisted of letters that I did not change in any way. I shortened them, of course, and I left out letters that were not germane to the dramatic task of the show. But they were all performed in the actual order in which they were written, and all the words were Pushkin's. This was very important for me — not to lie. I felt as though Pushkin would slap my hands if I were to transpose his letters or, God forbid, insert even a single word of my own. That was completely out of the question. Even his commas were crucial for me because I knew they expressed his intonation, they revealed the meaning he was putting into what he wrote. That could not be changed.

All of these letters begin with such salutations as "My Most Respected Sir" or whatever. In the style of the time, there was one salutation for a friend, another for an acquaintance of a friend, another for a person in authority, another for an elderly person and so on. There were salutations for women you knew and women you did not know. There were salutations for young girls. They were all different and they all revealed the character of the age. Pushkin, however, as a man of genius, found nuances even in the most rigid of phrases. Let us say he closed a letter with the words, "Respectfully yours, Alexander Pushkin." But we can tell by the context of the foregoing letter that he hated the person he claims to "respect." In fact, he was ridiculing him.

I loved seeing those kinds of nuances in these letters. Letters were structured very strictly at that time, especially to women. You could not say anything openly. In letters to passing acquaintances you had to maintain the proper distance, to say nothing of authorities on whom your fate depended. I mean that in the most direct sense — these people were in a position to send you into exile or deny you permission to do something you considered imperative. An improper intonation or an incorrectly used word might be perceived as an insult. This would give the offended party complete written justification for challenging you to a duel. This is the extent to which people were restricted by the epistolary structure of their day.

I loved that. Everything Pushkin wrote was squeezed into the proper form, but I could still hear what he really wanted to say. In the most impeccably polite letter to a woman, I could see how badly he wanted her. In the most courteous letter I could see how he despised the person he was writing to.

That is where the drama of *Pushkin and Natalie* emerged, in the form that forbade the direct expression of thoughts and emotions.

I want to say, "Go to hell!" but I cannot. So I express that thought through the context in which I write "Respectfully yours, Kama Ginkas."

This kind of thing is incredible! Formal restrictions provide a rich opportunity for dramatic development. When you play by the rules of the game, you cannot shout as you would like to. You are bound to maintain decorum. This is a tremendous source of tension, when you are forced to achieve your task not by a direct route, but in a roundabout detour to the essence.

My production was a play at letters. By which I mean to say it was a send-up of letters. That is, "I'm not Pushkin, I'm the actor Viktor Gvozditsky." The method of the show was this: "Of course we can play Pushkin. Let's try it. How would it be if we tried to play Pushkin?"

The show began with a short introduction of "the actor playing Pushkin."

"Let's see, how do I do this? Maybe like this? No, I'd better read something about him first — 'Pushkin had curly hair.' I'm reading a document here. That's how his contemporaries describe him."

Well, Gvozditsky has the curly hair. But Pushkin also had a bit of a bald spot. So, now, we already have our first discord. Or, Gvozditsky would declare, "He was . . . " — and he would proudly straighten up to his full height — " . . . very short." Then Gvozditsky would instantly scrunch down to make himself small. So now he's tugging hair over his bald spot and squatting down to make himself look smaller than he is.

Or, he would read, "Pushkin walked with a little bit of a limp." So, now, you can add that physical characteristic to the picture.

Then he would remember the most important thing of all. Pushkin might be anything at all, but he has to have sideburns! Without sideburns, Pushkin wasn't Pushkin! Major crisis time for the actor. Up to now, he has been able to imitate everything more or less successfully. So now he pulls some fake hair out of his small pocket and sticks it onto his cheeks. And he does a little pantomime, as if asking the spectators, "Well? What do you think? Am I Pushkin enough for you?"

Gvozditsky's efforts to be Pushkin, of course, evoked wild laughter. And they completely abolished any notions of trying to imitate a realistic Pushkin.

He began by pronouncing the title of the show: "*Pushkin and Natalie.*" Next, on a school blackboard, he wrote, "Pushkin — 1799 to 1836." That is, he erred on the last date for a minute, then erased it and wrote the correct one, 1837. Following that he launched into his awkward attempts to become Pushkin. After a time, he wrote: "Natalie" on the blackboard and picked up a tack and an old postcard. It was a bad-quality color reproduction of Karl Bryullov's portrait of Pushkin's wife Natalya Goncharova. Gvozditsky industriously pinned this cheap picture to the blackboard.

Having run through all these parodies, Gvozditsky began "performing" the letters. When Pushkin was trapped in Boldino because of the cholera quarantine, he tried explaining to his wife why he could not come see her. He told of trying to travel by various roads, but all were closed. Meanwhile, Gvozditsky is drawing diagrams on the board of all of the different routes that got Pushkin nowhere.

This is the method of playing a text that is not meant to be performed, a written text composed according to the strict rules of decorum. Dramatic tension arises for the very reason that it is not meant to be performed. Meanwhile, the psychological factor is genuine. This presents to the actor the task of existing in realistic circumstances while he is barred from expressing himself as he would like to. He wants to smash a cup, he wants to shout — but he cannot. People neither break cups nor shout in letters. In letters, they observe the proper etiquette.

This is where the drama comes from. This provided what I would call a new form of existing on stage. That which you see in *Pushkin. Duel. Death* or in *The Black Monk* are distant, pale reflections of what I originally discovered in *Pushkin and Natalie*.

Is that clear?

I can see that not only because I know *Pushkin. Duel. Death* and *The Black Monk*, but because I see you performing it as you speak.

In fact, having the advantage of historical hindsight, I can declare now that that was an innovation. It was the discovery of a new method of existing on stage.

Did this happen by chance, or could you feel yourself moving toward it? Or did it happen because you couldn't do anything else and this was the only means you had at your disposal?

It is true that my having to rehearse at home had some effect because if I had been able to do a regular show in a theater, I would have done something else. However, my theatrical bearings were already set during my work on Dürrenmatt. It was all there then. These were different efforts to set the same basic mechanism into motion.

In short: My actors onstage do not do that which it would seem they must do. They may say they are doing something, but they do not do it. They say one thing and do another. This gives rise to a breach between realistic, psychological acting and a nonrealistic, unnatural aspect of visuals and concrete actions.

After *Pushkin and Natalie,* I proceeded to develop what I had discovered. Having fallen into the trap of Pushkin, so to speak, I was unable to break loose of him. As if my father had commanded it, I began studying all of Pushkin and everything that had anything to do with him. I simply disappeared into the black hole of Pushkin. That is when I came upon the documents which later gave rise to *The Execution of the Decembrists.* I became fascinated with the whole era and, by chance, hit upon the material about the Decembrists. Here again, I wrote this play based not on live texts, but on dry reports, inquests, and the like. These were historical documents. People do not talk the way their speech is recorded in interrogations. I liked the fact that my characters would not be able to speak as a living person would. They must express themselves according to protocol.

It does not matter if the situation is one of great stress for the speaker. The speaker does not have the right to express himself emotionally. This is very difficult to get an actor to do, because the actor always wants to speak naturally.

In *Pushkin and Natalie,* I left in the spoken text all the salutations and even the dates and places when and where the letters were composed. Whatever Pushkin wrote went into the performed text. When a person speaks, he does not say things like that.

The first task for an actor who plays a text like this is to find his own personal justification as to why he is speaking such words aloud.

The Execution of the Decembrists was written in 1980. *Pushkin. Duel. Death* was written around 1982 or 1983. I did not stage them until the nineties, however.

What about *The Black Monk?*

I did not write anything there. That is staged exactly as it is written. It is another matter that I had wanted to do it for some twenty, twenty-five years. I had long ago marked up the story in my father's green Chekhov collection. I worked out the structure long ago. It is all there in dad's old book.

A show I have never been able to stage completely is one I call *Life Is Beautiful,* based on Chekhov. I have staged or tried to stage parts of it, but I have never done it completely as I would like. I include a certain irony or question mark in that title, but it is based on Chekhov. It includes the story "The Lady with the Lapdog," which ends rather tragically, and it includes "Rothschild's Fiddle," which is, quite simply, a tragic tale. They are what comprise my idea for *Life Is Beautiful,* based on Chekhov. I first had the idea of doing this show in the 1970s in Leningrad at the Lenin Komsomol Theater. However, the culture committee forbade me to do it. It was not the show they were suspicious of, but me personally. I was persona non grata.

When they asked me what I wanted to stage, I said, "Chekhov." Then they asked for the play. I said, "I'm not going to stage a play. I'm going to do something else." They did not like that because it was not something they could keep under their control. So they made me write a play based on the prose I wanted to use. I wrote lines like, "'The moon rose,' said one person. 'The river flowed,' said another." When they read that, they concluded I was making fun of them. These were not dialogues. So they turned me down. It was only twenty years later that I was able to stage the first part, "The Lady with the Lapdog," in Istanbul. Then I did another version in Helsinki although, as I say, I was not able to realize my plans for the second part.*

You engage in a certain kind of inbreeding in your productions. I mean that when talking about staging Chekhov you might say you were thinking of Dostoevsky, while when discussing your work on Dostoevsky, Shakespeare, or some other author you are liable to say you were thinking of Chekhov.

Well, using Chekhov, I worked out a unique method that I am very proud of in my production of Alexander Galin's *The Toastmaster,* a play about the guests at a large wedding. Imagine this: Fifty-two people are on stage at all times, eating, dancing, talking, walking around, each living his or her own life. But the spectator's attention was constantly drawn back and forth to the necessary location on stage, the most important of the many events occurring simultaneously.

The counterpoints existed all around at all times. I do not mean that they set up a realistic, lifelike background, but that they were actual counterpoints establishing contrasts or parallels to the main event at that specific moment. An action would take place at one end of the stage and it would be followed, seemingly without connection, by another action at another end of the stage. While that was happening, someone over in another corner was singing while in another location a couple was kissing or someone was killing someone else. They seemed like random developments but, in fact, they were all interconnected. The result was a very dense show even though it was a comedy, a tragi-

---

*Ginkas since has staged *Lady with the Lapdog* in Moscow at the New Generation Theater (2001) and at the American Repertory Theatre in September 2003. A production of *Rothschild's Fiddle,* created jointly by the New Generation Theater and the Yale Repertory Theatre, is scheduled to open in January 2004.

comedy, a philosophical comedy. It was extremely dense with what I would call earthworms digging everywhere.

The Toastmaster was the only show in which I have ever successfully applied this method. You can organize things scene by scene in film, using close-ups and long shots. In principle, you cannot do that in the theater although I did something similar in *The Toastmaster*. My models were *The Three Sisters* and *The Cherry Orchard* where Chekhov gives us the parallel existence of various characters. Of course there are far fewer characters in Chekhov's plays, and all of them were put into a web of simultaneous interaction by the author. I accomplished this on the level of the direction.

SHAKESPEARE

Your 1971 production of *Hamlet* and your 1997 production of *Macbeth* have been landmarks in your career.

Shakespeare, as literature, is another sort of foundation for me. Primarily it was *Hamlet,* but, since my approach was such a total one, Shakespeare as a whole was extremely important.

When I was a pretentious kid of seventeen or eighteen, I used to dream of the great shows I would do some day. Like a good, orderly Jewish boy, I ticked off all the great plays and asked myself what was the greatest of them all? Shakespeare's *Hamlet,* of course. So, I would have to stage *Hamlet.* And since I would have to do that some day, I began, even then, at seventeen years old, to make preparations for my future production. I was very industrious about it, very ponderous. I studied the play forward and backward. I bought and read all the books about Shakespeare I could find. I asked someone to translate what Jan Kott had written about Shakespeare in Polish. I still have those manuscripts, typed on loose pieces of paper with a bad typewriter. I bought and read books about the Middle Ages. I became fascinated by the way people lived then. Their music. Their customs. I did all of this because I knew I had to prepare myself, some day, to stage *Hamlet.*

In my youth I found Hamlet to be a wonderfully romantic figure.

He was all in black and he asked questions like "to be or not to be." I imagined him having a very tragic face and wearing a short velvet jacket. I even had my own Hamlet-style jacket that I used to wear. It had a thin waist and was broader in the chest. The sleeves were very wide. It had a collar sewed in that could be worn up high or folded down like the collar of a sweater. It was a very strange jacket that looked nothing like anything anyone else was wearing. It looked like something Hamlet would wear.

I began to see specific images in my head. Not scenes, yet. Just simple images. I saw Hamlet in every interesting person I met. I used to draw portraits of Hamlet. I still have my collection of these drawings. In some he wears a black beret. In another he looks like a young Dostoevsky. I have a Hamlet with a shaved head. This turned out to be of particular interest later when I staged Chekhov's *Ward No. 6* with Marcus Grott in Helsinki. Grott shaved his head, and I suddenly saw in him the same Hamlet that I had drawn many years before. It was as if I had done the drawing with him posing. He was not even born at that time, though.

Reading *Hamlet,* I came up with approaches and compared it to my own life, finding its echoes in my own personal experience. This went on for a long time. Figure I began around 1957 but I only actually staged it in 1971.

When I entered directing school in Leningrad in 1962, I immediately began working on *Hamlet.* This was extracurricular work. I invited my movement teacher to play Hamlet. His name was Kirill Chernozyomov. He was an extremely interesting person and a very talented actor. But he suffered from some ailment that attacked his bones. He was hunched over and kind of dragged his feet when walking. His long arms hung loosely at his sides. He had sunken cheeks. At the same time, he was quite adept at fencing. He was probably thirty-three at that time. In Grigory Kozintsev's film of *Hamlet* he was Smoktunovsky's stand-in for the fencing scenes. But he himself could have been a brilliant Hamlet.

When I arrived in Krasnoyarsk I had the freedom to do anything I wanted. Still, I did not have a proper Hamlet, a proper Ophelia, or anyone else. At least not by the standards I had at that time.

We lived a very difficult life in Krasnoyarsk. We lived on the other side of the Yenisei River from the city center, a place we never went. We lived in a hotel next to the actors' dormitory. We rehearsed mornings and evenings alike. If we had evening performances, we rehearsed after the shows were over. During breaks we ate and continued our rehearsals and conversations over our meals. After performances or evening rehearsals we would return home through the frozen city, passing by the thick walls of a silk factory. Naturally, our topic of conversation along the way was what we had just been rehearsing. In essence, the rehearsals never stopped. And when we would get back to our hotel room, within five minutes the actors would come over, Henrietta would make tea, and we would continue talking and rehearsing. We might have a few drinks and continue on into the night. That is how we lived there. It was like living in a commune or a monastery. Or maybe among a band of hooligans. Call it what you will, it was a bit of everything. It was a Theater. A Studio. All together in one.

That is when I came up with the idea of doing *Hamlet* as a show with and about young people. The troupe in Krasnoyarsk was very young. There was no one in it over twenty-five. They were mostly recent graduates of Moscow, Leningrad, or Kiev institutes although a few were from Krasnoyarsk. I realized this must be a production about boys and girls who were all brought up and educated in some centrally located, cultural center. Perhaps it was some place like Moscow or Leningrad where many of us had been educated. These would all be people who shared the same ideals until they were flung into an alien, cold, hostile place — Krasnoyarsk, for example. No matter how much these people try staying together, life creates serious obstacles and problems for them. They are forced to choose what they will do in life — deceive, sell out, kill, betray their own ideals, or maybe cling to something.

Shakespeare tells us that Hamlet studied in Wittenburg and that Horatio was his classmate there. Moreover, Rosencrantz and Guildenstern studied there with them. I did not think it stretching much to assume that Laertes studied there, too, although there is nothing in the play indicating that. Similarly, why could not Bernardo and the other guard be students from the same group?

As we rehearsed, it became clear that one of the actors was perfectly suited to playing Claudius. Since he was the same age as all the others, I realized what I wanted to do. It does happen, after all, that uncles are the same age as their nephews. You get nephews who are older than their uncles, so this was no problem. Hence, all of my characters would be of the same age. They all studied in Wittenburg, Claudius included. So here was the program:

Hamlet, Prince of the Danes.

Horatio, Hamlet's friend and classmate.

Rosencrantz, Hamlet's friend and classmate.

Guildenstern, Hamlet's friend and classmate.

Laertes, Hamlet's friend and classmate.

Claudius, Hamlet's friend and classmate; presently, King of Denmark.

You see the interrelationships — they all are friends. They all grew up with the same ideals. They ate the same food. They told the same jokes. They loved the same women. They drank together. They got into the same trouble as students together. Then, out of the blue, one of them is king and the other is a prince who has his claim to the throne.

When this notion came together for me, the whole show snapped into place. It added a new intensity to the play. I made no changes, no cuts. "To be or not to be" was still there as was everything else. Only everything became much more intense. Claudius, in this interpretation, was not just some thug who usurped the queen and drinks and carouses like all thugs do. He was a close friend, even a relative of Hamlet's, with the same sense of humor and the same general outlook, who, for some reason, suddenly does something that sets him apart entirely.

This was something we could easily understand at that time. Of all of us who had studied together, some invariably attached themselves to the Soviet infrastructure while others refused to do that. And once you took one step toward integrating with the status quo, that forced you to take another, then another, then another. It eventually led you, if not literally to murder, then at least figuratively: You ended up signing letters and denunciations whose ultimate purpose was character assassination. At student meetings, one student would speak out against another in support of expulsion from the institute or the Young Communist League or the Communist Party or the theater or whatever.

Galina Yelifantyeva as mad Ophelia in *Hamlet;* Krasnoyarsk, 1971. *Photo by Boris Barmin.*

This person might willingly bear witness against you in court — as happened to Joseph Brodsky and others.

The approach I took in *Hamlet* was very clear and understandable to everyone. I staged a show about a generation of people who grew up together with one mother, so to speak, one common alma mater. Then the sudden changes and life choices moved in and altered everything. After that, they had to continue living and try to survive.

It so happens in Shakespeare that individuals like Rosencrantz and Guildenstern, who choose to become toadies, are the ones who are killed. And those who choose to become killers and usurpers are, themselves, killed. And those who choose not to participate in that life at all . . . face a similar fate.

This latter method was Hamlet's choice and it was very close to the way many of us, dissidents and others, chose to live our lives in Soviet times. We did not participate in the official life. We did not struggle with anyone or anything. I, personally, never actively struggled against Soviet authority. I merely took no part in it. I was so adamant about not taking part in it in any way that, for me, even talking to a party bureaucrat was almost impossible. I simply did not know how.

One time I had to go to the local board of culture. It was an office full of bureaucrats. This was no simple office. It was the mouthpiece for, and an executive office of, the Communist Party. They fired people; they banned shows; they censored and crippled shows they did not ban. This was all done by the people working at the board of culture. In essence, these were our executioners. They were not acting entirely according to their own will. Among them were people we had gone to school with. I do not literally mean they were our classmates in Leningrad, but they were people of our time and our generation.

I had to go to the board to listen to a discussion of one of our shows, and I recall not being able to make myself touch the door knob. I had to put my sleeve over it to turn it and open the door. Can you imagine that? Believe me, this was not a public act of protest. Nobody saw me do that. Nobody knew about it. I just remember the reflex of having to distance myself from these people in some way.

I remember a cultured, refined, very genteel woman who once represented the Leningrad board of culture at a dress rehearsal of one of

Henrietta's shows. She had to give the show her OK before it could officially open. This was at the Maly Drama Theater in Leningrad, the one now run by Lev Dodin. At that time the theater was outfitted with these awful wooden seats that were attached to each other. It was not a big theater, and she sat right there in the middle to watch. It drove me out of my mind that she had the right to butt in on our intimate affairs and control them. And, of course, rehearsals are intimate affairs. So I grabbed the end seat in that row and started shaking it. I wanted her to feel it shaking. After that they started calling Henrietta and me "row-shakers." Now, whenever Henrietta says to me, "don't shake the rows," she means, "don't do those silly things you used to do when you were young." The woman, of course, did not understand why I was shaking the seats. But I could not help myself.

In *Hamlet* I wanted to maintain all the depth of Shakespeare's existential philosophy, but on the level of plot, on the level of concrete relationships among the characters, I wanted to create people who were extremely close and accessible to us. My show was a prophetic one. Our generation of theater artists was wiped out. People either left the profession or they left this life.

Hamlet avoids taking action of any kind for more than half the play. Remember that moment when Claudius is praying? There is no one around and Hamlet could easily kill him. He even takes out a dagger. But in the text Hamlet says that sending Claudius "to heaven" would be "hire and salary, not revenge." Brought up as an atheist, I found that hard to justify. My Hamlet, as a result, could not sincerely think like that. For me that moment was a ruse — Hamlet merely needed a reason not to kill Claudius. And he was right, because when he kills Polonius — even though it was absolutely by accident — he is sucked into a chain of events that ends with him killing a large number of people in the finale. After he murders Polonius, the insanity that he purposefully dons as a mask becomes the real thing. I emphasized that by having the same actor play both Polonius and the Gravedigger, of which my show had only one. You see how that works, then. When Hamlet approaches the open grave, he sees what appears to be Polonius coming out of it. His insanity consists of the fact that he loses himself; Hamlet who has murdered is no longer Hamlet.

Alexander Kovalenko as Hamlet and Yevgeny Pokramovich as the Gravedigger in *Hamlet;* Krasnoyarsk, 1971. *Photo by Boris Barmin.*

This is one manner of mental illness, when the personality breaks down. He is no longer himself. After that murder, it is not Hamlet whom we follow through the final quarter of the play. It is someone else.

Later I read where Jan Kott counted the number of people Hamlet kills. Claudius never dreamed of killing so many. Hamlet first kills Polonius. Then, in a sinister way, he sends Rosencrantz and Guildenstern to their deaths. Sure, they wanted to kill him. But he escaped and that should have been enough. He did not have to go through with the writing of that death letter and give it to Rosencrantz and Guildernstern. This is no longer the accidental homicide of Polonius, but is a sadistic, premeditated murder. Further, Hamlet is to blame for Ophelia's death. She goes mad because her father was killed, and the killer was her beloved Hamlet. That serves as Ophelia's death sentence. Beyond that, Claudius and Laertes die at his hand. The latter is coincidental, but that is not the point. Six people. Claudius did not kill so many.

This is the result of a total character breakdown. Hamlet feared that. He feared that if he were to begin taking part in life, he would break down. That if he were to join in the living of life, he would cease to be himself.

That is my conclusion based on my personal experience. I, indeed, avoided taking part in life for a very long time. Honestly, that was a great problem. I suffered terribly. I did not know what to do about it. Several of my colleagues, my classmates — they were not people without talent — became part of the status quo in Soviet theater affairs. They sold out although there was a certain balance you could strike. That is what people did. You sold out, but you also found ways to create art.

I could not do that.

That was a serious problem for me because I scorned my colleagues who had become a part of the status quo. I saw through the cunning and deception of what they did. I saw the effect it had on their shows.

I have always loved a phrase Andrzej Wajda uttered after he saw Grigory Chukhrai's film *Clear Sky*. Earlier, Chukhrai had made a wonderful film, *Ballad of a Soldier*, about his youth and the war. *Clear Sky* was, in part, about the difficulties of Stalinist times being replaced by the "marvelous" Khrushchev era. The film really did not say much, it just barely drew back the curtain on the changes of the times. A river that was frozen over ever so slightly begins to flow again — a man, who had only just thought he would be arrested, is shown to come out of some ministry carrying a Hero of the Soviet Union medal.

After seeing this film, Wajda said, "That is a place of no return."

It was a tragically prophetic phrase. After that film Chukhrai was not able to do anything. He made one very bad film after which he made almost nothing at all. It was said that the reason for that was failing health. Was that a coincidence? This kind of situation was something Henrietta and I felt extremely deeply. It informed my production of *Hamlet*.

Where does your production of *Macbeth* fit into your work?

The plot continued a theme I had pursued for some time: that of crime and punishment. Even when I staged *The Lady with the Lapdog,* I was staging *Crime and Punishment.* Chekhov's idea of crime is that a man had existed senselessly, without meaning. He lived forty years and was punished by Life, which brought him love.

Love as punishment. Love as a trial. As a test. As punishment. That is very Russian. And very much Chekhov. Gurov is crushed by love. He does not measure up to it. As we often fail to measure up to life's demands. Life demands that we live to the maximum degree possible. It expects us to measure up to the titan of Life! And to all of life's complexities.

Measure up! But we are not able to. We do it just a little and then we close our eyes. Life is off over there somewhere, and here we are existing over here. You have a wife, kids, job, card games, conversations and interaction with people of some sort — is that not life? Yes, it is, but not really.

For the first time ever, Gurov ran up against life in the form of love. Gurov, as we know, had many beautiful women. Now he meets one who is not all that pretty or intelligent. She is quiet, provincial, and a little silly. That is the humor and the paradox of Chekhov. Chekhov is a genius in that he never has goddesses of fate doing the punishing. It is not like Aeschylus. Nobody gets their eyes put out. Nobody sleeps with their mother or kills their father. There is none of that. Gurov is simply crushed when he himself does not measure up. I think that is brilliant. That is one of the types of crime and punishment.

That plot is in *Macbeth,* too. A man committed a crime and was punished for it. But this time it was not the crime or the punishment that interested me. It was not the politics, the problem of power, the struggle with power, court intrigues, what it means to be a good or bad ruler or a criminal on the throne. I was interested in the way life lures. Life lures. It is always giving us opportunities.

There is money lying there — true, it is not mine.

There is an apple you can pluck, but the garden is not yours.

You can climb Mount Blanc, but you might break your neck.

You can travel to the North Pole, but you might freeze.

You might be the greatest director ever, but you might fail. If you are modest and careful you will never fail. But if you have ambitions, imagine how painful it is to find out every time that you are not the greatest that ever was.

Life lures. It presents opportunities. And a person wants to express himself. Wants to realize himself. Wants to leave some sign about himself. I am Kama Ginkas who — and there is some sign there. I am Kama Ginkas who stages productions in Finland. I am the person who kicked the winning goal. I am the person who wears sweaters and not sports jackets. I am someone. I am the one who is different.

And then there is the matter of a person realizing his capabilities. "I can run, so I run." "I can't jump, but I'll try it. It turns out I can jump." To do that you have to overstep, to transgress something. As a Jewish boy I have to sit in the ghetto and not stick my head out anywhere. But I want to study so I cross the line. I transgress.

I am Adam. Eve and I are among the representatives of the herd of paradise. By twos, the bull and the cow, the he-goat and the she-goat, Adam and Eve. We all graze together. The wolf does not eat me. I do not eat the ewe. Everything is peaceful and calm. I am not any-one. I am Adam, but I am no one. I want to know myself, and so I know Eve, whom I was forbidden to know. And so I come to know myself. But I committed a crime. It was forbidden. I did not kill any-one. I did not rob anyone. I only knew her and came to know myself. But I was not supposed to do that and we were banished.

As I see it, we are sent here — damned to come here — to be born in pain. We are punished for the original sin. I can be a member of the herd, a no one, and grow like grass. But if I want to know myself fur-ther, I transgress, commit a crime. It does not have to be murder. It is just that Shakespeare is a crude playwright. He picks on crude, obvi-ous things. The parable of Adam and Eve is very beautiful, but it is not very clear: why all the prohibitions? What interested me was a man who commits a crime, desiring to know himself.

An individual is lured by life, by all of life's opportunities. But at the same time he is forbidden. You should *not* go to the North Pole. You might die. But you want to go because you want to know

Santeri Kinnunen as Macbeth and Anna-Leena Lyytikainen as Lady Macbeth in *Macbeth;* Helsinki, 1997. *Photo by Ken Reynolds.*

yourself. There are all kinds of silly things we do. Mother says, "Don't drink water from the faucet." I want to do it for the very reason that I was forbidden to. So I do it and I do not get sick. What have I done? I transgressed. I manifested myself. I am the guy who could do it.

Macbeth portrays a life that lures. Macbeth is a young man who loves his wife and she loves him. Basically, they are told, "You have an opportunity." It is very difficult to reject that allure. True, it is a crime, but that is easy enough to justify to yourself. My *Macbeth* was not about the crime. It was about *life* which lures and deceives. Lures and punishes.

Your production of *Macbeth* looked like none I had ever imagined.

I found what you might call a proto-habitat. Adam and Eve. But it had to be an abstract Adam and Eve. So I dreamed up a time and a place inhabited by barbarian tribes who live in herds with a leader. I wanted to peel away the civilized luster that exists even in Shakespeare. The luster of the Renaissance, of poetry, of Christianity. I staged it as a pre-Christian story. It was a story about a time when witches quite naturally communicated with people, as in Greek times the gods communicated with people. I was after that kind of consciousness, where our Christian, bourgeois perception of sin does not exist.

Remember? Zeus killed his father Chronos, the high god. And that is when he became Zeus. There was no problem in that. It was a time when it was natural to kill off the old wolf to make room for the young wolf. Otherwise the pack begins dying off. The old wolf cannot lead them to food anymore, cannot defend them. It is a natural law, an animalistic level of existence. Animals sleep with their offspring and there is no problem. But when Oedipus killed his father and married his mother, he put out his own eyes. Greek tragedy arose when such things were beginning to be perceived as sins. When people were beginning to become people. A code of laws began to arise for a human, as opposed to an animal, existence.

I went back to the tribes. I did not need a real one. Just as Shakespeare was not writing about England or Scotland. He did not write a history or a chronicle. He wrote poetry.

I was amazed to discover it, but Duncan is Macbeth's relative, an uncle. They were all aunts and uncles. That is how it was; only we pay no attention. We think, "Oh, it's just a story about a kingdom and it's only a coincidence that this guy is somebody's uncle." But this is a

Santeri Kinnunen, center, as Macbeth in *Macbeth;* Helsinki, 1997. *Photo by Ken Reynolds.*

single family. A single tribe. They all descended from the same forefather. Just as, I suppose, Scots descended from one forefather. The Germans descended from one forefather. The Jews descended from Abraham. Within this context, however, what interested me were not the tribal interrelations, but rather the sudden awareness of sin.

Next, there are certain elementary rituals and signs. Let us take a struggle for the throne. What is it? It is a struggle for a chair. A throne is a complex notion. It is really a chair. Or a battle for the crown. What is a crown? It is a piece of head gear. A hat. It is a battle for a hat. So, to move toward this proto-history, we have a certain hat which signifies you have the right to command me. It does not have to be a hat. In my tribe an old man holds a chicken. The chicken is dressed in peacock feathers. They are not her feathers; they have been put on her. She is attired. She is different. There are normal chickens in the show. They walk around and peck and drop droppings. But the leader's chicken is different. One of his sons carries a chair on his back. Whenever they arrive anywhere, he puts the chair down and the old man sits down on it.

Imagine what went into creating that chair! It is nothing less than an atom bomb! It is an amazing invention. You can sit in it comfortably. In the whole tribe there is only one chair and, naturally, the leader sits in it. Everyone else sits on the ground or stands. Plus, the leader carries a specially dressed chicken. It is obvious that when you become the leader, you will get to sit in the chair instead of on the wet ground. And you will get to have the outfitted chicken.

My *Macbeth* portrayed the life of a tribe like that.

Naturally, when the chair was put down, everybody bowed down to it. Because it is unique. Why do people make strange motions with their hands when they walk into a church? Just moments ago they were walking and talking normally and all of a sudden they make some furtive sign over their chest with their hand.

I took a lot of the things we do and looked at them anew.

The King says, "I want my eldest son to inherit the throne. And so I appoint him Prince Cumberland." At this point in my show the King suddenly hopped in the air. And then everybody else did, too. Strange? But why not? Why should everybody shout "hurrah"? Why not make some gesture with your hand or, even better, hop in the air? Who said it had to be "hurrah"?

You created an entire world with its own symbols and laws of existence.

That is right. It was very similar to what we know and at the same time very strange.

When Macbeth was still a general he had blue palms. The thane of Cawdor, who is defeated and succeeded by Macbeth, had yellow palms. In my show this is how that transpired: Witches appeared from beneath the ground between the legs of Macbeth and Banquo. They address Macbeth first as the thane of Glamis, then as the thane of Cawdor and finally as "King hereafter." Macbeth is angered and says, "The thane of Cawdor lives." The witches disappear. Warriors arrive and inform Macbeth that the King is pleased with his battle exploits and has appointed him the thane of Cawdor. They paint Macbeth's hands yellow. He shouts, "The thane of Cawdor lives: why do you dress me in borrow'd robes?" They reply that he will be executed shortly.

Duncan is the king, so his hands are white. When Macbeth kills Duncan, his hands are bloody red. Lady Macbeth offers to smear her hands in blood, too. But they wash their hands, which become white and they become King and Queen. Everything is washed away. Everything is fine.

What does it mean when someone wears three little stars in one place or one big star in another? It signifies a general or a captain or something. That's strange too. The thane of Glamis had blue hands. Now he is the thane of Cawdor so they are yellow. When he becomes the King his hands will be white.

Was *Macbeth* one of those shows that you had wanted to do for decades?

I had wanted to do *Macbeth* for about six years. I finally did it in Finland because the production side was extremely important. The strange, mummy-like costumes, for instance. There is a reference there, because Christ wore swaddling. It was also an ancient manner of burial. The actors were in these costumes that made them look like mummies on the one hand, and diapered babies on the other. That was very important for me.

There was a terrible scene when Macbeth confronted the witches. In Shakespeare they are boiling herbs in cauldrons. My version was different. My witches — who were wrapped only in part, their heads and legs were covered but their breasts were exposed — had black sacks. From the sacks they began littering the stage with pieces of paper and little babies — I used seventy lifelike dolls. Then they covered all that with trash. Since my witches appeared from out of the ground, Macbeth cleared away the ground and summoned them by knocking. They appeared and then a sort of erotic, sexual, shamanistic scene of ecstasy began. They squatted in very indecent poses. Then they began twisting and turning and pulling out from within themselves one baby after another. They gave birth to all these children. Then swaddled men appeared and lay down behind the witches. And, with terrible shrieks, the witches pulled the men from behind them as if out of their wombs, as if giving birth to them.

Your lighting in *Macbeth* was stunning, whipping in from the side like a gale force wind.

It indeed was stunning lighting, and I must say I did not design it. The remarkable Finnish lighting designer Juhani Leppänen created that.

Naturally, I established the task. The space was extraordinarily long and narrow. Abnormally so. The depth was very shallow, only seven meters. At the New Generation Theater in Moscow, for example, the length from the forestage to the backstage area is thirteen meters. That is a normal depth. Bigger theaters may have fifteen meters. Opera theaters may have twenty. The usual stage space is, say, ten meters wide and ten to thirteen meters deep. The depth for my *Macbeth* was just seven meters, while the width was approximately twenty-five. When the stage-left wall opened up, there was even another five or ten meters I could use.

Moreover, Sergei Barkhin's set for that show enhanced the sensation of length and narrowness. It appeared as a long hose or intestine that continued out into the offstage area stage left. In total it was approximately thirty-five meters long and only five meters deep. Imagine what that looked like. It was like a long worm.

That configuration was further enhanced by the lighting. The spots were set up at a low trajectory from offstage left, approximately at the same height as the actors.

As a rule, theatrical lighting is directed from above. Batten lights, strips of lights, and spots directed from the upper loges. This creates problems because you get shadows on eyes. That is why you also have footlights that cast light from below. Footlights are seldom used in contemporary theater because it is a "theatrical," unnatural light. Why do you think lighting from above is considered the norm? Because it is as if the sun were shining. It is as simple as that. So that is the traditional, usual theatrical lighting. Which, of course, means it is of no interest to me at all. What I want is to escape the common, realistic method of lighting. I want the spectators to sense something peculiar.

I may use footlights, only not as they usually are used in the theater. For example, I use them in *The Black Monk*. Why do you think you have such a strong sensation of the peacock feathers in that show?

In the dramatization of Chekhov's *The Black Monk,* Kovrin (Sergei Makovetsky) and his father-in-law Pesotsky (Vladimir Kashpur) talk things over in the latter's garden, represented in Sergei Barkhin's set with a field of peacock feathers; Moscow, 1999. *Photo by Ken Reynolds.*

It is because they are illuminated from below. In fact, the lighting there is established not so much to illuminate the actors as it is to fall on the field of feathers. Of course, the light also catches the underside of the actors' chins, the upper arches of their eyes, their nostrils and so forth.

In the theatrical tradition this is infernal lighting. In the opera when the devil used to appear from a trap door he was lit from below. Yury Lyubimov often uses an expressive lighting from below.

In *The Black Monk* I use it in a way that is devoid of special effects. It imparts a strangeness because it is neither the usual theatrical lighting from above, nor is it the infernal lighting. Its function is to give texture to the field of feathers rather than illuminating the actors. The feathers, in fact, cast shadows on the actors above them. So this lighting is very different from what we are accustomed to in the theater.

But, let me come back to *Macbeth.* The first time I was in Norway I was amazed by that country's unusual light. I was there in November or December when the highest the sun gets is on a level with the treetops. As a result, all objects, including people, cast very long shadows. This gives every object and every person a strange appearance. I was not used to seeing them in this way.

In Russia we see something similar when the sun goes down. But that is usually for a short period — perhaps an hour or an hour and a half. And the sun in Norway is white, while our Russian evening sun is a hot color, reddish or yellow. It comes in at an angle that seems to be about the same height as a human being. It evokes a strange atmosphere and it does not last for long.

Now, I did not think about this when I was staging *Macbeth,* but it came to me later: Look at the photos or the films of the Americans on the moon. They are illuminated by a very strange light. It literally is not an earthly light.

In *Macbeth* I needed something strange. I needed to avoid the usual, the normal, the typical. I wanted to evoke the sensation of a primitive, I might even say, a cosmic, atmosphere. What I mean by that is that I

A scene from *Macbeth;* Helsinki, 1997. *Photo by Ken Reynolds.*

wanted it to be clear that this was all taking place at a time when the earth was not yet illuminated by the earthly light we now know. It was a time when we still did not even know how light is supposed to shine.

That is why I had that specific lighting. I do not use side lighting everywhere, but there was a specific reason for it in *Macbeth*. Three-quarters of the light was like that in that show. It was very harsh, bright light, as it might be in the desert.

I was born and grew up in the desert, so that light was very familiar to me. I would say the lighting in *Macbeth* was very similar to the morning sun one sees in the desert.

Well, in *Macbeth* we created a desert. We did not imitate a desert but created the impression of a desert. The set was made of paper, so there was no imitation at all. No imitation of earth or sand. We needed to evoke the feeling that people were still alien here, that they did not yet belong to the land or it to them. They had not assimilated their surroundings yet. Similar to those astronauts who skipped across the surface of the moon, they were still strangers in their own land.

You say that one can play Shakespeare because he is a crude writer, but that Chekhov is another story.

That is true.

That raises a question that could lead us far afield, but I cannot pass up the chance to pose it now. You often seem to give words implications that are diametrically opposed to their dictionary meanings. When you use a word that we usually assume to have a negative connotation, I sense that for you it has a positive implication. The contrary is also true. Words that we are conditioned to perceive as positive often sound negative in your use. In fact, whenever you start saying "nice things," I always start doubting you.

Because of my irony.

So, when you call Shakespeare a crude writer, I sense you mean something else.

That is true. He is not crude in a general sense, of course. He is crude in the sense that his plays are constructed on a very simple basis. They are often detective stories. Court intrigues. There is always a murder. There is always some treachery of some sort. In terms of the action, in terms of what induces the spectator to follow what is happening, his plays are structured with very elementary components. Mad love, enflamed passions, jealousy. Shakespeare has people going mad, ghosts appearing.

Chekhov entirely avoids plots built on intrigues. Chekhov does not give us direct struggles between people. The more I think about Chekhov's later plays, the more I think he does not touch on the topic of love at all. At least not the kind of love that moves the play forward.

Even *The Three Sisters* is not given movement by the love between Masha and Vershinin or the love of Tuzenbach for Irina. Love in this play takes place backstage, so to speak, during the intermissions. Chekhov wrote no love scenes here. There is no jealousy at all. Kuligin might be jealous, but we do not see his jealousy. As a character, Kuligin is so minor that, even if he is jealous, that cannot have any impact on the play.

Solyony is jealous of Tuzenbach and Irina, but that is a different kind of jealousy. That is something very deep seated.

Moreover, it is not what moves the play forward.

In Shakespeare it is very clear. Jealousy is a motor of the play. Love is a motor of the play. Naturally, it ends with a murder. In fact, there usually are lots of murders. That is what I mean when I say crude.

However, Shakespeare is a genius as a poet. All his wealth as a writer exists outside his plots, outside the intrigues he spins. Even outside psychology. He is not the most subtle of psychologists. His wealth is his poetry in which his plots nearly dissolve. And, even when they do not dissolve, their crude structures making us follow simplistic actions lead us to the riches of poetry.

I have always thought that Alexander Ostrovsky is another writer of this kind of wealth. But, as far as I know, you have never staged him.

I have never staged him. I love him, but I fear him.

When I look at you, I can see the connection to Shakespeare. But I do not see a connection to Ostrovsky, although I do see a connection between Shakespeare and Ostrovsky.

There are several reasons, but the main one is that Ostrovsky is a very Russian writer and I am not a Russian. I am not English, either, but Shakespeare is so universal that he gives me the right to stage him. To do Ostrovsky, you have to have a very deep feeling for what is Russian. I do not have that feeling, and I can tell I would be faking it.

DOSTOEVSKY

One of your favorite authors has been Dostoevsky. It does not seem to have bothered you that he was a pretty hardcore anti-Semite. I asked you about that once and I found your reply intriguing: You said something to the effect of, "It wasn't that he didn't love Jews. It was that he hated anything rational." What I would like to know now is what your attitude to rationalism is.

First I want to say that Dostoevsky, indeed, did not like Jews. In many things, like all people, he was very primitive and simple. You can be a great philosopher and hate your neighbor whose snoring comes through the wall. In fact, it was not that Dostoevsky did not like Jews — he hated them. But he also hated Poles. He hated Germans. He could not stand the French. Americans for him were on a level with the Chinese.

I always like to recall that when Dostoevsky sends Svidrigailov off to kill himself in *Crime and Punishment,* he has him say, "Tell them I went to America."

You see? That is what America was for Dostoevsky: suicide. Because the idea of a Russian in America is suicide. But, Dostoevsky's anti-Semitic and Russian chauvinistic ideas are not grounded merely in an everyday hatred of Jews, Germans, or Poles. He was hostile toward those peoples' very ways of life, their rationalism.

You ask about my own attitude toward rationalism. I will tell you. Twenty years ago an acquaintance of mine in Lithuania read my palm. Whether she was right or wrong, she said I had excellent harmony between the rational and the emotional. That is very bad for a creative person. Any kind of harmony for a creative person is bad. The artist always needs something to overcome.

I do not like rational theater. When I was still a student at the institute, intellectual theater was very much in fashion. Sartre and Camus. Brecht. I always hated it. I had not staged Dostoevsky yet, but I had discovered *Notes from Underground* and had written my dramatization of it. This was at a time when most people in the Soviet Union, even among the intelligentsia, had no knowledge of *Notes from Underground.* I discovered it because I felt a kinship with it.

I do not like much of what is rational in me. First, because I am a Jew. Second, because that is my nature. What saves me, I guess, is that my life and my temperament are so irrational. That probably seeps through into my productions. What is rationality? It is believing too much in professionalism. In your schooling. It is knowing too well how to do something. It is trusting your instrument too much. Or the material. That all makes you too rational or it makes you a mere craftsman.

You did two similar productions of *Crime and Punishment,* one in Helsinki in 1990, the other in Moscow in 1991. They were not identical shows by any means, but they were based on the same text. Still, they were performed in different places with different sets by different actors in different languages for very different audiences. And, judging by what you have said in the past, you found one of the two productions much more satisfying.

What I can say is this: The difference in nature between the Western and the Russian actor worked to my advantage in my Finnish production of *Crime and Punishment*.

You would think that Swedes — my production was performed by Finnish Swedes in Swedish — have little in common with Dostoevsky. What does Dostoevsky mean? Dostoevsky means guts on the table and enjoying the fact that your guts are on the table. There is almost a sense of pride in knowing that your guts are on the table. Suffering in public. That is diametrically opposed to the Western way of life. And it is particularly opposed to the Lutheran and Swedish outlook.

For a Swede, the personal life is highly private. He will not wash his laundry in public nor will he complain publicly, to say nothing of the fact that he would never make a public spectacle of it. For the Swede that is the height of gross behavior. I do not only mean that he would consider it bad manners, he would consider it inhuman. They have a completely different measure of behavior, and I began to respect it greatly, the longer I was exposed to it.

The bottom line is that you yourself shall stand before God. You alone. You made your choices, now you answer yourself. There is a dignity about that which you carry before people and God. You ask the hard questions of yourself just as God will ask you later. This is the classical bourgeois outlook — each person is the maker of his own life.

So, with this in mind, who would think that Dostoevsky would be of interest to the Swedes? Their point of view is that God will ask of you what He will, not you of Him.

The Russian, Dostoevskian manner of wailing and railing at God is completely alien to them. The Russian weeps and howls: "How could you do this to me!? I can't live like this any longer! Well, if you don't care about me, I don't care about you either! And to prove it, I'll dance on my own spilled guts!" That is Russian and that is Dostoevskian.

That Russian manner is well known and has been expressed so often in so many ways that it has largely lost its power. It ceases to have an effect. It ceases to be a subject of art. Often it is overplayed terribly. That brings on the overkill of frayed nerves and hysterics. Through it all you do not even recognize Dostoevsky. Aside from everything else,

Dostoevsky is an intellectual. In his novels, he creates intellectual structures. He tackles problems of the intellect and the spirit.

Dostoevsky's characters are often neurotic, but he is not interested in medicine. He needs such characters merely because they are more expressive of what he is trying to say. In fact, everything he does is very carefully constructed. Look at his title: *Crime and Punishment*. It is a very neat construct. The same thing with *The Brothers Karamazov*, a novel in which each individual brother has his own unique path in life, his own unique argument. Only, it is not a linguistic argument, it is Dostoevsky's own argument with himself, a debate of substance. It is one that functions on a gut level, on the level of human fates.

When Swedes play Dostoevsky you will never see guts on the table. It simply will not happen. You can try everything in the book to get it out of them, but you will fail utterly. It is opposed to their nature.

On the other hand, the Swede is a live, sensitive person. He is sincere. And, as a talented actor, he accepts, believes, and understands the circumstances and logic that I, as the director, establish. Therefore we have a certain alienation or estrangement. Everything is happening as it should, but it has been shifted somehow. There is an added irony. It is as though the actor is examining himself at the same time that he is examining what he is performing. This is what produced such a wonderful, unexpected result in Helsinki, one that differs from what you would expect of Dostoevsky. He became more voluminous because his novel took on a sense of playacting.

It was in Moscow that I called the show *We Play "Crime"*; in Helsinki it was simply titled *Crime and Punishment*. But, in many ways, the Helsinki production was the more playful. That really is where we played at *Crime and Punishment*. Because there we had Swedes playing Russians in Swedish working with a Russian actress playing in Russian. The very nature of that project was conducive to playacting.

But in the acting, I would say that there was less "playing," that is, less faking it. Asko Sarkola's performance of Porfiry Petrovich was filled with playfulness and irony. He toyed with himself as he toyed with Marcus Grott's Raskolnikov.

Marcus Grott, in my opinion, did not perform all that well in

Helsinki. He was young at that time, and he did what he was capable of. I think he played better in Moscow. I went out on a limb when I brought him to Moscow to perform in Swedish. It should have been a failure because there were excellent actors all over town who could easily have played that role. And here I bring a Finnish Swede to Moscow to play Raskolnikov in a Russian show. Nonsense. But it worked because we were not *playing* Raskolnikov, we were playing *at* Raskolnikov. As a result, the audiences and critics not only forgave him his approximation of Raskolnikov, they perceived it as his great achievement. Because there was a distance.

The Russian spectator was able to watch this highly familiar role from an unusual distance. As a result of the playfulness which I introduced into the material, Marcus Grott did not so much play Raskolnikov as he played a Swede who wants to be Raskolnikov. In the Helsinki show, he was perceived by the audience as Raskolnikov without that added distance.

Porfiry Petrovich (Viktor Gvozditsky) sits on the floor as he interrogates Raskolnikov (Marcus Grott) in *We Play "Crime,"* a dramatization of Dostoevsky's *Crime and Punishment;* Moscow, 1991. *Photo by Igor Kravchenko.*

Asko Sarkola gave a marvelous performance of Porfiry in Helsinki. He played — everything at once. He played the fool. He toyed with his partner Marcus Grott, a younger actor. He was too old to play Raskolnikov by this time, but twenty years ago he probably would have been the one playing Raskolnikov. By which I mean to say that he knew everything about the path Raskolnikov had chosen. He played the tempter. If he did not exactly play a father figure, he did play an older authority figure.

An uncle perhaps.

An uncle. That is exactly right. He played an uncle delighting in playing tricks on his nephew.

In Helsinki there was a sense of joy about it all. There, Porfiry Petrovich toyed with Raskolnikov to attain and impart knowledge. He wanted to share part of the journey with this young man whom he probably even liked. He wanted to help him learn something, to attain some understanding. The main thing that imparted volume to the Helsinki show was the sheer love of life that Asko brought to his character of Porfiry Petrovich.

This is very important because Dostoevsky has almost no character who can be said to really love life. If there is such a character, it is usually a criminal, one who violates norms. Take Svidrigailov, for instance. But you cannot call him one who loves life, really. He is more a cannibal. His love of life is the love of ingesting live flesh. That is not really a love of life. So, when Porfiry Petrovich becomes a person possessed of a great love for life, this work acquires a new dimension. It is played in a new key.

You cannot play love of life in the theater. In the theater, you can love to perform on stage. You can take pleasure in the fact that you are on stage and are engaging in the "pranks that are characteristic of theater." The sum total of that is an approximation of the love of life.

The fact remains that in *Crime and Punishment* and *We Play "Crime,"* I wanted to stage a tender production about a father and a son or a writer and his character. About the fact that they are bound by love even though they torment one another. In the Moscow production, my actor playing Porfiry did not have that delight. The tricks he played on Raskolnikov were evil and wicked. They really were not tricks, they were mocking taunts. That is a big difference. And with that change, the show lost that voluminous quality.

Ever since I staged *We Play "Crime,"* it has been a part of my conscious desire to develop the aspects of sensitivity and delicacy in my work. I did not achieve it in that show, but I wanted to stage a tender show about a father and his child. The "child" is Raskolnikov, the young intellectual who murdered a "useless" pawnbroker to make a philosophical point, but ended up killing the old woman's innocent sister to cover up his ugly crime. The "father" is Porfiry Petrovich — and the author of the show, if you will, Kama Ginkas. He is not a sentimental father or author who fusses over his child. He is strict and severe. He must be that to keep his son from making the same terrible mistakes he has made. He batters his son. He actually puts his son through the same terrible conflicts that he went through himself. The difference is that he did not know then how to react to these conflicts — now he does. He wants to force his son to go through them so as to be able to say, "Don't do it that way! Don't make the same errors. We have already been through that. We already know that! When you go through these conflicts, draw different conclusions!"

But as always, young people believe nothing and must experience everything themselves. That is what the father — the author and Porfiry Petrovich — comes to realize. He is horrified at what his son must go through and yet, at the same time, he has the most tender emotions for him. It hurts him more now than when he went through it all himself because now he knows what needs to be done. He pushes his son toward the next conflict, knowing full well how his son will cry out in pain. He thinks, "My poor child!" He thinks, "How funny! How his reactions resemble mine! He has the same gestures, the same intonations. He does the very same things! Just as I did, he sticks his hand in the fire and then blows on it to cool it off!"

Every second of the Moscow production should have been infused with tenderness — my tenderness and that of Porfiry Petrovich for Raskolnikov. For all the cruelty, all the provocative nature of their relationship, Porfiry Petrovich should have adored Raskolnikov. I believe it did not happen properly in that show for several reasons. Perhaps I merely failed to achieve what I wanted. Perhaps the relationship between the actors Viktor Gvozditsky and Marcus Grott got in the way. There were a lot of reasons.

You came back to the same novel a third time in *K. I. from "Crime,"* only on this occasion you focused strictly on one single character — the seemingly minor figure of Katerina Ivanovna, the widow of the drunken Marmeladov. In other words you took an author famed for his polyphonic novels and distilled him to a single voice.

K. I. from "Crime" has an extremely complex internal structure. Perhaps one of the most complex of any I have done. It is built according to the Stanislavsky school. Consider his term, the *inciting event.* This is the event that moves the action forward. In other words, it is what happened *beforehand.*

The direction in which a performance progresses depends upon how the director determines and defines the inciting event. If the director says the inciting event of *K. I. from "Crime"* is that Katerina Ivanovna is hungry and must find some way to feed her children, it becomes a very different show than what I staged. I would say that almost nothing in my show could remain if it were to be restaged as a show about hunger or a show about how Katerina Ivanovna was evicted from her apartment and ended up on the street. If that were to be the inciting event — Katerina Ivanovna being evicted from her home — we would have an entirely different set of actions and tasks. What does she plan to do? What does she do? She begs to get money for food. That is one thing. She defends her human dignity. That is another. She provides for her children's future. That is a third. Those are all different productions. Do you sense that?

When we create an event that incites, it sets off a complex chain of actions and reactions. Take, for example, the death of Katerina Ivanovna's husband. But even that means almost nothing by itself. That is just a label. For every person, the death of someone close is a tragedy. Everyone experiences that tragedy in their own way and then they get on with their life. So that tells us nothing new.

This, then, is crucial: What does Marmeladov's death mean for Katerina Ivanovna?

Here is what I explained to the actress Oksana Mysina: Your husband was a drunk and he used to steal all your money. In other words, you are free now that he has died! You have been liberated. Why suffer? Life should be easier now!

Why, then, does Katerina Ivanovna die after her husband dies?

Well, there are physical reasons. Dostoevsky wrote that she is ill — that is true. But if the determining factor was Katerina's tuberculosis, she could have died before or after her husband. And this is Dostoevsky — which means that the sequence of deaths is no mere coincidence. Dostoevsky created a dramatic structure.

That brings us back to the question: Why is Katerina's death caused by the clumsy, silly death of her ridiculous, worthless husband — a man who really only gets in her way? Essentially, Marmeladov is a flaw in her life; he is her sorrowful burden. But, still, his death, her liberation from him, is what brings on her own death. What does that mean?

What I explained to the actress was this — Marmeladov was Katerina's reason for being, he was her obstacle to overcome. True, even without him she had plenty of obstacles. Every day was an obstacle to her. But she perceived Marmeladov as the source of all her misfortunes. You see? *He* was the source of her misfortunes. And when you know the source of your misfortunes, when you can strike out at it as one would at a wall with a fist, when you can point at it and say, "Here it is! Here it is!" — then you are alive, you can live.

You overcome. You struggle with your obstacles. You are alive.

When that obstacle disappeared, the reason for Katerina's being disappeared with it. It does not matter that she only *imagined* he was the reason for all her misfortunes. Losing that perceived source of misfortune was what brought down on her real misfortune in all its naked horror. That is something she is in no position to overcome.

So, you see? That means death has come to her.

It turns out that everything else she constantly complained about was merely a buffer between her and death. It allowed her not to see what was coming. That gave her something to struggle with, something to blame everything on. What is left now is emptiness. Total, naked death. Death in all its nakedness and immutability.

Now, there you have the inciting event for *K. I. from "Crime."*

Beyond that, Katerina must do something to survive, to prevail. But this is an event, against which, by nature, you cannot prevail. So what can she do? This is not a wall. This is *emptiness, nothing*. A wall you can break down. I say that all the time; that you can break through a wall. You may smash the bones in your hand while you are at it, but you *can* break down the wall. You can break down a wall with your head. You can scratch it with your fingernails.

You cannot do that with emptiness.

What does Katerina do? She begins grasping at the emptiness around her. She attempts to fill the emptiness with phantoms. All of her efforts are directed toward not seeing that she has lost the object of her fury. She tries to make an end run around it. She simply acts as if Marmeladov did not die. That was someone else who died. She makes something official of it, as if she were burying a faceless bureaucrat who worked for many years in a generic office. She pretends it is not really happening to her.

You see this happen to people in a state of shock: "See, I have a piece of paper here confirming the fact." A statement or action like that instantly puts a distance between the person and whatever event has befallen them. It allows them to remain off to the side.

Explaining this to the actress was very difficult. And doing it, for her, was even more difficult. Because the obstacles are not concrete. It is one thing to try opening a door when the key will not fit. In that case you have a specific obstacle and tools to work with. You struggle and struggle and then — there! — you did it. But in the case of Katerina Ivanovna, the obstacle is a chimera. It is there, but it is not! The task here is to grasp at nothingness; but what can you grasp at? How do you do that?

My explanation to the actress was a story that I often use. It is the tragic story of my father's funeral. This requires a substantial digression.

My father Miron was the first and only man in the life of my mother Fruma, whom everyone always called Manya. After she met him, she never imagined there could possibly be any other men more interesting or attractive. There were three children in our family, and father, essentially, was the fourth child among us. Father was like me, nervous, explosive, and authoritarian. He was a leader, a manager by nature. But for Mother he was the fourth child. Moreover, he was the most important one among us. No matter how much she loved us children with all her Jewish love, Father was still the most beloved. We knew that, we understood it, and we had no problem with it. I could not imagine Mother surviving Father's death.

At the funeral, Mother sat where she was supposed to be. She was constantly busy with little tasks, making sure people were seated or standing in the proper places, ordering flowers to be put in specific locations, or making sure that Father's hair was properly combed if a hair fell out of place.

What, in effect, was transpiring? Throughout their lives together, Mother never allowed Father to — how do I say this correctly? — Father never knew what he would be wearing the next day. Let us say he had an appointment at the ministry. Mother, of course, knew he was going to the ministry. Therefore, in the morning, his suit was already laid out. All the papers he would need were already set out. In his pockets she had put the exact amount of money he would need. His passport was there; his papers were there; his handkerchief had been slipped in place. Sometimes she would chase after him and give his hair an extra last-minute brushing. His tie, his shirt, his suit, she took care of all that.

When Father died, she continued doing the same thing at the funeral. She primped his handkerchief, brushed back his hair, rearranged a flower. If the music was playing a bit too loud, she asked them to turn it down. There was a cold breeze, so people had to be arranged so as not to catch cold, and so on.

I could not understand what she was doing! It was driving me crazy. I had it in my head that all that was left my mother now was to die herself. Instead, here she was, full of activity.

My father's body was carried out and put in the hearse. My mother, my aunt, and I accompanied it.

My mother and my aunt had a curious relationship. My aunt had no children before the war because she was afraid of what was to come. Mother, however, had her first child. After the war, my aunt thought it best to wait some more because peace and stability still had not come. My mother, meanwhile, gave birth to a second and then a third child. My aunt never did have children.

My aunt always considered my mother simple and uneducated. She did not quite consider her worthy of her brother. He was an intellectual. That was the basis of the curious relationship between my mother and my aunt. My mother with her three children, her job, her husband, her household all on her shoulders, quietly despised her frivolous, bohemian sister-in-law. My aunt wrote poetry, attended the theater, was always in the middle of company, spent hours on the telephone.

When my father's casket was carried out, my aunt asked me, "Kama, where is Papa?"

Everybody called my father "Papa." They did not use his name. He was just Papa. That was because we kids naturally called him Papa.

So my aunt asked, "Where is Papa?"

Something was wrong. My father was being carried out in a casket and my aunt was asking, "Where is Papa?"

I said, "Aunt Sonya, I'll explain it later."

And she said, "Now don't you forget to explain it to me."

I said, "Don't worry, auntie, I'll explain it to you later."

The casket was put in the hearse and my aunt and mother sat down on either side of it. Again Aunt Sonya asked, "Kama, where's Papa?" My mother heard the question and began to howl with laughter. Right there next to the casket. She was thinking, "Oh, that actress! That bohemian sister-in-law is playing the fool."

I said, "Calm down, Aunt Sonya. I'll explain it to you later."

And she said, "Now don't you forget to explain it to me."

In theatrical terms, we are dealing here with the evaluation of an event in its purest form. You have an event that must be evaluated in some way. Your evaluation depends upon your attitude toward the event. If the event is important to you, you evaluate it one way. If it is unimportant, you evaluate it differently. If you are in a complex relationship with the event — say, it is important to someone else but not to you — then your evaluation might be paradoxical.

My Aunt Sonya's evaluation of the event of my father's death was one of such power that she was internally incapable of accepting it as a fact. She excluded it. It was as if she had turned herself off and banned the information. It had not happened.

I am not making this up. I saw it happen. The casket was right there. People were walking around, looking into it. And Aunt Sonya was asking, "Where is Papa?" Her organism and her consciousness rejected the fact of my father's death. That was one kind of logic, the logic of a global evaluation of an event.

Now I will tell of another. My mother was fine. She just laughed. She made fun of Aunt Sonya. But what happened with her after that? Absolutely nothing. That began to irritate me. One day passed, another, a week, a month. But Mother did not seem to be affected. She had not shed a single tear. True, she would travel to the cemetery once a day. Summer, winter, no matter, she rode the bus to the cemetery. At first, every day, then at least once a week. She would spend thirty minutes or an hour there. She would keep the mound of dirt clean, keep the weeds out in summer and brush the snow off in winter. She would put things in order and then ride home again. This went on for a year. Finally, we had a proper gravestone erected.

That is when my mother began to die. Literally. She could not get up until two o'clock in the afternoon. She could not eat. She could not speak. My father had been a doctor, so there were plenty of people to turn to. But nobody could find anything wrong. We would put her into the hospital for three or four days and she would come around. We would bring her home and it would start all over again.

She was the kind of person who was incapable of doing nothing. Even as she got older and weaker, she was always occupied with something. I explained how she kept herself busy even around my father's grave, but now she was powerless. She could not do anything. She was dying.

Then she received an invitation to visit her brother in Israel. She had never been there and had not seen her brother since before the war. My brother said, "I think she ought to go." I said, "You must be kidding! She can't even move." He said, "True, but she wants to go." I said, "She'll die in the airplane." My brother is a doctor and he said, "She's in such terrible condition, what is the difference at this point where it happens?"

In short, although it was a terrible strain, she went.

Ten days later we received word that she was doing wonderfully. She was visiting old friends — an enormous number of her old school mates were living in Israel by then. She spent two months in the wicked Israeli heat and could not have felt better. She came home healthy, and, shortly after that, she and my brother immigrated to Israel where she lived a while longer before her death.

That, now, brings to an end my long story. What theatrical conclusions can we draw from it?

I have described two evaluations of a single event, both of which are equally profound and powerful. Both my mother and my aunt refused to accept my father's death as a fact, although in different ways. Look at the depth of those evaluations! And how paradoxical they are!

I attempted to construct the logic of behavior in *K. I. from "Crime"* on the basis of that experience from my own biography. When I told that story, my actress began to sense what I was after.

However, that was still not enough. Beyond that, I had to come up with specific objects that she could grasp. You cannot grasp at air. It must be something concrete. This is where we came up with numerous little pieces of paper, a tiny photograph, a shawl, and the little articles she has in her purse.

But the most important thing, I kept telling her, is the contact with the audience. I told her, "As long as you are interacting with the spectators, that is the reality; that *something* that you can grasp onto. You are alive as long as you are making contact. The instant you lose contact; that is when you must die."

The most important thing in the business of theater is contact or interaction. It is *lethally* essential. The instant you lose that, you lose your safety cord and you are sent into a downward spiral. That is the end.

Those are the origins of Katerina's strange, unique relationship with her partners in *K. I. from "Crime."* By her partners, in this case, I mean her little pieces of paper, her photo of her deceased father, her little dried flower, her little handwritten signs, her children who are standing by. Those are real things she can grasp onto.

Death, which lurks on the other side of the door in the form of the unseen corpse of her late husband, does not concern us in this production. It simply is not there. There is a scene where Katerina is talking to her daughter Polya and she suddenly asks, "What's that?" What *that* is, is the bloody body of her dead husband. But Katerina's task is not to see that, not to admit that it is there, so she immediately becomes involved in some activity.

The inciting event, the foundation, of this production is the death of Katerina's husband. But the actress must understand what the death of a husband means. That is, how the death of her husband differs from the death of some other relative or close friend. What does it mean for *her*. This is crucial. Because this is the very thing that determines the character's personality, logic, manner of action, and very meaning. What choices do you make? What does that mean?

I have mentioned that for someone the death of a drunkard husband might be liberation. But that is not Katerina. That would be someone else entirely, with a different personality and a different reason for being. It is even a different genre of performance.

Another thing. An event occurred. Katerina wishes to nullify that event. Why did my Aunt Sonya keep asking, "Where is Papa?"? She had to invalidate the event. As if to say, "Papa just went off somewhere and he'll be right back." And it was important for her to receive my confirmation that she was right. What if I had said, "Papa died"? Can you imagine what might have happened? She was not capable of hearing that. She was searching for something else in my eyes. And when she asked her question, she essentially was providing her own answer in the very manner and intonation that she asked it. It was as if she were saying, "Give me the answer I need to hear."

That is precisely the kind of contact Katerina has with the spectators in *K. I. from "Crime."* She approaches someone and asks, "Do you understand me?" But before the spectator can say no, she has already moved on because she has no need of that answer. She has no interest in answers; she is already off on another subject.

In other words, the manner of preemptive interaction in *K. I. from "Crime,"* whereby the actress is constantly appealing to the spectators but rarely allows them to respond, is more than just a device with which to keep the performance from descending into chaos. I suspect many spectators — and I along with them — assumed that this form of one-way communication was strictly a provocative device that allowed the director and his actress to keep control of the performance. Obviously the show would fall apart if spectators were allowed to respond all the time. But what you are saying is that the actress's behavior is not only a mere manifestation of theatrical form, it is also a carrier of meaning.

Absolutely. Although it is meaning primarily in terms of the character's logic. She has no need whatsoever of a partner — in this case a spectator — who will respond in any way.

Some people may think, "Oh, this show is just a happening." But it is not. I may employ some elements of a happening, but nothing more. In a happening, the most important element is the spectator. He is provoked into doing something or responding in some way by the actor who is of secondary importance. If you get the spectators to run around in a sack or crawl into soapsuds or sing in unison then you have a happening. That has absolutely, categorically, nothing to do with *K. I. from "Crime."*

Several of my shows, *K. I. from "Crime"* most of all, are designed to contain unexpected developments. The actress in *K. I. from "Crime"* has been taught to respond to all problems, accidents, and unanticipated incidents as if they were a part of the show. There are times, for instance, when a spectator enters late. The actress responds to this immediately and uses it as a new event. If she gets off track during any one particular performance, these unexpected developments dependent on outside forces, not on her, can get her back on course. Her partners, here, are the spectators and they are a help to her.

What is important — I mean in the director's work, not in that of the actress, whose job it is to keep the character on course by doing whatever the character is supposed to do — is continually to be turning something over inside the spectator.

Let us take the notion of theatrical conventions.

Is there a fourth wall in *K. I. from "Crime"* or not? That is a question I ask myself as a spectator. In other words, am I going to watch this performance as if it were a picture, or am I going to be taking part in it? I constantly talk to Oksana about that. The actress must constantly work with the spectator in a way that brings results. The spectator should have sudden emotional responses, maybe even be moved to say something. Then, just as suddenly, he should realize he has transgressed some limit of behavior and feel sheepish about it. The spectator should constantly be deceived in the rules of the game. A comic example of that is when Katerina invites everyone into the next room but slams the door in their faces when they get up to follow her.

That is a literal example of deception, but I want that very same thing to be happening on an internal level. Katerina opens herself up emotionally and lets the spectators into her internal world. Then, instantly, she closes up and shoves them back out. As soon as the spectators again grow accustomed to the distance separating them from the actress, she must again come back after them and draw them into her confidence.

There must be an atmosphere of discomfort in the hall; the absence of comfort; the absence of peaceful contemplation of a theatrical performance. It should be the very same sensation that you have when an unbalanced person approaches you on a street corner. These are situations in which you cannot possibly respond adequately. You cannot respond to this person on the same level because he exists within his own particular form of logic that is inaccessible to you.

I would like to dig around in your past for a moment. You once told of a shaft of light that always fell on a certain part of the floor in your house. You would huddle there in that light because it was warm, while in the shade it was colder. But even more important was the way you described the scene visually. I could not help but think of the very specific, very expressive lighting of your shows. We have talked about the side lighting you used in *Macbeth*. It seems to me you often use angled lighting of some sort. You certainly did in *K. I. from "Crime"* and *We Play "Crime."*

I do not believe I use side lighting all that much, although it is true that lighting, in general, is a crucial element of every one of my shows. The visual side of theater has always been very important to me. When I was studying to become an actor and was living on a minuscule stipend, I saved my money to buy a very expensive book. It cost 30 rubles at a time when the average worker earned 100 rubles a month. It was an album of Picasso's paintings. That was my favorite book. I would delve into it at least three times a day. I lived by that book. It was a part of my life. It was a big, fat book published by Knaur. I still have it at home. That was a part of me.

A visual image is often determined by the light that falls on an object or objects. Of course, in my productions I am not fashioning a sculpture that I can bend and shape and make abstract in some way. I am always working with a live person. One live person. Next to him is another live person. And then a third. In different shows the people may be the same, but the shows are not. The atmosphere is different, the content is different, the style is different, the genre is different. The tension is different.

So, in terms of visuals, what can help me express the specific style, meaning and tension that I am after? Set design, of course. Costumes. But often enough, these elements are rather modest in my shows. Nothing to speak of, really.

Light draws contours differently.

The same person and the same object appear in a different form thanks to the lighting. Depending upon the light, you may see an actor as gloomy or sad. You may see him in an ethereal space or in an obscure space. In a dead or live space.

When I was still a student, I had already become fascinated by a certain kind of lighting that I have often used since. I found it in the building of the Leningrad State Institute of Theater, Music, and Cinema, which is located across the street from the famous Tenishev School where the poet Osip Mandelshtam studied before the Revolution and where Vsevolod Meyerhold staged his famous production of Alexander Blok's *A Puppet Show*. In our building there were two very high old windows. I liked the way the light came through them into the room. And I always wanted to find a way to use both theatrical lighting and the natural lighting that came in those windows. As you know from many of my Moscow productions, I often use light that comes in through windows.

The rehearsal room at the institute was lit with those "daylight"

Katerina Ivanovna (Oksana Mysina) shakes her son Kolya (Oleg Rayev) as her youngest daughter Lida (Anna Rayeva) looks on in *K.I. from "Crime,"* a dramatization of segments of Dostoevsky's *Crime and Punishment;* Moscow, 1994. *Photo by Ken Reynolds.*

fluorescent lamps. They cast a strange, dead light. I liked them because of their unreal quality. You see, once again, there was my desire to overcome the realistic, psychological lighting that would accompany a typical genre scene. I used that light in *K. I. from "Crime"* and in *We Play "Crime."*

The lighting of a show depends on the genre, the method, the language, the design, the space of the show. As a rule I look for light that does not imitate anything. I never forget that I am working on the stage. It is very important for me that the lighting not merely be some manner of illumination or tinting that creates an atmosphere. It must be something that is real, independent, and natural for this production.

When you stage a show in a room, you cannot imitate light. The spectators are located in a room and they know that. There is no point trying to make them think they are at sea. That is nonsense. They are in a room and the lighting must be the kind of lighting one finds in a room. That is why in *K. I. from "Crime"* the actress turns the lights on and off herself. My one compromise there was that I outfitted the room with those daylight fluorescent lights that give that flat, unnatural, deadening light.

Floors are not white. Walls may be white and ceilings often are white. But floors are not. In *K. I. from "Crime"* I had the floor painted white. I had the table painted white. I had the chairs painted white. And the lighting is white. I wanted it to be unnatural. That is, it is *natural*, but it is *too* natural. It is not incidental or random.

Another of my objectives in *K. I. from "Crime"* and *We Play "Crime"* was to create the effect of an operation or dissecting room where nothing is superfluous. Where every microdetail is of the utmost importance. The inside of an eye. The inside of an intestine. The inside of a heart. Where a hair is plucked out and studied under a microscope. My task was to make a clean break with realistic detail, with everything habitual and routine. At the same time I wanted everything to be somewhat shocking or irritating. Everything was *too* white, *too* bright. The eye does not like that. It gets tired.

I purposefully changed the lighting at the end of *K. I. from "Crime."* That is crucial for me. After I have long tormented the spectator in this "operating room," I suddenly change the lighting at the moment of the tragic resolution. You see the paradox there? It is tragic and yet it is also a resolution. I impart to that a certain artistic quality. Up until that point there has been nothing "artistic" in the visual aspect. When I change the lighting, it has a liberating effect on the spectator. "Finally!" thinks the spectator. "My eyes can rest after straining all night long!"

Then, in the finale, I add music. There has been no music for the duration of the entire production. The actress plays on the violin a bit, but that is not music. I only give music in the finale. And the spectator drinks it in as he would water in the desert. The music here liberates the spectator, it is his salvation, just as was the change in the lighting a short time earlier.

With the new light, the spectator begins to see shades and perceives that as something beautiful. In fact, the lighting is quite simple. It is merely a spot from outside the window that casts a shadow into the room. That is all. A ray of light falls on the wall. But for the spectator there could be no more beautiful light at that moment. If you were to give him blue or pink or green or flickering light — that would ruin everything. First of all, the ray of light casting a shadow is lifelike. It reminds us of life.

Why is it like life?

Because the earlier flat, even light is not what you see in life. It is what you see in an operating room. It is a calculated light that the director uses to torment his spectator. You may not notice that at first, but you begin to as time goes on. The eyes even begin to hurt from it. It is an impossible kind of light when everything is white. Then consider the contrast of the black coats that Katerina Ivanovna and her children wear. The light becomes too harsh, too white. It is not a living light that gives contour to the actress's face. It is everywhere flat and monotonous, illuminating everything equally as if everything is of equal importance.

But people do not want everything to be of equal importance. We want to focus on details. We want to see close-ups, then long shots, then medium shots. That kind of variety reflects human nature. My white room in dead, white light does not reflect human nature. Do you see what I mean?

And when I change the lighting — when a ray of light seems to shine in the window in a haphazard way — that is *life*. That is something living, something new, something beautiful. It has a palate of hues and shades. It is not oppressive.

Let me repeat myself. The spectator perceives this shift as a gasp of fresh air, a gulp of water. He eats it up as he will the music shortly thereafter. He gulps it down.

That is important to me because this scene is about death and resolution. Deliverance. It is freedom.

"I am breathing!" says the actress.

That text was added by Oksana. It was not part of the script. But during rehearsals we constantly talked about the fact that she had to breathe. And so here she finally is breathing, she is breathing!

It is as though Katerina Ivanovna is saying: "There it is! Freedom! Freedom! I have the right! There it is! I am breathing! I am breathing freely."

In fact, she is dying of tuberculosis.

In the course of rehearsals the actress added those words as a realization of her own internal text. And it became a part of the play text. Most of the time the text that actors add gets in the way. As a rule, you cannot allow them to do that. As a rule, internal text should never be pronounced. But this was a case where it did not get in the way. In fact, it enriched the performance.

You touched briefly on the function of music in your shows.

The contact of the actor with sound and music is a very complex area. Often enough, actors respond weakly or not at all. Only an extremely sensitive actor will react in some way to music. I am not talking good or bad here. I just mean that there are specific types of actors who are more susceptible to music. In the schooling I received, the musical sphere of a production is essentially a new and independent character. It is not just music. It is a constituent that has an added and highly specific impact.

As a rule, the music in my shows is me. It is my voice. It leads and provides direction, and it offers a view, as it were, from neutral territory — an objective view. Music provides something of a cosmic or divine view. Perhaps I would be better off just calling it the point of view of a certain power.

Of course, I exist outside the show; I do not take part in it. I am not the gardener or a neighbor or the groom in *The Black Monk*. Who am I? I am an ephemeral presence who is fascinated by what is transpiring. I arranged a whole series of provocative acts to see how they might help me understand who these people are and what is occurring among them. I am like the guy who pokes a fly with a needle to see how it will wiggle its legs. I am curious to see what will happen if I bring my fly closer to a candle flame or if I dunk it under water and let it rise to the surface.

That is what I am like as director. Only at the same time I am not indifferent to these people. I know I could be in the place of the fly or the cockroach, of Katerina Ivanovna or Macbeth. I know I could be there.

On one level, then, I am poking myself with a needle. On another, I have the opportunity to sit off to the side and watch. I can observe you flailing your legs and swimming to the surface, knowing what you do not: that up ahead is a no-exit situation. So the music that plays is saying, "You're not going to get out of this."

I can play Bach or Mozart's *Requiem* in which a different harmony is heard, something that essentially has nothing in common with the action. I can play a gay polka that will mock your struggle to swim to the surface.

Music and, to a lesser extent, sounds comprise a peculiar independent character who may be considered me, the director, or perhaps even something more consequential, a higher power of some sort. It observes the goings-on from afar with interest, with empathy, and with great irony. Actors often have great difficulties with this character. They may respond as I ask them to, but down inside it is not easy for them to find their own motivated response.

Oksana quickly and naturally responded to the music I put into the finale of *K. I. from "Crime."* The finale of that show always works when she is able to hear that music as a powerful, counteracting force, one that might be considered that scene's main character. What I have always told her is that at this culminating moment, the moment of death, Katerina Ivanovna must be thinking, "OK! Here we go! It's all just beginning now!! Finally, I have achieved the right to confront what is really important. And I will! We'll see who is boss! *I'm* the one who is coming! It's *me*! *I'm* coming! I don't care about all your righteousness. Even if you're right. So let's stand face to face! One on one!"

She is staring down death, now. That is *freedom*. When the actress demands and achieves *freedom,* then the spectator is triumphant with her.

This is a moment of failure. It is the death of the character. But it is also a moment of extraordinary power. The character's extraordinary confidence evokes in the spectator a certain fearlessness. And that is where the catharsis comes in. The belief that, damn it, I am not a bug, I am not weak, I am not what Dostoevsky called a "quivering creature." That goes for the spectator in the hall as well as for Katerina Ivanovna. On the surface it would seem the difference is minuscule. But in fact, that minuscule difference changes everything.

There you have the crossroads of light, music, and meaning. And how they interact with the performing artist.

Obstacles Are Our Saviors

I would like to wrap up our discussion of literature by quoting Alexander Tairov again. You have already said you have little in common with him, and I am not in any way trying to establish some kinship between you. But once again I find an isolated phrase of his seems to illuminate an aspect of your work. He said that periods of great growth in theater tend to happen when theater leaves behind the written text, when theater turns to literature for material.

That sounds like something I could put my signature to. Tairov tended to work with highly sophisticated literature. And he worked with it as a kind of basis, as a starting point.

But both literature and material are important here. That is, not just literature as literature, but literature as a material to be worked with. That is how I understand it, anyway.

I have begun to be rather impertinent when people ask about my relationship to the authors I stage. I say, "They are a pretext for the show I am doing." I stage Dostoevsky, Shakespeare, Chekhov. And I use them as a *pretext* for what I do. They are the initial impulse for my shows. I am interested in seeing to what extent the author is capable of helping me do my show. That is, I am not staging the author. I am staging the literature he offers me. I know this is impudent, maybe even provocatively shameless. Of course, I am exaggerating a bit. Because I love and I study Chekhov. I do not just use him to make shows. The same is true of Dostoevsky and Shakespeare.

Nevertheless, when I am in the process of creating a production, all of my powers are directed toward that creation and not toward Chekhov. I am staging my own show. A show that was born thanks to the impulse that Chekhov or Shakespeare or Dostoevsky gave me. Thanks to what I learned or knew about this person and his work prior to commencing my own work. But when my process of creation begins, that is no longer what occupies me. I am now given over entirely to my own show.

But there is no such thing in art as just doing whatever you want. If you, as a director, do not have an author setting limits for you, then you yourself set the laws you must abide by. These laws are inviolable. The laws you establish for yourself and which you accept of your own free will, ultimately, are what make art of what you do.

This is what I tell my students: "Obstacles are our saviors." If you have no obstacles, no limitations, then you must find them. Man is not man without obstacles. It is in the overcoming of obstacles that character, both in life and in theater, is revealed.

Anything is possible in the theater and spectators know that. You can make a hole in the stage, add a paper flame and a figure in black and there you have a devil. That will not surprise anyone at all. But that is the whole point. My job is to find a way to surprise and frighten you when my devil appears. My job is to make that a terrible experience, as it would be in actual fact.

You must create laws that limit you. You must establish theatrical taboos which, in turn, force you to overcome them. And you must make the spectator aware of these laws, so that they exist within their bounds as well. When they feel that law acting upon them, or they sense you attempting to overcome it, that is when you get spectators shivering with goose bumps. On one hand, the spectator knows it is all make-believe. On the other hand, he begins to accept the set of rules you have established for the show.

In *The Black Monk,* the spectators enter and take their seats on the balcony where a stage has been erected. They look out over the empty orchestra and see the theater's empty stage down below. They think nothing of it. A stage like any other stage. This is a theater, after all. Then the action begins to unfold up here, in the limited area on the balcony that I have set aside for the performance. The spectator becomes caught up in this specific space. He forgets about everything else. But, after a while, something suddenly happens down there on the actual stage. And you can feel the spark, the tension ripple through the crowd.

What happened? Nothing of importance at all, really. But the spectators' attention had become concentrated on what was happening here on the balcony. The scope of their visual and psychological awareness was limited to this space alone. Suddenly, way down there, far away, something happened.

Some spectators have told me this is a moment of cosmic proportions. Because they came to accept the small world on the balcony as a representation of the earth, while the space down on the empty stage seemed to them an approximation of outer space. Thus, the interior of the theater took on the dimensions of the universe.

I created this effect quite consciously. I knew the spectators would exist in this small, limited space on the balcony and would grow used to it. So, when I gave them something to respond to some thirty feet away, the difference strikes them as enormous. That is a natural, human, psychological reaction.

Laws and limitations are essential. You establish them for yourself. If you are a poet, you say, "I will write in five-foot iambs." Why would you do this? Because that is where art comes in. But look what Akhmatova does — she holds strictly to the meter right to the end and then suddenly breaks out of it. It is a shock, a gulp of fresh air!

Or a poet starts out writing trochaic verse and suddenly, in the middle somewhere, switches over to iambs. You are thrown out of your rut! Big deal, right? It would seem nothing really happened at all. But, no! That is a change that you feel physiologically, with your whole being.

This is all connected to what I have been saying about literature. A key for me was discovering the opportunity for shifts in Dürrenmatt. I could have staged him as written. Somebody spits, so I have him spit. Somebody hits somebody, so I have him hit somebody. But this writer and his play revealed themselves to me when I set myself limitations, when I forbid myself to do certain things. Moreover, these limitations were suggested to me by the relationships existing within Dürrenmatt's play.

This is what makes art. This is what opens up new dimensions. This is what allows you to work not with ideas, but with aesthetic aspects. This is what exists outside the play's meaning or plot.

7

Digressing and Surviving

One of my favorite phrases is from J. D. Salinger's *The Catcher in the Rye*. It is a phrase that has become my own in many ways. The young narrator says he especially does not like getting up in class to make speeches because as soon as anyone strays from the topic, the whole class yells at him: "Digression! Digression!" Then the speaker is required to get back on the subject again. The boy says, "The trouble with me is that I *like* it when somebody digresses. It's more *in*teresting and all."*

That is a stunning phrase. Brilliant. I came to understand it very late. Life, essentially, consists of going off on tangents. The vector of life is clear and unchangeable — death. But what make up life itself are all the digressions, all the forays onto side roads where you occupy yourself with topics that are "off the subject." That is what comprises the richness of life. That is where you are apt to see best what a person is like — not when he is sailing down the straight and narrow.

I have mentioned that there are those who think I stage productions about that unchanging vector, about death. They are grossly mistaken. The more a production strays from that central, inevitable topic, the richer it is.

This is more difficult, of course, because it is much easier to draw a straight line. But to show how a person wanders and meanders off

---

*J. D. Salinger, *The Catcher in the Rye* (Boston: Little Brown and Co., 1991), 183.

into all kinds of murky places — without losing the thread — that is what is tough. You still have to bring the spectator back to center and show that, for all the digressions, the character still is moving down that unchanging vector. That is art on its highest level.

I think of Pushkin's *Eugene Onegin*, which essentially consists of nothing but digressions.

There is almost no plot at all in *Onegin*. That is a work of genius. You can declare the plot in three lines. And yet, as it has become customary to say, that novel is an "encyclopedia of Russian life." Moreover, not only of that era, but of all eras. And not only of Russia, but of everywhere. That novel does everything. It is life. It is life. Because Pushkin is fascinated by everything he sees along the way — no matter whether it is a butterfly, a woman's foot, or some sort of aberration that it turns out is a part of life, too. Everything. Everything interests him. Life is rich and interesting. To be able to do all that and at the same time not forget to wrap up the story you are telling — that is high art.

In that sense, Salinger is a genius in *The Catcher in the Rye*, as is Pushkin in *Eugene Onegin* and all the rest of his works.

Do you not think that the idea of plot in general has faded away over the last few centuries?

No. That is not true. You cannot go anywhere without a plot. You see, we are programmed on that vector. We know what lies at the end. We are hell-bent for death. You cannot just pull that out unless you do it at some given moment for the shock value. To shake up your audience and force them to think, "How can I live without my vector?"

It is just that contemporary literature and, to a lesser extent, drama have found a way almost to erase the contour of plot. Or perhaps the plot line is so thin that a whole work consists of something like: "Well, she did turn her head in my direction after all." But without that minimal, negligible plot, everything around it would cave in.

You see, it would have been impossible for Pushkin to write *Onegin* without its silly plot. She falls in love with him, he does not love her. Then he falls in love with her, but she cannot reciprocate. That is the plot. That is it. Just a humble yarn. Pushkin does not even pay it any attention, really. But none of what goes on around it could be there without that plot.

Tovstonogov, drawing on Stanislavsky or Nemirovich-Danchenko, I do not remember which, taught us about the cone of ideas. Every work of art can be depicted as a cone. It has a single point of origin — the simplest, most basic concept.

More often than not, it is one of the notions expressed in the Ten Commandments. Thou shalt not kill. Thou shalt not commit adultery. Very simple notions. If that is all there was to it, it could be a newspaper account that says, "Mr. So-and-So killed Mr. Thus-and-Such. He was caught, punished, and sentenced to prison." In other words, nothing of particular interest.

But Shakespeare wrote *Macbeth*. What is going on here? An enormous number of details are piled on top of the central concept. An enormous number of deviations. An enormous number of corollary ideas and observations that have no relation to the original notion. That is when that single point at the bottom begins to grow into a wide, three-dimensional cone of ideas.

Look what happens with a great writer like Chekhov. Or Leo Tolstoy. Tolstoy wrote *Anna Karenina*. The point of origin is "Thou shalt not commit adultery." But you barely even perceive that when you are reading the novel. You become immersed in something incredibly lifelike, a meaty broth of life. Look how much is going on in that novel! Most of it has nothing to do whatsoever with that point of origin. But it all adheres and holds together.

The narrower the cone, the more primitive the work of art. If it is very narrow, it will be nothing more than a moral admonition or a newspaper article. The wider it is, the richer the work. And in the finest works, you almost lose touch with the origin.

But, as Tovstonogov said, the cone is always there. And then it depends upon the level of the spectator or reader. A simple cook who has never read much at all might say about Anna Karenina, "That slut! She shouldn't have cheated on her husband! She had a son, she had a husband. So what if she fell in love? If she had not cheated, she would not have ended up under a train."

A more educated reader, with more imagination, experience, and subtlety, will be capable of appreciating the riches of the work on various levels. And, in fact, the gradations of levels are unlimited.

That point of origin — the plot — is crucial. That is what everything grows out of. If there is nothing in particular there to start with, it might turn out to be nothing more than a spindly little twig. On the other hand, it might grow into a lush, thriving tree with such exotic leaves, blossoms, and fragrance that you will not even notice the trunk.

This talk of tangents brings up a topic that is distantly related. When you tackle themes in your shows, you always approach them any way but directly. You sidle up to them or you sneak up on them from behind, but you never attack them —

Straight on.

Straight on. Which brings me to the following two-pronged question. I do not know much about your dramatization of Ray Bradbury's *Fahrenheit 451*, but I can imagine many would assume you must have used it to mount a broadside attack on Soviet censorship. I, on the contrary, cannot imagine that is what you did.

Second is a question I have long wanted to ask you. It is so simplistic I almost fear asking it, but it is purposefully simplistic, so I will forge ahead. If you were a Western director, you most certainly would have staged shows about the Holocaust. You would have staged shows about how people survived or did not survive it. I think I know why you have not done that, but it might seem strange to someone else that you have not.

That is a very good question. Let me answer the second part first.

I do not know whether I would have staged shows about the Holocaust if I had lived in the West. What is important is something else.

When I was still young — that is, when I was fourteen or fifteen — I imagined myself staging, not something about the Holocaust, but about something I knew well: the story of our family, as it was bound up with the Holocaust. It was to be a story about my father, my mother, and me when I was little. I very much resembled my father then, as I still do now. My idea was to play my father. I did not think yet about who would play my mother, but I assumed my future son would play me. I imagined it all very clearly. I saw it almost as a documentary. Later, when I grew up, I did not become an actor and the idea faded away. Anyway, you could not do anything on this topic at that time.

On the other hand, I would say those critics are on the right track who say I do nothing but stage shows about this topic, even if that is not what they say in so many words. Everything I create is about that. Naturally, I engage many different themes. But, to one extent or another, that theme exists in everything I do.

You remember the basic situation in Chekhov's *Ward No. 6* — living people are held in an enclosed environment. That was also an image of Soviet reality. You might say I have lived a Holocaust most of my life. It was not entirely the same, of course. In my lifetime the Soviets did not kill people the way the Nazis did. But the differences were only a matter of degrees.

Take, for example, the end of the second act in my *Ward No. 6*. I created a scene in which Nikita the watchman enters the closed room to wash the people living there. It is called a "bathhouse day" in Russia. Everyone must wash; the sick, the dirty, and the infested must be washed. In my show the patients were frightened of this intrusion into their space. They were frightened like little children who are dunked in water. Their fear increased as Nikita brought in a tub and then a bucket. Their fear grew into panic and they began running around the room, hiding in the corners. But there was nowhere for them to hide, the performance space was an empty square.

One of them, shaking with fear, began to undress. Another refused to undress, so Nikita grabbed him and stripped his clothes off him. Eventually there were five or six men of varying ages standing there naked. One was very old, another was fat, another thin, another all shriveled up. All of these naked men were forced up against the wall,

Inmates being prepared for a bath by orderlies in *The Theater of the Watchman Nikita,* a dramatization of Anton Chekhov's *Ward No. 6* (rehearsal); Helsinki, 1988. *Photo by Rauno Träskelin.*

and Nikita splashed them with water from the bucket. He did not actually wash them; he merely got them wet as if he were covering himself in case anyone should ask.

There is a photograph of this scene, of the men standing pushed naked up against the wall. This image is a reflection of scenes in the large number of photographs I collect — of naked people being stood up against a wall to be shot. I have a photograph from Kaunas on the first day of the war. It shows how the Lithuanian Greens, nationalists, bandits, patriots, whatever you want to call them, slaughtered Jews who had gathered at a bus stop to leave the city. I am not even sure what had happened just before the photo was taken. Whether they beat them with crowbars or whether they took the huge hoses for washing the buses and shoved them down people's throats, I am not sure. But the scene involves water and these hoses in some way. I do not know why. In this photo there is a whitish wall and some near-white cement slabs lain out in place of asphalt. They are covered in water and off to one side is a water spout from which water is gushing and flowing over the slabs.

It goes without saying that the photo I have from my production of *Ward No. 6* is a quote of the photo taken in Kaunas. In my production, all the inmates, after having been washed, stood in a line to get into the bath. This created the image of naked men standing in line, some covering themselves out of shame, others not bothering. As I say, some were old, some fat, some thin — all were what we would call unattractive and all were terribly, frightfully vulnerable. They were waiting their turn for a bath.

What do you think that is? Obviously, it is that theme again.

Were I to work at it, I could recall an enormous number of scenes — both literal and so oblique as to be known only to me — that derive from that theme. They may be very internal, not visual at all, and, therefore, not obvious to others.

This theme will never leave me. It is a part of me. It may be the largest part of me.

Why do I need to stage a show about the Holocaust?

As for *Fahrenheit 451*, I could not have staged it as a direct commentary on Soviet reality because, even as it was, this work was impossible to stage. This is a work about burning books and that was a time when real literature could be read only in samizdat, which was liable to be seized and destroyed. The parallels were direct. Moreover, this was a time in which unfavorable books were removed from libraries or offending pages were torn out of books or pasted over with blank sheets of paper. Entire chapters were cut out of books. Any person living at that time in the Soviet Union knew about this and understood what was going on. You might take a book from the library and find a photograph in which one man's face had been blacked out. Who was this person? Someone they did not want you to know about. He no longer existed.

I might have even wanted to stage *Fahrenheit 451* as a direct commentary on all this, but I could not have done that. It was impossible. What I could do was stage a show about American life. There was something even fun about that. In this regard I recall a production I did of Maxim Gorky's *The Final Ones*.

I have wanted to ask about this. I cannot possibly imagine the combination of Kama Ginkas and Maxim Gorky.

Quite simple. First of all, I threw out half the play.

Then I can at least half imagine it.

I moved some of the text out of the body of the play into a performed epigraph.

The spectators entered the hall not knowing what they would see. Before the hall lights dimmed, a calm, cold, indifferent voice was heard: "We lie on a road of people, as if we were chunks of a fallen building, perhaps a prison. We wallow in the dust of destruction and obstruct people's forward motion."

That is a quote from Gorky's *The Final Ones*. If it were to be spoken within the performance, it would sound silly and pompous. In my show it was an epigraph followed by a pause. The audience was confused. The show had not begun yet. To whom did those words refer? To them? The voice had said "we" — was the audience to understand it included them? The implication was that they themselves were from a prison, wallowing on a road and obstructing the forward motion of others.

After the pause in which those mental questions inevitably rose, the voice continued, "Gorky. *The Final Ones*." Another pause, followed by the words, "This play was written in 1908." In other words, I was stating, "No hints are implied here." But, of course, the more I denied the hints, the harder the phrases hit.

This epigraph caused my first big conflict with the authorities. It was banned. Following a huge war, the epigraph was thrown out and the show was allowed to be performed. However, after just the tenth performance, the show itself was banned.

I did *Fahrenheit 451* as a show about a woman who is killed for attempting to save books, culture, and knowledge and about how books were burned — although I did not have book burnings on stage. I did not know what would happen when the authorities came to pass judgment on the show. A dress rehearsal was attended by a specialist in ideology from the Krasnoyarsk regional headquarters of the Communist Party. After the show, he literally jumped up and down, spattering spittle as he spoke excitedly.

"What a blow!" he enthused. "What a blow to imperialism!"

That was my blow to imperialism.

You must have loved that man at that moment.

I was thrown for a loop.

Standing next to him was Marina Sidorova, the head of the Krasnoyarsk board of culture. She was a genius, a Party bureaucrat and a genius. She is the one who had organized the theater, the city's Young Spectator Theater. She is the one who came to the theater's defense every year, every six months when the authorities wanted to close it down. This was a long and unending battle. She not only came to the theater's defense, she was intelligent and authoritative enough to be able to beat back the constant attacks.

Anyway, Marina Sidorova stood staring at me quietly with intelligent eyes while her colleague shouted about blows to imperialism. Her gaze clearly said, "Don't say a word!"

My most important task in *Fahrenheit 451* was to come up with a definition for the firemen. Who were these strange and fantastic figures? And who or what was that mechanical dog that set everything on fire?

All of my individual firemen, including the main hero Montag, lived in iron boxes. There were a whole series of these small boxes making up one great big huge box. They were similar to tiny little tin garages with doors on bolts that squeaked when they opened and which were on wheels and had handles by which they could be pulled and moved.

People lived in this city of fantastic metal boxes. The main hero also lived in a box like that. At the same time, this looked something like a fire station. When the firemen had to go out on a run, the doors would open and they would ride out. I did not have any actual fire truck on stage, of course. The point is that there was no difference between the fire station and the dwellings that people inhabited.

Who were the firemen? They were individuals, but when they set to work, it was as though they were observing a ritual. They had a captain in charge. He would seize a fire hook and begin uttering rhythmic grunts or chants. The rest of the firemen — supposedly dressed like Americans, but, in fact, wearing nondescript khaki uniforms — would move around then line up in a row. Suddenly, from behind each of their backs a series of hands would protrude and begin moving and feeling the contour of each fireman. At a certain point, the people standing behind popped out into view. The captain continued to incite everyone with his rhythmic, militaristic grunts. The firemen began moving in unison. These were not dances, but rather something like what soldiers do when they are being trained to stab the enemy with bayonets. There was an element of that in it.

They all stood in a circle. In the middle was the captain with the fire hook. Like dogs, they stood waiting to see who he would give the fire hook to. He continued to incite them with his grunts until he singled out the one who would receive the fire hook. The chosen one took the fire hook and — there it was! — *he* was the one who would do the killing. The rest, like a herd, fell in behind him. They rolled out a narrow, vertical iron box on wheels. They turned it around and revealed a woman standing in it — she was the one who was protecting the books.

The captain began to roll the box back and forth, pushing and pulling it, pushing and pulling it. It was almost as if he were teasing the others with it as one would tease dogs with a piece of meat. The woman was still inside as he rocked her back and forth and the herd ran and jumped around her, all the while growing more and more excited. When the excitement reached a culmination, the box was turned, its narrow, nichelike opening hidden from the audience. The captain reared back with his fire hook and plunged it into the back wall of the box.

Of course, the actress had moved to one side before the captain drove his spike through the wall of the box.

That was one of the scenes I had.

That was not about American life. It was not about Soviet life. It was about something animalistic, the ferment of something bestial. The excitation of sexual, murderous impulses.

How typical was this of what you were doing at that time?

My first productions, everything I did from 1967 to the mid-1970s, were terribly focused, even castrated. Everything was directed toward the one single image or idea that was at the center of my conception. Everything worked toward that goal — the set, the music, the blocking. I am exaggerating, of course, it was not that obvious. But I essentially discarded everything that did not in some way illuminate my main conception, what Stanislavsky called the through-line. My shows at this time were intense and quite imaginative, maybe even more so than now, since I was young at the time. Their form was often extremely far-out for that era. But their content was heavily concentrated on one thing.

What I am saying is that there was very little life in them.

You see, life is randomness. Life is not the train you are riding on. It is the scenery you see whizzing by outside the window. That is where life is. Not in the train car that is speeding off to a specific destination. When I finally discovered that for myself, I realized I had been living wrongly. I had been living with a focus that was much too tight. I was not interested in anything outside my profession or anything beyond perfecting myself within my profession.

Basically, life did not interest me. I did not know how much bread cost. I did not know how people lived. I figured, "People must live, somehow. Some better, some worse. Some people probably love someone. Somebody's probably dying. But none of that is important." That even goes for my attitude toward love. It did not interest me in the least. I thought, who cares about love? It's just a detail. I thought lots of things were just insignificant details in life. My attitude was that anything which failed to touch on the "great questions" was superfluous. That is how I lived and that is how I created my art.

The result was that, essentially, I was impotent. I did not know the aroma of life, of relationships, of love. I did not know the aroma of nature. I knew nothing. I knew my profession and I continually moved deeper into it. I knew it very well. I knew very well its torments and its pleasures. I knew literature and the delight of plunging into it. I knew painting and I loved drawing. I loved looking through art books, going to exhibitions or talking to artists. I loved poetry and I still do. But none of that is life. Those are all mirrors of life. Reflections of life. Not life itself.

I knew nothing about life itself.

To comprehend this fully, you must understand that Henrietta and I were very poor. Neither one of us was working. And we never took second jobs. I was a rather haughty person and I was not going to stoop beneath my dignity as a director. I even refused to take jobs with amateur theater groups. That was a common way an out-of-work director could earn a little money. But I considered myself a major talent, and I believed that was beneath me. True, I did end up having to do that, although it was complete torture.

So, how did you end up making your acquaintance with life?

There was this popular café in Leningrad called the Saigon. It really was not even a café and its name was not the Saigon. That is just what people called it. It was a dinky street-corner place, maybe thirty square meters, with no seats or tables, where they served lousy coffee. It was basically just a dirty little hole. You stood at these elbow-high counters to drink your coffee, which cost a couple of kopeks, or you brought along something stronger of your own. It was on the corner of Liteiny and Nevsky Prospekt. If you look down Nevsky toward the Admiralty, it would be at your left on the farthest corner from the center. It was around for a long time, into the late 1970s, before it eventually fell apart. This semi-underground place attracted alcoholics, unemployed people, dissidents, crazies, and geniuses. It brought together all of Leningrad's outsiders with an intellectual and bohemian bent. The KGB naturally knew all about it. Its agents were always there listening to what was going on.

Everything avant-garde in Leningrad was connected to this spot in one way or another. It was a place where all the rejects of the Soviet era congregated. They did not have their own apartments. They often did not even have their own room. Or they did not have a residence permit giving them the right to live in the city.

The way people with no means would get a place to live was to rent the corner of a room from some landlady. However, she would not let you bring guests home. So you had to go out somewhere to socialize. The notion of renting a whole room to yourself was way beyond most of these people. Only people making good money could do that. None of these people even thought about having a whole apartment to themselves. Anyway, there were very few individual apartments in Leningrad; most were communal apartments. That is how everybody lived.

So, the question was: Where are you going to meet? This was not Paris where you can go sit in the Luxembourg Garden or at some cheap café. There was nothing like that. So, it all happened at the Saigon. This is where I was forced to go out and mingle with people.

Another major incident in my life was finding a stray dog on the street. That is a whole chapter in my biography, about how I brought home a stray dog. More important, however, is that, having taken the dog in, I now had to take it out for walks. That was totally abnormal for me. I never went for walks.

On this topic I remember a conversation I once had with Lev Dodin. He was never out of work. He always had something going. Nobody knew anything about him, of course, he was still a nobody then. But he was always able to earn a little money working as somebody's third or fourth assistant. It was only much later that he would become a world-famous director. Anyway, I remember him once telling me how he and his wife had taken a day trip to the suburb of Pavlovsk. On a Sunday.

I was astonished. I was shocked. Dodin takes time out to rest! For me, that meant he must have no personal or professional problems. How else would he be able to pick up and take a day trip to the park at Pavlovsk? I could not imagine Dodin and his wife walking around the park at Pavlovsk for three hours. That sounded insane to me. Absolutely insane.

I bring that up as a contrast to the image of me taking a dog for a walk. That was just unheard of for me. On the other hand, I had nothing else to do. I had no job. My life consisted of getting up in the morning and waiting for the Actors House to open at 11 A.M. or noon. I would go down there every day and talk with people about all kinds of things, usually about the latest shows or about literature. About my ideas for future productions. I would hang out there for two or three hours and then go home. Perhaps some unemployed actor might drop by for a visit and we would talk about literature and theater. Sometimes we would rehearse something.

It happened on occasion that my actor friends were not happy with the way their directors were rehearsing with them, so they would come work with me at home. I would help them out. There were a lot of scenes being played in Leningrad theaters that Henrietta or I staged for actors in our home. The directors of those shows knew nothing about it. I am exaggerating the importance of my input, naturally, but those rehearsals were good workouts for me.

Also, I would sit at home and write the scripts that I would be able to produce only many years later. A good number of my shows that are currently running were either written or sketched out way back then. They include *Pushkin. Duel. Death, The Execution of the Decembrists,* and Chekhov's *The Lady with the Lapdog.* Much of what I wrote never saw the light of day. Another play, *The Famous Adventures of T. S. and H. F.,* based on Mark Twain's *Tom Sawyer* and *Huckleberry Finn,* is usually considered to have been written by Henrietta. In fact, we wrote it together.

Every day I wrote something. I read something. I drafted something. I rewrote something. I fantasized something. I drew something. And I talked a lot. It was a kind of creative masturbation. And it lasted a long time — over ten years. Every once in a blue moon, when I would get a chance to stage a show, I would be afforded the genuine pleasure of the real thing. I am talking now about the period from 1967, when I graduated from the Leningrad State Institute of Theater, Music, and Cinema, to 1981 when I came to Moscow.

Anyway, by getting out to walk the dog, I was forced to look at people. I would sit on a bench and watch the dog run around the park doing its thing. Next to me there might be an old lady who was watching her dog run around too. I would look at her. I would see how she was dressed. Then she would say something. And I would respond. This was insane for me. Even today I still do not make contact with strangers easily, but back then that was doubly true. There were whole classes of people and strata of society that I knew nothing about and cared nothing about. Thanks to the dog, I began coming into contact with these people and talking with them. The result was that I began to notice life. That is what I want to say. You understand? I began to *notice* it.

And then, little by little, I began to appreciate it.

Only much later — I would say it happened only in my Moscow period — did I cease balking at love as a theme for a production. It was only much later still, in Finland, that I really saw nature for the first time in my life. This was only around 1995. I began noticing there how nature changes. The Finns are extremely close to nature, they are part of it. When the color of the sky just barely changes, they react to it instantly. There is so little sunlight there that when a ray of sun appears, they will run to stand in it. They see light. They touch nature. They tend their gardens. They are part of nature.

Once, during a break in one of my Finnish rehearsals, I went on doing what I always did — I kept on thinking about what we had been doing. But since my actors went outside, I went out with them. This was when I was staging *The Seagull* on an island near Helsinki in the mid 1990s. I was still completely wrapped up in rehearsals, but my actors were not. They were engrossed in something else. I began wondering what they were looking at.

It was the sun they were looking at. It was spring, April, and the sun had come out for just half an hour. They stood drinking it in, some of them standing by a tree. I began to observe the sun with them. Nothing like that had ever happened to me before.

In sum, I did not know life. I was not interested in all of its varieties and riches. Basically, I had not lived. As a result, my productions were, to an extent, castrated or distilled. As though the life had been bleached out of them. The mold, the mildew, the bacteria of life was missing. I had ideas. I had grand existential problems. But the mildew that clings to these problems and either turns them into a disease or into some carrier of new life — this was absent. Mildew, as you know, can give rise to a new organism that fosters new mildews and fungi, which give way to grass, which gives way to trees that produce oxygen, and so on and so forth.

When I realized that about myself, I began to combat this weakness. I began to take an interest in life — especially within my art. I became interested in everything that had nothing to do with Stanislavsky's through-line. I abandoned my fear of digressions, of getting carried away — true, always taking care to come back to the main thing.

I suspect that is the greatest art. To be able to stray as far as possible from your topic and to be able to delight in the details of digressions. You stray from the path because one thing attracts you, another draws you farther, and a third entices you even farther. But the key is to know how to find your way back. And when you return, you are profoundly enriched.

No matter how smart you are, that dry twig at the center, that dead outline does not do anyone — myself included — any good without the riches, the mildew, and the life-sustaining microbes. That is, without randomness; without life itself.

All right. The Saigon café is where you made your connection to life as a person. Where did it happen in your work?

It probably began happening back when I directed Rustam Ibragimbekov's *Resembling a Lion*. This essentially was a melodrama about a man who wanted to, but could not, leave his wife for a woman he loved. When he finally brings himself to do it, he finds that his lover has fallen ill and has returned to her husband. In the end, he dies of a heart attack. That is the basic melodramatic plot.

In this rather charming and precious play, there was one scene I could not make any sense of. It occurred at the moment when the hero finally decides to leave his wife. He comes to tell her of his decision, but she does not understand what he is saying. He says, "I'm leaving." And she says, "OK, eat first and then you can go." He says, "No, I'm going for good." And she says, "Fine, fine. Only first drop by and pay the phone bill." She does not understand because he is not the type to go chasing after women.

At this moment, a plumber arrives to fix a pipe. Over the course of two or three pages, he tells some story. It is a big monologue, a funny, charming tale about himself or a child, I do not even remember now. I thought this was nonsense. The whole plot came to a halt. And this plumber never shows up again. I could understand it if a plumber

Vadim Yermolayev and Kirill Dateshidze in Rustam Ibragimbekov's *Resembling a Lion*; Leningrad, 1974. *Photo by Nina Alovert.*

showed up for an instant and had a few colorful, comic lines. But this guy has a three-page monologue that has nothing to do with anything.

I did not know what to do. I would have just tossed it out — I can be pretty brazen — but at the same time I could sense that there was something marvelous in it. It was very funny, very lively, something very touching. But it had nothing to do with the topic of the play or the character of the hero. I struggled terribly as I tried to figure out how to deal with it. I knew I had to understand why it was there, and I knew it was my task to fall in love with that scene. Until I could do that, I would not be able to stage the show.

In fact, this scene is what determined the genre and the meaning of the play. Suddenly, thanks to this scene, it becomes clear that the hero was capable of leaving his wife. However, at first she does not understand, and then, when she does, she throws a tantrum. But since he was, by nature, an honest, straightforward person, he would have gone ahead and left her. Nothing could have stopped him once he made that decision. If his wife had tried locking him in, he would have broken down the door. Or he would have jumped out the window. Even if it was the fifth floor. That is the type of person this man was.

However, when the plumber begins talking to him and telling a personal story, he cannot excuse himself and leave. He cannot say, "Sorry, I've got my own problems." He is bound by his nature and his upbringing to sit and hear out the person who is talking. Even when it is a drawn-out, nonsensical tale that has absolutely nothing to do with him. So he sits and listens to the plumber. In fact, he listens for so long he ends up never leaving.

What I understood in this was that the real obstacles for a person, especially a person of culture, are not cement walls. You can break a wall down with your head. Or you might crack your head open, which, for a person of cultural and spiritual leanings, is an equally satisfactory result. That was a favorite theme in Soviet times — the man of culture destroying himself in an effort to knock down obstacles. But cotton wool is another thing. A wall of cotton, one that gives you no resistance at all, is the one you cannot break through. You get bogged down in it. And that is what happened to the hero of *Resembling a Lion*.

I began to realize that the entire show must consist of minute, nonsensical details, of a whole series of cotton-wool obstacles that had nothing to do with the theme of the play. Without this aspect, the play would be a very primitive melodrama. But it becomes something else when all those inanities are piled up one on the other.

I came up with the idea of having the wife buy a whole bunch of chairs. And my designer Eduard Kochergin used that in his fascinating set. He gave the space the appearance of a large room that was melting and bending. As a rule, on the stage, you have a room with two squared-off corners in the back. Here, however, they were stretched and bent, as was the ceiling above. The walls and ceiling had a liquid, flowing feel, although everything else was perfectly realistic. The floor space was covered with chairs. That is, as the husband explained that he was preparing to leave his wife, she methodically carried in all these chairs she had bought and placed them all over the stage. In fact, she would hand them to him and he was forced to help her. So, he was constantly busy carrying and moving and shifting these chairs, while she kept going out to bring in more or pay off the delivery man or whatever it was she was doing offstage. As a result, he was forced to wander in zigzags through all these chairs, because there were so many now he could not walk anywhere in a straight line. Essentially, he could not get out of the room because of all these stupid chairs.

That was a great discovery for me — both in terms of my life and in terms of the theater — when I learned that big problems become transformed. They take on completely different forms, often very silly and inconsequential.

Where does this discovery stand in regards to your production of _Pushkin and Natalie_? We have discussed this show already, but you have not come close to exhausting the subject.

I have already said that I changed fundamentally and that I became me both as a director and as a person when I staged _Pushkin and Natalie_. Everything changed with that show. The director Kama Ginkas that you know was born in _Pushkin and Natalie_.

This show began as a person by the name of Alexander Pushkin began sending out letters — that is, reciting their texts — on various themes to various people. One might be a request for a loan. Another might be an invitation to go for a drink. Another might ask whether someone had passed on another letter. Another might be that tonight we have a meeting with a certain female. Another still about the fact that a different female is jealous and wants a meeting at the same time. Another about the fact that he made a bad choice of words in one of his poems and now the tsar is angry at him. Another about problems at home. And on and on and on.

Some of the topics were important, some were not. But none had anything to do with each other. All were appeals addressed to different people, although the actor playing Pushkin was alone on stage. That is, he never received any responses to the letters he was sending out. He would send — that is, recite — a letter and there would be no response, so he would immediately switch over to another and then another and then another. All the while he was getting no satisfaction because none of his questions and requests was eliciting responses. He threw himself into each new one with renewed passion, but it did him no good.

He might attempt to address some important problem but, instead, become bogged down trying to explain something different to someone else before breaking off because a third or a fourth topic that was even more crucial would crowd in on him.

Let us say, someone had misunderstood an earlier request: He needed to borrow three thousand rubles, not three rubles. He would tell us that and then go back to his original topic. But before he could say anything of substance, he would be interrupted by another thought and he would shout, "I don't love you! We were just lovers!" And then it was back again to, "OK, three thousand rubles is what I meant. I'll pay it back later. When I get the money." And then he interrupts himself and declares, "Listen, I have every respect for the tsar and his government. I'll admit I was a bit harsh in that article I wrote, but . . . Sweetheart, listen. You were a great lover. A great lover. But I can't marry you. . . ." And so on and so forth.

In this show an enormous number of problems that seemed important — maybe some even were — became hopelessly entangled with all the folderol. It was one huge snowball that could be called "the problem of Pushkin's life." But he cannot get at the essence of that problem. It is all heaped together in one pile. He cannot extract any one problem from all the others.

The problems facing the character named Pushkin in my show could be as petty as someone misunderstanding a word, or a letter he sent being delivered to the wrong person, thus creating some trivial confusion. But suddenly it turns out that his whole future will be determined by this absolutely trifling matter. "That's it! I've had it!" he shouts. "I'm destroying everything! Breaking off with everyone!" All because he put a comma in the wrong place. The enormous piling up of problems, events, duties, objectives — usually trivial — is what brings us to some sort of resolution.

"I want to tie my shoelace, but you keep interrupting me. Every time I bend over you come in with something new. And I keep bending over and you keep interrupting me and I never get around to tying my shoelace. And then I explode: 'Damn it! Leave me alone! I want to tie my shoe!'" The problem here is not a shoelace. The problem is that you and I — if you and I are the characters of the dialogue — are not understanding each other. But my response might be that I rip my shoelace out of my shoe.

That was a part of *Pushkin and Natalie*. Everything was a digression, a straying from the subject. What was the subject? I do not know. I guess I would say it was "*finding* the subject."

"What is my life?! What is my theme?! What do I want?!"

Basically, the story of the play is how Pushkin wants to get married; all the problems that he keeps encountering because of the wedding. That is what he keeps coming back to. He wants to get married but he just cannot do it. For one thing, there are all kinds of rumors about him — all the women he has had. Then he has no money. Then that problem clears up and he runs into other problems because of some careless word he wrote. Then he and Natalie cannot seem to meet up with one another, but they finally do agree to meet. That meeting does not come off either, however, because Natalie is in Moscow and Pushkin is quarantined in Boldino because of a cholera epidemic. No matter how he tries, he cannot seem to get the deal done. There are problems with his inheritance and he cannot scrape up the money. He hopes to get some cash by selling a statuette of Catherine the Great.

The point is that all the problems are silly, insignificant.

At first Pushkin was stuck in Boldino because of the cholera epidemic. Then he sent a letter to Natalie which did not reach her because the mailman confused the address and delivered it to the wrong place. Natalie, as a result, was offended by his silence and broke off the engagement.

Completely monstrous obstacles.

In one of his letters Pushkin wrote how he had visited the Countess Golitsyna in an attempt to find a way to reach Natalie. Then he gets a letter back from Natalie saying, "Oh, so you're spending time with Countess Golitsyna. Now I understand!"

Pushkin writes back, "Golitsyna is a hundred years old!"

True, that would not have held Pushkin back. He could easily have flirted with a hundred-year-old woman. In my show, Pushkin shouted, as if he were writing back to Natalie, "Golitsyna is a hundred years old and fat! In fact, she is as big as your entire family taken together — myself included. I was just there visiting!" I had my actor Viktor Gvozditsky hesitate when he came to the lines — "she's fat" — to indicate, "So what if she's fat? That wouldn't stop me." I had him speak the line not to indicate that he was not guilty as accused, but to indicate that maybe he was guilty after all.

Obstacles, obstacles everywhere.

I explained to Gvozditsky that this was a battle with fate that would lead to a known, predetermined conclusion. Because seven years after Pushkin married Natalie, he would fight a duel over her and die. In other words, all of the obstacles that Pushkin faced in the show were obstacles to the eventual death that would come from his marrying Natalie.

In my interpretation, Pushkin knew what was coming. I included fortune-telling songs from the Christmas folk tradition that clearly tipped off everything that was to come. One song augurs death, another augurs a long journey, another augurs separation, another wealth, another poverty, an argument, prison. Each section of the performance was accompanied by the singing of these fortune-telling songs. My Pushkin character heard them and understood unequivocally what they were saying. He knew he ought not to be pining for this marriage. But he did anyway. It was the case of a man choosing his own destiny and destiny leading him on. More often than not, fate appears not as a monstrous divine image with fiery red eyes, but as the mailman who mixes up addresses or the cholera quarantine that stops people from moving freely. That is; it appears in the form of cheap, silly, vulgar, quotidian images.

While working on this show I came to realize that the exalted is seldom revealed in the lofty. More often it appears in the ridiculous, the simple, the common. That is the charm of it. And that is the wisdom of Pushkin. I came to understand a great deal through Pushkin. He believed in the power of fate, of course, but he did not understand it in a primitive form, as something mystical or as in something so simplistic as "a rabbit crossed my path."

Pushkin and Natalie marked a renewal in my biography. It was a turning point in my creative life and in the evolution of my mentality.

"I was reborn in my entirety," as one of the lines in the play says. That is from a letter Pushkin writes after he is married. In it he says, "I am happy. I do not want this to end. And I feel as though I have been reborn in my entirety." In fact, that line is a quote from Pushkin's play *The Stone Guest*. Don Guan says to Donna Anna: "I believe I have been reborn in my entirety." I did not know about that connection at the time. I learned that later when I was reading an essay by Anna Akhmatova. She is the one who made the connection between the line in Pushkin's letter and in his play.

Pushkin was reborn when he married Natalie. He wanted to be reborn. He wanted to change. He wanted to live. He did not want to whine; he wanted to live the way others lived.

Don Guan was reborn.

When I made that show, I was reborn.

To a certain extent you have been answering my next question. But I will pose it anyway. The question is this: What does it mean for an artist to wait?

You are an artist who has spent a great deal of time waiting. Decades. You may not agree, but my impression is that Kama Ginkas became Kama Ginkas in the 1990s. Obviously, before that you were in a valuable preparation period that included such shows as *Resembling a Lion* and *Pushkin and Natalie,* but my impression is that you essentially stood up and took off in the late 1980s. I am not talking about your becoming famous, as you did in the 1990s. I am talking about you finally having the opportunity to realize projects that you had begun conceiving in the 1960s and 1970s. The artist who sat down to write the script for *Notes from Underground* in the 1960s was only able to stage it in 1988. If you had been able to do that when you composed it, you and it both would have been different. We do not know what you would have been like and that is not important. However, and this is what interests me, you are who you are in many ways because of that lag in time, because of those twenty years you had to wait to realize some of your most important ideas.

So, what does it mean for an artist to wait?

I will tell you what it means: It means a great deal.

Not everyone withstands it. They break down. They dry up. They evaporate. There are many who do that. They are no less talented than others. That is not it at all. It is just that — as in love — there must be give and take. It is unnatural for an artist to go for years without seeing his ideas realized. It is the same as the perversion of a person who is deprived of love — he may become a psychopath, may grow mentally ill, may become evil. That is not his nature. He may be a good, kind person who becomes depraved.

Usually, an artist who is forced to wait too long is broken or destroyed. That is, his potential for creativity may be destroyed entirely. Most often, the artistic gift is crippled and distorted.

Obviously, I am who I am because I went through that period of waiting. Perhaps not entirely, but to a large extent. Would I have been any better without the delay? I do not know.

When Henrietta sees the freedoms we have now in Russia and sees that young people are able to do whatever they want, she often says, "Thirty years ago you were doing what they are discovering today." The problem was that I did not have the opportunity to make known what I was doing. What she has in mind is the inner and outer structure of a show, not its themes or its meaning. She means the way a show is put together — its muscular system, its method, its appearance, that is, what it looks like.

During my early years a great deal of what I saw, imagined, planned, and wished to do, was impossible to realize. I am not even talking about the fact that there were no plays or texts that suited me; I am talking about the fact that the kind of theater I was imagining did not yet exist. I was greedy. I had thousands of ideas. I suppose that is true not only of me, but of any young person with talent. An enormous number of these ideas and perceptions may be faulty. But you have to make those mistakes and you have to make them in their own time. You cannot make errors that you have outgrown. You cannot have lessons in naiveté when you are middle-aged. All of this must happen at the proper time.

I did not have that luxury. I made a lot of my errors very late. Because, ultimately, you have to make your mistakes, whether it is late or not. It is not enough to make them mentally; they must be made and experienced in reality. You must feel them in your bones.

Perhaps I missed the opportunity to make discoveries for myself that might have led me in a different direction. Perhaps I would have emerged very different than I did in fact. No one, including me, can say today whether that is good or bad. But I believe that the ability to wait is part of a creative person's talent. I do not mean simply having patience. No. It is not enough to *be* patient, you must *know how* to be patient, how to put that wasted time to use.

I was patient, but I did not sit around doing nothing. I was always up to something. It was not what I wanted to be doing. It was a form of masturbation. But at least something imitating the process was going on. In one way or another I was engaged in the creative process. As I mentioned, I rehearsed scenes with actors for other people's shows. That was nonsense, of course, invisible work. But, still, it allowed me to flex my muscles.

The most important lesson I received in my time of waiting was to learn not to become bitter. There is no less creative stimulus than bitterness. Anger and bitterness destroy the creative impulse. When you hate your surroundings and everyone around you — including yourself — you end up hating what you are doing. When you let hatred in and you blame someone or something for that, you lose everything. You lose everything. I know that and I know it absolutely.

Many of my colleagues, very talented people, perished in bitterness. They had good reasons to hate. There was nothing trumped up about it. The conditions in which we lived were monstrous, inhuman, anticreative. There were people and circumstances deserving of hatred.

I cannot explain what happened with Henrietta and me. Maybe it is because we were together. Maybe it was enough that we could exercise the creative process before one another, for one another. We hated Soviet reality. We truly hated it. But that was something different. As directors we just did not accept it. We ignored it. Perhaps it was because I came from Lithuania, had grown up with Lithuanians, had gone to Lithuanian schools and was considered a patriot of Lithuania. My attitude to the Soviet way of life was not actively hostile, I simply disregarded it. It is like this table here: It is standing here and there is nothing I can do about. I cannot stretch my legs out because this table is in the way, so I just sit here with my legs tucked up. I do not struggle with the table, but I do not especially take it into account either. That is the way Henrietta and I existed in Soviet times.

Bitterness arises when you begin trying to break down the obstacle. I, on the other hand, was busy ignoring it.

One thing waiting requires is a belief in yourself. That is no easy thing, believing in yourself. Let us say you make some gesture with your hand that you think is graceful and elegant, but everybody laughs at you. How are you going to believe in yourself after that? You tell a joke and only one guy snickers out of politeness. His snickering only increases the sensation of your failure. How do you believe in yourself when there is no reason to? I do not know.

I suspect that talent has its own rights. I mean talent here as something independent of the person who has been blessed with it. You do not guide your talent, it guides you. It can easily be killed off. But talent believes in itself. It is not a matter of me believing in my talent, for my talent exists independently of me. I cannot explain that exactly, but I know it is true.

I often admit that I do not know where I get my ideas. In the middle of rehearsals I will tell an actor, "Now sit! Now pause!" Why do I know the actor should sit and be silent right here? Where does that come from? It is something that exists within me. Talent. Experience. Professionalism. Maybe certain creative reflexes have developed. They are what dictate what happens, not I. Most of the time it is not I saying, "Well, now, it would be better if you would do this . . ."

Where do visual images come from? How do I know something should look this way and not another? I cannot say.

So, how can you say, "Believe in yourself"? You cannot sit there and repeat over and over "I can do it. I am talented." That is nonsense. Nevertheless, you must believe in yourself. You must do it, no matter how you do it.

The first rule of waiting is not to give in to bitterness. The second is to believe in yourself. Third, if you believe in yourself and your ideas keep flowing freely — even if there is no rhyme nor reason to them — it will not matter whether the results are any good. That is not the point.

The point is that your imagination has not surrendered. Sooner or later, it will latch onto something, it will gain intercourse with someone or something — an actor, an author, a space of some kind — and it will bring forth fruit. But you must be ready for that all the time. I know from many of my colleagues, actors and directors, that you can honestly justify inaction by blaming the hostile circumstances surrounding you. That is a comfortable situation to be in — "It's not my fault I'm doing nothing."

But then, when an opportunity does arise, this person does not recognize it. He has lost his keen eye. His ear has dulled. Even if he does realize that now is the place and the time, he is no longer in shape to take advantage. His organism no longer functions properly.

You must work constantly. It does not matter if it is wasted work. It is agony. Believe me. It is agony to work in vain for ten, twelve years. It is agony, it brings on nervous exhaustion. You are working with nothing but the air. No partner. No anything. I called it masturbation a moment ago and that is just what it is. It is nothing but a quick check to see that the system is still working.

There are various stimuli. None is real, but at least it is something. Your imagination is working. In fact, it becomes extremely inventive. To the point that when you have no reason for seeing the possibility of work, you see it any way. You want to, so you do.

Take, for example, the year 1981, just before my being invited to Moscow to stage *Five Corners*. By this time I had essentially abandoned my profession. I had had no professional productions for three years and had done little more than take my dog for walks. You would think I would recall this period now with horror, but it comes back to me as a period of calm. I assumed I had merely made a mistake; that my father was right and it was folly for me to think of a life in the theater. Apparently, in my pride and vanity, I merely imagined that I was someone. Now, I thought, I could see I had been wrong.

There was nothing painful about it. It was a period of resignation. I became resigned to the fact that — as Kovrin says in *The Black Monk* — I was a mediocrity. Kovrin insists that he must be satisfied with his mediocrity. And he is. Because every person should be satisfied with what he is. It is a terrifying thought — that you should have no ambitions to be more than what you are! That you must be satisfied with what you are. It is a tragic thought. One steeped in wisdom, but terrible nonetheless.

I always tell my actor Sergei Makovetsky to break that line into pieces: "Everyone — must. be. satisfied." Period.

A person must be satisfied. That means if you are, you have no choice but to be satisfied that you exist. Even if you are small and insignificant. But that is what you are, so be satisfied with it. You are bound to be grateful to God or to whomever or whatever, for that trifling little that has been given you.

It is horrible. But you must admit it is true. That is resignation, acquiescence. It is meekness, a key quality of Christianity. *To submit* — that is a verb of extraordinary width and depth.

So there I was: I had had creative ambitions. I had thought I was different from others in some way, in my creative powers. But it seems I had been wrong. I became resigned. I grew calm and took my dog for walks. I sat on park benches and talked with old ladies. There was nothing strange about it. I was not yet forty but I felt as though I was just like the old women I talked to. I still had a certain number of years left to live, but that is the way everyone lives. You can live like that. I wondered why it was that I used to think I should live some other way, as if I were different.

There was something I did not formulate for myself at the time, but which I felt deep inside me very clearly. Chekhov has a way of identifying the most gloomy, tragic, and, at the same time, wise thoughts. In "The Lady with the Lapdog," after a problem has been resolved, there is a phrase something like, "But there is a long, long life ahead to live." In another work, I cannot remember which right now, Chekhov writes, "There are another twenty years to live." In other words, what a long, long time left to live.

When you have a goal, when you are engaged creatively — and I do not mean only theater or literature — when you are busy doing something, creating something, then you are alive. And it seems that this time is short. But without that, imagine living twenty years! Twenty years of nothing! That is a terribly long time. Chekhov pinpointed that with fantastic, terrifying precision.

I came to understand that myself. I was not yet forty. My ambitions had come to an end. And I would live out my long years like everyone else. I did not quite understand how I would do it. But I assumed that every day I would have to do something. Walk the dog. Sit and wait. A long time. A half hour. Talk with an old woman or a drunk. Sweep the floor. Do something to earn a little money. In other words, do what 99 percent of humanity does. This did not strike me as anything terrible. I entered into it calmly.

And I believe this is when I was actually reborn. This is when I began to work on *Pushkin and Natalie*. I just did it to do it. There was no purpose for it. I had no intentions of showing it to anyone, performing it anywhere. Even if I wanted to, there was nowhere to play it. I had no access to a theater. It was an aimless, pointless bit of work. As if certain of my reflexes had not yet atrophied entirely. It was as if I still had the remnants of a few creative impulses and I had to do something with them to get them out of my system.

So *Pushkin and Natalie* was a turning point. But it was rarely performed and seen by very few people. That was not enough to bring you out of limbo on its own. What else helped you turn the corner?

After spending three years outside my profession, the news came that the Mossoviet Theater in Moscow was going to stage *Five Corners*, a play by Sergei Kokovkin. This was a melodrama about an aging ballerina whose much younger lover cheats on her. It was not the type of play that would usually have interested me with all my fascination for grand questions. What could there be in a story like that for me to stage?

I essentially created the show on the theme of the life I was living at the time. Roughly, the plot is this: The ballerina has a fan, a captain, who often comes to see her, but she pays him no attention at all. Meanwhile, she increasingly senses that her popularity is waning as time passes. This creates problems with her younger husband and he begins to cheat on her. But off to the side is this strange figure of the captain who was probably in love with her. He often brought her flowers and he occasionally wrote her letters. At the end the ballerina receives a letter informing her that the captain has died. Basically, that is it.

I added my own aspect to the play. In my interpretation it becomes clear that while this man was dying, he had experienced a great — yet unrequited — need for the ballerina. This, then, forces her to think back on what she had been doing while he was dying.

In the show the ballerina had a barre at which she often would stand and do exercises. She was no longer performing, but she was still maintaining her good form. In other words, she was doing what I myself had been doing. She was constantly working, constantly setting herself tasks although there was no point to it. She realized that when the captain had been dying, she had been working. She *had been working*.

And at this point she began attacking the barre to which she had dedicated her entire life. Ever since she was five years old, she had been working at that barre. She was inseparable from that barre, as if they were nailed together. She knew nothing in life other than that barre. It was firmly attached to the stage floor but she began pulling at it and

Nina Drobysheva, as the ballerina in Sergei Kokovkin's *Five Corners*; Moscow, 1981. The mirror that fell and shattered during the performance hangs above the barre that the actress ripped out of the floor in a fit. *Photo courtesy Kama Ginkas.*

ripping it up out of the floor. She ripped down the posters advertising her past performances. It was as if she were attacking herself through these objects. The subtext of her actions was: "What are these? Pieces of paper! Worthless! Pointless!"

It suddenly dawns on her that everything she has been doing is worthless. She realizes there is a life out there about which she knows nothing at all. There are living people out there who need to hear a word or two from her, people who have need of her help. She did not even have to say anything to the captain; it would have been enough simply to sit alongside his bed. But she had been too busy with these silly posters — nothing but a piece of paper!; and with this barre — nothing but a stick of wood.

Were I to do the show again now, I would do it essentially the same, only I would do it a little more boldly. As it was, the ballerina ripped the barre up out of the floor and she stripped the walls of all her posters, throwing all of that in a heap. If I were to do it today, I would have her set that pile on fire.

I staged *Five Corners* about my own realization that I had spent so many years working to the exclusion of my own life. That is what I saw in this melodrama that had been written about something else entirely. As usual, I arrogantly tossed out half of the text. Kokovkin had this literary device of a narrator which I jettisoned. And I added words of my own. Everything I have just described was added by me. I turned the meaning of the play to something that was of importance to me. And at that time I was obsessed with the notion that I had not lived, but had only worked. I then thought that was a terrible, tragic mistake.

8

Provoking the Spectator

Some people believe theater can exist without spectators. I am not among them and I do not believe you are either. Your theater is unthinkable to me without a vital, responsive audience.

I do not mean to ask who is a good spectator and who is not. A spectator is a spectator. But I suspect you work a great deal with your spectator. I know your actors do. I can imagine all kinds of problems that you and your actors must deal with.

The question of spectators is one of the most all-encompassing questions in the theater. It touches all aspects of theater. I do not even know where to begin.

Then let me quote from one of your interviews. You said, "The spectator is categorically mistaken in his opinions and verdicts. But in his emotions, the spectator is invariably right."

Let me decipher what I had in mind.

What is an opinion? — "Brilliant!" "Terrible!" "That's art." "That's not art." "That's profound." "That's not profound." "That's contemporary." "That's old-fashioned."

I do not give a damn about any of that, about your opinion. I have my own opinion and I stick to it.

Opinions often depend upon education or upbringing. Upon which arts or theaters you were exposed to in your formative years.

Maybe you were exposed to none at all. Opinions depend upon the ideology you subscribe to, the newspapers you read, the clichés that have sway with the public at any given time. These may be clichés of language or they may be clichés of thought that are formed in schools and institutes, through television, newspapers, and other mass media.

There is nothing worse, nothing more loathsome than that. That is always the greatest obstacle to honest communication between the artist and the public. They are separated by these clichés. These clichés do not allow the spectator to open up fully and approach the work of art in an unprejudiced fashion. So, the first obstacle you confront is seeing to it that the clichés do not block your ability to reach your audience. That is precisely why most of my productions have been provocational in nature. Because my first task is to remove the spectator from the comfort of what he already knows.

The best spectators are those who never go to the theater — or children. They are able to see what they see.

This brings to mind a great story about a student discussion of my production of *Hamlet,* in which, you will recall, all the key figures were former university buddies. One student jumped up and passionately began criticizing Grigory Kozintsev's film of *Hamlet,* which had just run on television. "What a disgrace!" this young man proclaimed hotly. "How could Kozintsev distort a classic so!? His Claudius was an old man but, as everyone knows, Claudius and Hamlet were peers and classmates!"

I was thrilled. This young man had accepted my version as the real thing. On the other hand, the most difficult, unpleasant, and, I would say, nontheatrical spectator is the one who considers it necessary to attend the theater from time to time. This person is certain he knows theater. He knows Chekhov and Shakespeare and how they must be staged. This spectator comes in as he is accustomed to doing, sits down in his seat, and says, "OK. Now show me Shakespeare."

But wait a minute! What do you know? Even if you do know something. Even if you are very well read. Even if you are nothing less than a Shakespeare scholar. You still do not know Shakespeare because Shakespeare is as heterogeneous and profound as life itself. It all depends on who, at present, is telling us about this life. In this case, *I* am doing

Strolling players perform *The Murder of Gonzago* at court in *Hamlet;* Krasnoyarsk, 1971. *Photo by Boris Barmin.*

the telling. But I tell about Shakespeare differently from others. Even if you know everything there is to know about him. Maybe I do it superficially or badly. But I am still the one doing it. Hear *me*.

Someone is bound to say, "That was silly." Or, "That was stolen from someone else." But that is another step. What I need is to get the spectator to hear *me*.

That is why most of my shows begin with a provocation or include provocational episodes. I want to keep the spectator from falling back on his clichés. Sometimes I parody the spectator's clichés. *Pushkin and Natalie* is a good example. I began by parodying the common perceptions about Pushkin's physical appearance. It was as if we came out and said, "You want Pushkin? We'll give you Pushkin." I mount an assault on their preconceptions, prejudices, opinions, and verdicts. Because what I want to get at is the spectator's emotional response, his associative memory.

This, incidentally, is where the spectator is always right and I will tell you why.

Let us say one spectator's range is small. It is my job to find access to his potential for responding. I must rely on my profession and my talent to locate where he is susceptible and then work on him to make him respond. Maybe he has no associative memory. He knows nothing at all. He just knows his own world. Well, it is my job to awaken him.

I recall touring the Caucasus with some shows I had staged in Krasnoyarsk. We performed in Grozny, the capital of the republic of Chechnya, and Ordzhonikidze, the capital of the republic of Ossetia. This was really wild. Women sat in the audience stuffing their faces with pastry and shaking their heads. They would point at the actors and talk among themselves — "He's got a beard." "Yeah, that one's laughing." "Listen, that one over there's making noises." One of the actors on stage would say hello, and people in the audience would discuss it among themselves — "That guy just said hello." No matter what was happening on stage, they would instantly repeat it, name it, and discuss it.

That is what these spectators were like. That was their natural, external response to what they were seeing. It was my job as a professional to interest them so that I could do with them what I considered necessary. My job was to make them laugh when I thought it was funny. I had to make them cry when I thought it was sad.

Spectators may give you more or less in return than you expect. They may not actually weep tears, but their concentration may grow more intense. They may not laugh as freely as you want, but they may smile. That is all a matter of their temperament, their upbringing, and many other superficial elements.

But they are not in control; I am in control. I have to find the way to bring them to where I want them to be. If I am not able to do that, that is my fault, not theirs.

Often enough it happens that spectators will laugh and cry during a show, and then they will walk out and mutter, "What a bunch of crap that was!" Or they will laugh and cry and walk out saying, "What the hell was that? I couldn't make heads or tails of it! Who was that story about?"

But that is another question. That is a matter of their perceptions.

There is no theater without spectators. That probably sounds terribly ironic coming from me, a director who in the last fifteen years has worked for such a small number of spectators. But theater, basically, should appeal to twenty thousand people at once. I would like to do theater like that, as in the ancient Greek theater. Or at least one thousand people as it was in Shakespeare's time or even in big, contemporary theaters.

On the other hand, I do not believe that a tiny fifty-centimeter by twenty-centimeter painting by Bruegel is any less important than a monumental, multistoried wall mural. I know that is true. Art is art. There may be different types and genres, but the value of art is not determined by size.

I am reminded of an article I ran across recently about the French director Didier-Georges Gabily. In it, he is quoted as saying he is not interested in theater as a place to achieve consensus, but as a place to create friction. You would probably call it a place for provocation, but I do not think the specific word is what is important. In any case, I do not believe that you or anyone else could attract an enormous number of spectators to come view a provocation. That is a different kind of theater. People come to the theater in large numbers when they can sit comfortably and watch a nice show about a nice person and then go back out on the street afterwards and say, "Oh, what a nice person I am." That is not your theater. It is not the theater many of us crave. Well, maybe not many, but there are plenty of us.

This also reminds me of something you said several years ago. When I heard it, I laughed and assumed you were putting someone on. What you said was that you "dream of a velvet curtain." I did not believe you. But that is almost what you are saying right now. That you would like to work in a big, traditional theater with a velvet curtain.

Still, I do not believe you. You do not dream about that.

No, no. Let me explain what I mean. Now, and for the last ten years, I have not been in favor of a theater of confrontation. I am for a theater of cooperation. A theater of interaction where the spectator acts on me and I act upon the spectator. I am not interested in proving that I am right and he is not. Nor am I interested in telling the spectator in advance that I agree with him and giving him what he wants so that on that basis we, *comme il faut,* like very polite people, communicate on a level where I do not bring up topics that are unpleasant to him and he does not demand anything too difficult or unpleasant of me.

That kind of art exists, of course. It is always very popular and always has success because it never offends anyone. If it is challenging in any way, it plucks those sentimental strings that make us ache so pleasantly. It does not strike those chords whose sound makes us really go down deep inside ourselves.

It seems to me that true art, great art, always offends. It touches on what hurts, on what is irresolvable, on what we do not want to think about, but which, in fact, exists. Great art is always honest. It is not blind. That does not mean it must be gloomy. It can come in different shades. Most often it is not gloomy, because even in the horrible you do not descend into horror. It is not at all necessary to plunge into horror itself upon recognizing the horrible. You can experience aesthetic pleasure merely from the knowledge that such dilemmas exist. There is courage in recognizing that. You can achieve self-respect through your ability to know; through the discovery that you are not blind.

I am not for a theater of confrontation. I am for a theater of cooperation. I would like to share with my spectator everything I know about myself and life. And I would like the spectator, through his reactions, to be amazed by the fact that I am showing him something unexpected, regardless of whether he agrees with me or not. I like it when a spectator responds, "I'll be damned. I didn't know I had that in me! Thank you!"

Maybe that something is terrible, but it is true.

I would like to achieve the kind of cooperation that leads to mutual enrichment.

I should quote Gabily directly. He said, "On the one hand there's spectacle, which is essentially consensual, and, on the other there's theater, which has to do with friction, which doesn't stoop to a mere celebration of unanimity . . . "*

Well, your inexact quote incited me to formulate my thoughts, which, as it turns out, partially coincide with those of Gabily.

I want to say that in recent years I have sought to avoid struggle, resistance and antagonism. What I want is interesting, deep, sincere communication. Better yet, let us say contact, interpenetration, interaction. Mutual enrichment. It is all right if you must go through friction or even resistance to achieve it. But I am not interested in merely seeking conflict.

As for the "velvet curtain," or, to use my exact words, "velvet seats," that is, a theater of comfort in the style of the Italian theater of the nineteenth century — what a magnificent idea! Magnificent because it implies a warm, though large, community.

In the past, my relationship with reality was one of disappointment that the world was not as I would have liked it to be. I dug into the negative aspects of the world order. And I was, I would not say infuriated, but plagued, by the fact that the world was not as I would have liked. I wished to communicate that despair to the spectator in the same defiant tonalities in which I perceived it.

Now, I do not close my eyes to any of that. As in the past, that is still more or less what I am busy doing. However, thanks to Chekhov and, perhaps, to my advancing age, I have come to a wiser point of view. The essence of it is that our existence is monstrously imperfect. Monstrously. I am not talking about social problems; I am working on a much simpler level. We live for such a short period of time. We are weak. We are clumsy. We spend so much time on nonsense that we waste most of the time we do have. The most terrible aspect, of course, is that we are mortal. That is horribly unjust. It is just horrible in itself. It is so horrible it would seem to nullify everything else.

---

*Quoted in "Writing for the New French Théâtre d'Art: The Example of Didier-Georges Gabily (and one or two others)" by Michael Sadler, *TheatreForum*, no. 16 (Winter-Spring 2000), 4.

But then you realize what has been granted you. That short piece of time. Given to you, Kama Ginkas. Unbelievable! It might not have been. There might very well have been no Kama Ginkas, no short period of time that makes up his life. What difference if it is very short, very silly, very unjust, filled with much that humiliates you, hurts you, cripples you, wounds you? Constantly.

But it does exist, that short piece of time. Unbelievable! What incredible good fortune! How could you have been so lucky? Think of all the possibilities by which that life might not have been! The percentages are stacked heavily against you! There is no way you should have existed. But you do. Amazing.

The warmth and tenderness — the wonder — of which you are speaking is very clear in, say, *The Black Monk*. And yet, inside that remains a very daring production. You will always be a daring director.

That is a different topic. That is my character.

I would pose this question: What predominates?

When I was younger I was less well-off. More to the point, I was more daring simply because I was younger. I was more decisive, more uncompromising, more foolish, more superficial. Plus I had fewer possessions and I had less satisfaction in my profession. So I was unhappy with that, as well. What predominated was my daring. My mordancy. My despair. The other aspect, the warmth and tenderness, was barely evident.

But, as time passed, I was drawn to do something else. In *Crime and Punishment* I terribly wanted to achieve a supreme tenderness that, essentially, is unnatural for that work. Yes, it would be painful, even tormenting. But I did not want it to be harsh. I envisioned the tone of that production as extremely gentle. Two people are bound by love and tenderness. But look how they flail at one another! Why do they . do that? I wanted the spectator to see in it something terribly charming and attractive.

If you think you will ever gather crowds of one thousand people — to say nothing of twenty thousand — for a show like *Crime and Punishment*

or *We Play "Crime,"* you must have an extraordinary, unimaginable respect for your spectator.

No, I know I cannot draw crowds like that. I know that. What I am saying is that I would like to. I wish I could.

Let me come back at you from another angle, then. Right now I am thinking of the first night of your production of Oleg Bogayev's *Room of Laughter.* That show was attended by huge numbers of fans of the famous and popular actor Oleg Tabakov who was playing a senile old man living in squalor and struggling with the demons of his own personal life and of the complex historical era in which he lived. Many spectators came armed with bouquets so enormous they had to peer around the flowers in order to see the show. The show was not more than twenty minutes underway when several of these spectators — mostly women — began standing up and leaving with their bouquets. There must have been a dozen at least. They left behind them a theater full of people without bouquets who, at the end of the show, applauded and shouted "Bravo!" Those spectators who came hoping to achieve a consensus with the actor ended up leaving.

I did not know that. That makes a wonderful tale very much in my genre. A parable with a moral. That is a clearly stated picture of my relationship with my spectator. My spectator is unique.

I cannot say that I respect my spectator and I cannot say that I do not. I have no relationship with him at all. I suspect there is some spectator out there. I would say that I address *myself* sitting out there in the auditorium. That is all. I respect myself and I relate to my spectator as I would to myself.

But what I have been talking about is that I find it very frustrating that there are only a few dozen spectators out there like me. Or, in the case of *Room of Laughter,* that only 400 of the 600 understand me and the other 200 either get up and leave with their bouquets or sit it out and stumble out not understanding why they bothered to come.

In fact, this torments me. It hurts.

In my youth I never let myself think — the way some did — that

I was so original and profound that nobody else was capable of understanding me. I was never condescending with my spectator. I never patronized him. Not when I was younger and, all the more so, not now. I believe that the spectator is the person who is out there tonight. Whether he is a Chechen, a Lithuanian, a Finn, a Russian, or a Jew. Those spectators who came tonight are the ones you have. He came to see your show. Maybe he even came by accident. He thought he was going to get one thing, but, in fact, he got another.

That, of course, is a very unpleasant situation. Unfortunately, it happens. It tends to happen more with *Room of Laughter* because many are coming expressly to see Oleg Tabakov. It happens less with my small shows because usually those spectators know what they are getting into. I do not get many random spectators at these shows.

It is a problem when the spectator comes not knowing what he will see. Someone once said that coming to my shows is rather like winding up in a gynecologist's office when you thought you were going to the dentist. All I can say is sorry. It is not my fault if you come in the wrong door. That has nothing to do with me. It is your job to know where you are going.

You see, I am not inviting people into my home as guests. It is not a situation where I must do people favors. I invite people to the theater for a conversation. It is the spectator's job to find out with whom they will be conversing. Obviously, I cannot achieve communication with everyone. That is perfectly normal. That neither insults the spectator nor the theater. That is merely the nature of interactive communication.

That triggers a thought I have had in connection with your production of *Crime and Punishment* in Helsinki. You believe that an actor can perform in a language other than that which the spectator knows and yet the spectator will have no problem understanding what the show is about. I take that to mean you believe that the most important thing in a performance is the idea that exists behind or between the words. And that a good actor, or, at least, an actor you feel is suited to the role, will be able to express what is essential through means other than language.

I would like to take issue with one word you used: *idea*. This word irritates me. First, for a person brought up in the Soviet Union, it has too many ominous connotations. But, more important is the fact that I do not have "ideas" in my shows.

But, yes. I believe that any spectator who does not have a command of the language an actor speaks on stage can understand or feel what is essential thanks to *what is occurring with the actor*. Something always must be going on, some process of some sort.

Let us say that we see an accident on the street from a third-story window. People gather. We do not hear anything they are saying, but we see what is going on. We feel the tension involving what has happened. We clearly grasp who is a friend or a relative of the person who was just run over. We clearly grasp who is there just to see what is going on. We sense who is taking charge of the situation. Maybe it is a policeman or maybe just someone taking authority into his own hands. We sense who among them is the driver who ran the pedestrian over, perhaps because he is clearly explaining that it was not his fault or perhaps because he is in a state of shock. People are appealing to him, but he is unable to respond. And on it goes.

We sense all of that. We may not understand the details. We do not know the exact words that are being spoken. We do not hear the obscenities that the friend or relative of the victim is using. But we understand what is going on. And we understand what each of those people down there is doing.

Activity. Action. That is the essence of theater as it was understood by my teacher Tovtsonogov and as it is understood by me. *Action.* We spectators do not focus on what the characters are saying; we focus on what they are doing and what is happening to them. Action.

Furthermore, for the most part, I am talking about internal action. Not just any old activity that an actor might be engaged in. I mean internal action, internal movement. This is what lies at the heart of Russian theater. This is primarily what is meant by action in the Stanislavsky system.

I just remembered an observation of Meyerhold's that was a revelation for me when I first encountered it. He said something to the effect that he could look at men and women, and, without hearing a single word that is being said, he could determine who among them was in love, who was falling in love, and who had fallen out of love. He could see all of that in their behavior.

Of course. That is exactly true. These things are all sensible, they are expressed. Therefore, you do not have to know the language that actors are working in to understand a production. Since you are a person, you are capable of understanding what happens to other people, regardless of whether they are of a different race, religion, creed, and even language. There are no two ways about it — all people jerk their hand back when burned. They all have hatreds, they all fear death, they all want to eat and drink, they all want to find love. These basic characteristics may take different forms in different cultures and languages. The rituals surrounding them may differ. The costumes worn when engaging in the rituals may differ. But the essence remains the same.

These are the things that the dramatic line of any show is built around. Nuances may change and we may miss or misconstrue some of the subtleties if we do not know the actor's language. We may fail to grasp certain details because of our own lack of sophistication, because of our own personal blindnesses. But you can throw all of that out and still sense what is happening to a person. It may seem to a spectator that a character rambles excessively if he does not know the language. But, if something is going on there onstage, we cannot help but get caught up in the flow. This is why we have no trouble watching a production in a language that we do not know.

I often talk with foreigners in Moscow who say they love the theater but do not go because they lack the language. Or they prefer to stick to *Uncle Vanya* because they know the plot. I tell them that Russian theater is rich in many languages besides the one we speak in. I say, "Go and trust your feelings. At first you will understand nothing. By intermission, you will know who loves whom. And, by the end of the show, you will know everything you need to know."

There are different kinds of spectators, of course. Some are more curious, others are less so. Some are more prepared to make themselves get to the bottom of what they are seeing. This is work.

More often than not, spectators are merely looking for entertainment. They want to be spoon-fed. That kind of spectator naturally needs to know the language and everything else. That spectator is satisfied when seeing something that corresponds to what he or she expected to see. If it does not correspond, then it was a bad show. In that sense, I am sure that your exhortations seldom achieve what you want.

Negatively attuned spectators, like enthusiastic ones, send out contagious vibrations that are passed on easily among other spectators. When one person laughs, it affects others nearby. The opposite is equally true — a hostile spectator can kill the mood for several rows around him. Obviously, you do not have control over this kind of thing. However, I suspect you do try to anticipate things that will affect the audience response.

As I have said, I do not merely try to do that; I am bound by my profession to do that. It is another thing that I do not command that skill entirely. I am not always able to provoke the reactions I am after. As a rule, that concerns comic responses segueing into dramatic responses. I have been doing this for many years. And I can point out several recurring errors purely on a professional level.

Take my production *The Execution of the Decembrists*. This show is intended to begin with a whole series of comic elements, and many more comic moments are supposed to arise throughout the performance. For example, somewhere along the line, someone lost the crossbeam on which the prisoners are to be hung. That cannot fail to be funny. It is a totally absurd event. A huge number of people in a major affair of state spent a large amount of time preparing an execution, and then it turns out that the most important item making the execution possible has either been lost or stolen. In any case, it is not here where it is supposed to be. That cannot fail to be funny.

But the spectators at this show do not always laugh where I want them to. And when the spectators do not laugh, this production

Igor Gordin as the prison warden Berkopff in *The Execution of the Decembrists*, written by Kama Ginkas on the basis of historical documents; Moscow, 1995. *Photo by Ken Reynolds*.

becomes oppressive. It cannot be perceived as I intended it. Without laughter, all of the tragic elements, all of the physiological elements, begin to weigh down on the spectator. There is much that is tragic in this show and that is as it should be. But it is all *delivered* in a playful manner.

Characters play with the nooses, with the ropes, with the lard that will grease the nooses, with hooks, with wooden beams. All this gives rise to some very playful scenes. It is as if these people are playacting at an execution, not preparing to carry one out. But, at times, the spectators only smile crookedly. They do not laugh.

After a certain period of time had passed, I understood what I had done wrong. And in *Pushkin. Duel. Death* — a show that is very similar in structure and method — I corrected the problem at least to an extent.

It is quite simple, actually. One of the great clowns — maybe it was even Chaplin — said that before you come out in the ring, you have to announce yourself and immediately do something funny. Fall or whistle or fart. Something.

One, you immediately must let the spectator know that what is to come is funny. You must give the spectator the right to laugh. That is very important.

Two, you must tip off what kind of humor it will be. You must guide the spectator, let him know what direction you are moving in, let him know what style you are working in. Is it English humor? Armenian humor? Eskimo humor? Is it an abstract joke or is it a joke based on smut? The spectator must know what kind of humor is coming.

I did not do that in *The Execution of the Decembrists*. The first thing that happens there is that a large group of frightened people shuffles out on stage as if they are going to be shot or led to gas chambers or as if they are about to face the final judgment. This is accompanied by tragic, powerfully spiritual music. Several people enter wearing signs bearing their names. This instantly calls up numerous tragic associations. The atmosphere is dark and tense. The character of the Narrator bustles out and curtly puts everyone in their place. Add to that the title — *The Execution of the Decembrists* — which has attuned the spectator in advance. After that there is no getting to the spectators with humor.

But you have forgotten the funny, handwritten signs that the spectators encounter before the show begins. You set it up so that, as they walk to their seats, the spectators pass numerous signs announcing, "This way to the execution!" Those are very funny.

That is true. I have not forgotten that.

I mention it because I once again cannot help but wonder if maybe you are too respectful of your spectator. Perhaps you assume he will make connections that he cannot.

No, and I will say it again: It is not a matter of my respecting the spectator. I appeal to my spectator as I would to myself. So, I am not even talking about my spectator when I describe *The Execution of the Decembrists* here. I am talking about myself. I think about how I might laugh at those signs before coming into the auditorium to take my seat. But as soon as that music starts, I switch onto a different wavelength and it would be very difficult for me to get off it again. That was an error in strategy on my part.

On the other hand, when we performed this show for an in crowd of actors, theater people, and friends, everybody laughed freely. You see, this is a freer crowd. They are not afraid of being wrong. Why do you think the average spectator does not laugh? Because he is afraid of laughing in the wrong place. Of laughing at something that is very deep, philosophical, and tragic.

This reminds me of an incident that took place many years ago in Leningrad when Valery Fokin brought to town his famous Moscow production of Dostoevsky's *Notes from Underground*. Since I had long before written my own dramatization of this novel but had never had the opportunity to stage it, I was curious to see it. I was just a nobody at the time; I had to sneak into the Leningrad Actors House where the performance was held. Only the city's elite were being allowed in. All of Leningrad's best actors, all of the city fathers, all the directors were in attendance.

I sat and watched from somewhere up in the last row. And when the actor playing the Underground Man said, "I am a spiteful man. I am not a pleasant man. I think there is something wrong with my liver," I burst into laughter.

At that, one of the top Leningrad critics of the time turned around and shot an icy stare at me. The show continued and everyone proceeded to watch with a great deal of seriousness and attention. Then the actor spoke about how he never goes to doctors although he respects doctors very much. I laughed again. And after that, whenever I thought it was funny, I would laugh. Because for me Dostoevsky's text and everything about it is very funny. After the third or fourth time the critic had shot icy stares at me, she hissed, "You should be ashamed of yourself! This is *Dostoevsky!*"

That was a critic speaking. An intelligent, intellectual critic.

The spectator has come to see a dramatization of Dostoevsky. The very name Dostoevsky means something gloomy, oppressive, profound, intelligent. The spectator has performed a great deed, has forced himself to come see this dreary Dostoevsky. He has prepared himself in advance to withstand all the dark desolation that this author will heap on him. Now it is the spectator's duty to soak it all in.

But what happens if you show him something else? What happens if Katerina Ivanovna pops out of a door, does a jig, disappears, and slams the door again? In *K. I. from "Crime,"* there is a great deal of clowning. And by the time the spectators have been fooled several times over as they repeatedly fall for the actress's tricks — at one point she invites them into the next room but slams the door in their faces when they begin to follow — they cannot help but laugh. Even if the actress and I have not been able to attune them to the clownery in the early going, by the time the door gets slammed in their faces, they have no choice but to give in. This is such an elementary thing that they must laugh. They feel relief. And from there on out, if the actress is working as she should, the spectators laugh constantly.

Later she will transfer them onto a different wavelength. And then back again. And then back again in the other direction. That is what I do — change voltage constantly, jerk back and forth between styles. That is what I love to do. And that is what I would like the spectator to do.

It is our job to alter the spectator's state. It is the spectator's job to be altered, to be sent back and forth. It is a lot of work. On one hand, the spectator finds all of these shifts quite pleasurable, but on the other, they can be very painful. We are constantly jerking him back and forth. Plus-minus. Funny-terrible. I am laughing then suddenly I am crying again. These are very intense shifts.

That is the game I play. In it, an actor — or else, I — might err. Basically, I always consider the errors mine. For it is my job to see to it that even an actor's minor slip-ups will not change the overall picture.

In *The Execution of the Decembrists* I was slightly off in my strategy. It is not the actors' fault when the spectators do not laugh. I attuned the spectators to one thing and they cannot be swayed from it. It just is not possible.

Even *Pushkin. Duel. Death* has a risk to it that can cause problems. The show begins when several actors in gloomy, black tailcoats carry a black table into the room. The spectators know the title of the show, and so they make the association that I want them to. All the more so because the actors lower the table onto the floor slowly and then stand by it as if in mourning before somberly taking seats. You do not have to be a particularly great director to be able to create the mood that reigns at this point.

But this is where I have an actress burst in all full of joy and life. She titters on about what a wonderful, gay person Pushkin was, what long fingernails he had, how he laughed, how he was always eating bread rolls. And how handsome he was — true, he had a small bald spot, but still, he was quite handsome.

That is not easy for an actor to come out in a completely different state from everyone else. You need talent, great confidence, and skill to be able to pull it off. When it works, the show runs as it should. When it does not, the performance can be long and difficult.

In *Pushkin and Natalie* everything was easy. It was clear from the very beginning that nothing was serious. First of all, neither death nor even seriousness was among the givens of the show. The given was Pushkin. Who was Pushkin? Pushkin was lots of things. He was airy and light. The title was *Pushkin and Natalie,* probably a love story, maybe even a little bit of smut. In other words, a completely different tuning process. Instead of coming to the theater and finding a big, involved set and, say, an organ solemnly playing, you are crammed into a seat in a little room. You even have to scrunch up your knees or twist to one side to fit in there. It is almost as if you are not in a theater at all. Almost as if what is happening right now is nothing important — probably just a prelude. Maybe the real theater will begin later.

Then an actor came out and started going through all kinds of comical gyrations as he created his fake sideburns and hobbled on crooked legs — all the while solemnly insisting "this is Pushkin."

The prologue to *Pushkin and Natalie* was a big one running five to seven minutes and consisting entirely of jokes. Its entire purpose was to set the tone of the genre. Later the tone changed drastically. But, by that time, the spectators understood the rules of the game — back and forth, back and forth. The actor's talent was crucial here. Another actor may not have been able to do this. Viktor Gvozditsky was stunning. And even then, some days one part would be more successful; some days another. It is the same in *K. I. from "Crime."*

You must find the one specific mode of communication with your audience, the one and only mode of communication that you need for this specific production, the one and only approach required for this specific audience that came to you tonight, in this country, in this city, in this theater, in this space. You must appeal specifically to that spectator who came today, not tomorrow's or yesterday's, but the one who came to you today, whether it was by chance or by design.

Perhaps your spectator today came on purpose to see something by Dostoevsky and so he has already furrowed his brow in advance. He has no idea what show he has come to see, and only later does he figure it out. Perhaps he has purposefully come to see a show by Kama Ginkas and so he knows that everything is going to be dreadfully serious. Or he has come with flowers for Oleg Tabakov, or perhaps he was able to sneak in at the last minute and does not even know what he has come to see. Perhaps he saw a television program or maybe he looked at the marquee and saw the title *Room of Laughter* and so he came to laugh. The spectator may not get what he is after. Or, perhaps he does.

Finding contact with your audience is a profession, an art, a craft. Not only in the particular show on which you are working, but also with the specific audience that has come to see you tonight. You do not choose your audience; your audience comes to you and it changes all the time. Naturally, there are many potential problems and pitfalls.

It is no coincidence that I keep referring to the beginning of a show. If you establish the rules of the game properly at the outset, if you find the necessary mode of communication for this show that you are staging, and for this audience that has come tonight, then you will have no problems. Beyond that, the material will lead. But if you are off — even if you are right in the vicinity — that communication will not happen. That is tough for the actor and it makes things uncomfortable for the spectator. That discomfort is very different from the one I often seek to evoke in my audience.

I suspect that my shows are of interest to spectators because yes and no invariably exist in them at the same time. Yes and no. No and yes. That goes for any aspect of my shows. It could be some realistic aspect. Of course, my shows are never about realistic, everyday occurrences. What realism there is in them exists as something that is there in the margins. The spectator always senses that distance. In *K. I. from "Crime,"* a spectator does not know whether the actress is actually addressing him or not. She says something, he starts to respond but by the time he gets around to it, his response is no longer necessary. The actress has moved on. In my other shows that do not have that kind of direct appeal to the audience, this aspect is expressed in different ways. But it is crucial nonetheless.

Your production of Oscar Wilde's *The Happy Prince* seemed to cause consternation when it first opened in 2000, not because of its actor-spectator symbiosis, but because of its unusual form. That long prologue of people wandering around making funny noises appeared to grate on some.

There was some confusion right at the start of the run, although that passed quickly and the show now enjoys tremendous success with audiences. The reason for the early baffled responses was that *The Happy Prince* contains elements I had never employed before. Some critics did not understand why I should try doing anything that is uncharacteristic of me. Others found things in the show that simply were not there and they cried, "Oh there he goes again! Doing the same old thing!"

I sensed bewilderment — I would call it "respectful bewilderment"— on the part of critics immediately after the first two dress rehearsals to which I invited a small number of critics. I sensed their respect for me and what I do. But I could tell they thought something was wrong. Some people were disappointed because they wanted to see what they had seen me do before. Others did not like what they saw because there was too much of the same old thing that they never liked to start with.

Arina Nesterova as the Swallow held back by Alexei Dubrovsky as the Reed in Oscar Wilde's *The Happy Prince*; Moscow, 2000. *Photo by Ken Reynolds.*

What I found unusual was the show's use of time. And this became much clearer after the show opened, as opposed to the dress rehearsal I saw. The show develops almost excruciatingly slowly. I would say it is aggressively slow. We come into the theater from outdoors where the twenty-first century is in full swing. We are all in a hurry, caught up in hyper-rhythms, and we take our seats still in a huff. And then this almost belligerently slow show begins. I could feel people around me shuffling and shifting in their seats because they were out of rhythm with what they were witnessing. Some were never able to get in sync. I was hardly different. I came into the theater from the same twenty-first century as everyone else, and I kept waiting for something that you were not giving me. Then, all of a sudden, I began perceiving not that which I had come to see, but that which you were offering. At that moment, the magic of this production snapped into place.

I had not thought about that. That is an intriguing observation. I have said that as a rule, my shows begin with a provocation, with some sort of aggression. They also usually begin with a clear-cut rhythm and a high-speed tempo.

K. I. from "Crime" begins with the actress running in and out, slamming the door. The spectators are taken aback completely; they have not had time to figure out what is going on but the show is already underway. And before they get accustomed to that, she is inviting them into another room, then slamming the door in their face and making them sit back down and on and on. Half that show is gone before the spectators know what has hit them.

The Black Monk also begins with a commotion of sorts. A man comes out on stage and, after staring around for about forty seconds, he leaps over the edge of the balcony. Almost immediately, and just as unexpectedly, he reappears again from below. The actors run about, joking and teasing. The rhythm of this beginning is very tense.

The Execution of the Decembrists begins with a pause that lasts for nearly a minute. But as soon as that pause is over, the rhythm and tempo pick up quickly. *Pushkin. Duel. Death* begins at a very fast pace. If it is being performed well, it also has a very buoyant tempo.

The Happy Prince is different in this sense. You might say this show begins with a seven- or eight-minute pause. It is a seven-minute pause in which people move about the stage very slowly and very strangely. They listen to themselves, to the space they inhabit and the sounds that arise from within them. These sounds surprise them and allow them to enter into dialogues of sorts. This lasts seven or eight minutes before the first words are spoken.

I am also intrigued by your observation that the spectators were trapped in their own inertia in some way, although I am not certain you are right. My observation was that the audience reacted well. It laughed and applauded a lot. That meant the show was getting through to them.

I created several scenes that are supposed to evoke a deathly silence. They last a long time. I took a risk with them. Henrietta even advised me to shorten them. One example is when the prince's dead body is lowered from his perch on high and removed from the gilded cage. This takes a good ninety seconds while nothing else happens at all. There are numerous scenes like this, wordless pauses when it would appear nothing is happening. In all these cases, the audiences sit in what I would call ringing silence. That means the audience is, in fact, caught up in the show.

It is another matter that, after the show, the spectators themselves do not know how to explain what they have experienced. I have talked about this common occurrence with my shows. If the show is successful, the spectators are locked in whether they want to be or not. Maybe much of what they see is unclear to them, but they never really get around to asking themselves just what it is that is unclear. In *K. I. from "Crime,"* is Katerina Ivanovna a clown? Is she crazy? Is this an actor or a sick person accosting us? Which husband died, her first or her second? What is this — theater or what? What the hell is it?! Of course, the spectators who are coming to see the show now, many years after it opened, have at least heard something about it. But for a long time people did not know what to make of it. They were perplexed by the very method of the performance.

When we played *K. I. from "Crime"* in Tbilisi, Georgia, the audiences were shocked by the extreme intimacy of it. We learned that no one in Georgian theater had ever performed so closely, literally, to the spectators. I thought that was curious, because contemporary theater often breaks down the distance between spectator and actor. But they had not seen that before. They were shocked by the actress's hand stretching out to them right there.

Where the confusion arises is when spectators start trying to explain things to themselves. The show is on and it would seem the actors are performing well. The audience is hanging on every word. When it is all over, the spectators are still caught up in what they experienced. But then they start trying to explain things to themselves, to their wife or girlfriend. That is when they get confused. It even happens that when spectators begin trying to analyze things, they find they disliked what they experienced. Their analysis leads them to conclude that something was wrong with the show.

They have the feeling something was wrong with what they saw even when they were engrossed in it. It is as though they were exploited to some purpose. The director explained nothing. And they like things to be explained. They suspect they have been taken for fools. They are indignant. How dare that director do that to me?!

The highest evaluation I can receive is when spectators tell me that they have not been able to shake the impressions of the show. In fact, I am not as interested in how spectators respond during my show as in how they respond after it. I am pleased when someone tells me that my show will not let them go, that it has remained with them for two days, a week or even more. I consider that my biggest accomplishment.

There may have been some confusion about *The Happy Prince* early on. But right from the start I could see the reactions. The spectators were caught up in the show. They did not cough, they did not rustle packages, they were not bored. That penetrating silence I heard meant the show had gotten to them.

Silence is not always the reaction you get in some shows. Your productions are capable of really getting under people's skin.

K. I. from "Crime" is interesting in this light. The first shows were extremely shocking for audiences. There were cases of people running out in hysterics. The whole hall would be red-eyed and wet from tears — something that continues to this day. There was a time, however, when the spectators who wanted to see Ginkas and/or something out of the ordinary began to thin out. That is when a different group of spectators began coming and they were not prepared for what they saw. These spectators did not know how to respond and their reaction was complex. There was a period — maybe a year, maybe six months — when we had trouble getting audiences in, even though the show only seats sixty people. Then something happened and it is obvious now that, in terms of audience interest at least, this show could run indefinitely. The case of *Pushkin. Duel. Death* is similar. We raised the ticket prices but people keep coming.

This says something about how shows attract their own public. The media send out various signals to the public and, over time, a kind of natural selection takes place. The audiences that attend these shows after they have been running for a while are completely unlike those that attend at the beginning of the run. This is a sturdier spectator, more committed than the critics or professionals who attend only premieres.

I have the impression that your spectator is changing nowadays and is changing rather quickly. Maybe that is a matter of the historical changes we are experiencing. Soviet life and theater, and the audiences they attracted, were pretty much monolithic. That is an exaggeration, of course, there was the underground that stood in contrast to the so-called official culture, but, still, the status quo was much more stable. Nowadays, things change quite rapidly. With the passing of each new year, we find we are living almost in a new country. New generations have appeared that know nothing about what has been in the past, while, in some cases, older generations understand nothing about what is going on in the present. I have the feeling that, in connection with all this, your shows are sending out new growth, sprouts and buds.

I would be dead if that were not happening. But it may not be as a result of audiences. It may be because I am changing. This may sound banal, but it may be a result of publicity. Soviet publicity was a very specific thing. In the first years following the collapse of the Soviet Union, publicity, in general, seemed to cease to exist. In Soviet times it was more or less like this: If the papers trashed something, you knew it was worth seeing. Now it is like this: If the papers write anything at all, good or bad, people will go see it. Thank goodness we are not like Europe yet, where people go to the shows critics praise and avoid those they slam. I find that abhorrent.

It is true that I have entered a new phase in my life. There really are a lot of people writing and talking about me and showing my face on the television. This encourages the public to be receptive to something that, perhaps, they would not be otherwise. I can imagine them saying, "Well, I guess that's something we ought to see." That is how fashion works. That is how women begin walking around baring their bellybuttons. They see one, two, three people doing it. Then they even see some famous model whose name they cannot remember doing it. So they figure they ought to do it too.

I think that is a little what my popularity with the public is like right now.

9

The Theater of Biography

You once declared that a Jew must destroy himself and his father, too. You were talking about what maximalists Jews are and you said your father was no less a man of obsessions than you are.

As was my father's father. I do not know about my mother's father. He died of tuberculosis when he was in his mid-30s, far from his family. He was a leftist Jew, a communist sympathizer who went to live in the Soviet Union. He spent his last four or five years in the Crimea. Mother was around twelve or fourteen when he left.

His name was Kalman Zingman. I am named after him. My full name is considered Kalman, but no one has ever called me that. Translated from German and Yiddish, Zingman means the singing man. If my maternal grandfather was anything like my mother, he was patient, calm, smart, and ironic; a lucid, radiant man. In personality that would have meant he was completely unlike the Gink line. ("Ginkas" is the Lithuanian form of my family name.) Kalman Zingman was a writer who wrote in Yiddish. And he kept a small store. First of all, that is what Jews did, and, second of all, you could not support a family writing. Who is going to read or publish you? Writing was a calling or a hobby, but you lived by other means. So he ran a small bookstore. I do not know whether he worked the store himself, but probably so.

He was a poor man. He probably had a small room where he traded in books.

The first time I was in Israel, I visited my uncle Abram Zimrani, that is, the older son of my grandfather Zingman. He had lived in Israel since 1939 and can be considered one of the builders of the Israeli nation. He was a teacher by profession, a philologist, although by this time he was around 90 years old. My uncle went to his big library and pulled out some books in Yiddish. And he said, "Here are the books of your grandfather." Somewhere in used bookstores or through book collectors, he had found my grandfather's published books. What was most surprising was that one of the volumes was a collection of plays. That just stunned me.

My uncle told me the plot of one of the plays. I think it was written around 1921 or 1922. Or maybe it was even as early as 1919. It was an ironic comedy about what life would be like in the year 2000, when communism had been victorious. Certain elements reminded me of the allegories that Bulgakov wrote, such as *The Fatal Eggs* and *The Heart of a Dog*. He had another play involving some futuristic machine. Obviously at that point, still a young boy, really, he had not discovered Bulgakov yet. But these were things that were in the air at the time — a time of the fantastic and the utopian.

Have you never wanted to stage one of his plays?

Unfortunately, I cannot read them. If I had really wanted to do that, I would have had them translated. At least to find out if they were written with talent or not. I suspect no one ever really read them. It is obvious he published them himself, probably in Kharkov. My mother was born in Kharkov in 1917. She was born during the evacuation that was going on because of World War I. My grandfather and all the Jews were moving deeper into Russia.

My paternal grandfather, Avram Gink, ended up in Dnepropetrovsk during that period, from 1914 to 1920. There was the revolution, the constant changing back and forth of power, the pogroms. My dad, who was born in 1912, weathered all those catastrophes with his huge family in Dnepropetovsk. His two older sisters, who were finishing school at that time, remained there in the Soviet Union. My grandfather and his younger children moved on to Lithuania. Then the borders changed, Lithuania became a different country, and it was difficult for the family to communicate. One sister went to live in Leningrad. The other, Reveka Gink-Lokshina, stayed her whole life in Dnepropetrovsk. She became a famous professor and pediatrician. She was a very wise, beautiful woman. She looked very much like Akhmatova in the last twenty years of her life, which is the only way I knew her. She was very regal, well-educated. On the Ginkas side of the family, I suspect she was the only one who was really so cultured, so highly accomplished and educated. Others, including my father, may have held professional positions but they were mostly of a local scope.

My grandfather Gink should have lived longer, but he was shot in 1941 in Panevezis. He remained alone there when the war began. His older sons worked in Kaunas, and his daughters were in the Soviet Union. His younger son, my father, had just graduated from the university and was sent as a doctor to the German border, in Taurag.

Was your grandfather shot by the Germans or the Russians?

The Germans, of course. As a Jew, he was sent to the ghetto and shot. As was my grandmother on my mother's side in Kaunas.

Let me clarify the picture for you.

My father was in Taurag. My mother had just given birth to me and was living in Kaunas. The war began at night and the Germans entered Taurag within a half an hour. My father described all this in his memoirs, which he wrote in Lithuanian. They were published in Yiddish as translated by my uncle. I think the book's title is *Road through the Barbed Wire*. I cannot read it.

My father described the beginning of the war this way: "A bomb fell on the central square of the small town. A pit formed in the earth there. Lying dead in it was a horse or a cow."

That is quite a picture.

Yes. Father did not understand what was going on although everyone

Marcus Grott as an inmate in *The Theater of the Watchman Nikita,* a dramatization of Anton Chekhov's *Ward No. 6;* Helsinki, 1988. *Photo by Rauno Träskelin.*

was expecting war to begin. Many Soviet soldiers were wounded immediately. The war began on a Sunday and the chief doctor had left for vacation in Kaunas. So my father, who was still a very young, inexperienced doctor, was left alone to tend to the wounded. He had never done any surgery of any kind nor was he trained to. Now he was pressed into service as a surgeon. So he pulled out his book and did what he could.

However, there was not much he could do because, before long, the Germans simply barged in and shot all the wounded. Father quickly realized what lay ahead because everyone knew the Nazi attitude toward Jews. This was common knowledge. The future was clear.

I was six weeks old at this time, and Father quickly resolved to take action. On foot he traversed half of Lithuania — about two hundred kilometers from Taurag to Kaunas. It took him a couple of days. He walked at night and hid during daylight to avoid the German troops that were moving through the territory.

On the first day of the war a large number of people who had been hiding in bunkers made their appearance. The name you attach to them depends upon your point of view. Some call them bandits, others call them murderers, others call them partisans, some call them patriots or nationalists. In other words, call them what you will. These were people who had remained in hiding in the woods or in basements during the six months following the annexation of Lithuania to the Soviet Union. They were waiting for the arrival of the Germans.

The war was only five or six hours old, but they were fully informed. The Germans were not in Kaunas yet, but these people had already come out of the woodwork. They were shooting the Russian soldiers who were attempting to organize evacuations. But the first thing they did was to occupy the bus station. I have already described the photographs I know of this event. A large crowd of Jewish refugees had gathered; I do not know if it was hundreds or thousands. There were countless old people, women and children. They were waiting for buses on which they could escape. But these partisans or patriots or ideological defenders of a free Lithuania — they began gunning down everyone at the bus station. And, essentially, there was some sort of heinous cruelty involving water. What I know, I know from people who saw it or were nearby when it happened. And I remember the photos of dead people lying in water.

So, in the very first hours of the war, an enormous number of Jews were slaughtered.

The Germans appeared on the second day of the war. They announced that if the Jews wanted protection from the — to use a Soviet phrase, "the righteous anger of the people" — they must go live in the Jewish ghetto which was already being built. There, soldiers would protect them. There was no choice. It was an order masquerading as advice. Moreover, it truly was dangerous to remain outside the ghetto where there was no protection. So, in a matter of a week or so, the Jews moved into the ghetto.

I do not know how many people lived in Kaunas then, and how many of them were Jews. There might have been three hundred thousand people, half of which were Jews. Kaunas had always been heavily populated by Jews. Most of the small Lithuanian towns and villages were three-quarters Jewish. Lithuanians worked the land, they lived in the country. There was a small Lithuanian petty bourgeoisie and intelligentsia in the cities, but not much. Jews never lived in the country; they were always concentrated in the towns and cities. According to the pale of settlement that was established in the late nineteenth century, Jews did not have the right to live in Russian sectors. They were allowed only to live in the Polish, Lithuanian, Belorussian, and Ukrainian areas.

From all over Kaunas, people threw what they could into small wooden carts or sleds or even baby carriages and began to gather in a place called Vilijampole on the outskirts of town. This was a kind of working-class slum. The people that lived there were moved out to make room for the Jews. Barbed wire was put up, guards were brought in, gates were erected, and yellow stars were pinned on the inhabitants. And there you have it.

I do not know for sure, of course, but I picture it this way: the Ginkas family lived in one, maybe two small rooms. This would be my father, my mother, me, my grandmother, and her younger son. Add to that my father's brother and my mother's aunt. I was six weeks old. I was still being breast-fed.

In fact, my biography can be told quite simply, as a series of anecdotes which may or may not be rather depressing.

The first anecdote is how I was six weeks old when — as my mother used to tell me — Hitler came to Kaunas to kill me. That is what mother used to say. She would say, "Hitler came to Kaunas to kill you, Kama."

Seemingly, Hitler did a great deal in his efforts to kill me. He built a ghetto. He killed thousands and thousands of Jews from the city of Kaunas. He later transported Jews from other small towns into Kaunas to be shot. For the entire four years that Kaunas was held by the

Marcus Grott as an inmate being subdued by orderlies in *The Theater of the Watchman Nikita*, a dramatization of Anton Chekhov's *Ward No. 6*; Helsinki, 1988. *Photo by Rauno Träskelin.*

Nazis, Jews were being shot. Very few Jews were left there after that. However, it so happened that Hitler could not have me killed.

As my mother used to say, "Kama, you are alive in spite of Hitler." And that is true. I, indeed, am alive in spite — if not of Hitler, then at least of those people who wanted to destroy me, who wanted to destroy *us*.

I sense that. I know that. An internal account of some sort exists inside of me.

For many years I lived with the knowledge that I was only one of four children to survive that ghetto. It is fascinating what has become of these children, all of whom are more or less my age. One woman is a famous pianist, a laureate of the Chopin competition. Another is a famous violinist. I have forgotten the third and I was the fourth. Each of us has become accomplished in the arts and has achieved a high level of quality in our given fields.

The first time I ever traveled abroad I went to Berlin. This, for me, was a very troubling experience. Let me put it this way: I could not imagine what all the devils must look like in hell, but I could easily imagine what they would look like in Berlin. Berlin represented everything hostile to me. It was as though I was allergic to it. All I had to do was imagine myself being in Berlin and my skin would crawl. I could not imagine how I would be able to walk about this city.

Obviously, I understood that this was a different Berlin, a different era. I knew that the Germans had accepted their guilt for what they did. I knew that they repeatedly spoke about that and that they were doing everything possible to make amends in financial, political, and moral terms.

That meant nothing to me.

I knew I soon would be there in that city and I did not know how I would do it. I was extremely nervous.

This was when?

It must have been 1986.

I will skip over the psychological aspect of what I experienced when I arrived in Berlin. How I walked the streets and was affected by how beautifully the Germans — especially the German women — were dressed. They were very elegant. Everyone around was so polite and so kind. There was nothing false about it; they were clearly kind by nature. But I did not know how to respond to that. The trip lasted only three days, but it made a tremendous impression on me.

One of the impressions was this. I got talking to one old Jew. We were speaking in Russian because he had come from the Soviet Union, Lithuania, in fact. I happened to comment that I had survived the ghetto. He said, "Really? But hardly anyone survived the Kaunas ghetto." I said, "Well, I know that I and a few others did." He said, "I know someone else who survived it, too."

I was flabbergasted, because I thought I knew everyone who had survived. He took me over and introduced me to a beautiful woman who was about forty-five years old. She was a famous artist who had exhibited her works in London and Berlin and had survived the Kaunas ghetto as a child.

Do you know these people's names?

The pianist is Esther Elenaite. Her father was a well-known Yiddish writer. Her mother was a musician. The violinist's last name is Pomerancaite, I do not remember her first name. Pomerancaite was sheltered in the home of a famous Lithuanian tenor, a national hero — Kipras Petrauskas. He sang with Chaliapin, he sang at La Scala. A famous, very handsome man. He and his wife, also a beauty, sheltered that little girl. The other names I do not remember.

But to continue the story, an organization called Child Prisoners of the Ghetto was founded around 1990 in the new Russia. Its purpose was to help people appeal to the state for help. As a relatively well known person, I was asked to speak at the first congress. I would not have agreed, except for the fact that I wanted to bring to it one of the women who had sheltered me. Her name is Antonina Vaiciuniene. I wanted people to see her. When I learned she was going to be able to come, I enlisted one of my friends to film it for her. So, when I spoke at the congress my short speech was captured on film. And there is in this film a place where I said I had always thought that only four of us children had survived the ghetto, but since then I had learned there was a fifth in Berlin. That is when someone in the hall yelled out, "I am the sixth."

Now, how do we continue the narration of my biography?

The first anecdote consists of, "I was born and Hitler came to kill me." That anecdote comes to a close with the words that Hitler was not able to kill me, as well as four or five others. What is especially interesting is that all of these people are highly qualified professionals in the arts. There would appear to be a certain quality in our people that makes those who remain wish to shout or cry or sing or draw or perform for those who perished.

I sense that. I feel that.

It was relatively easy to leave the ghetto because they drove people out to work. They did not feed them, but they made them work. There was always something that needed to be done in town — after bombings things had to be picked up, rebuilt, carried, moved, whatever. The Jews would all be wearing the yellow stars, and ahead of them and behind them would walk Lithuanians carrying sticks. Sometimes they had guns. So, imagine this group of hundreds, maybe even a thousand, people walking along. It was not all that difficult for someone to slip off his star and sneak out of the crowd. The Lithuanian guards did not care about this at all, because everybody knew a Jew had nowhere to go. No matter where he went, he most likely would be reported or shot. Or the Lithuanians themselves might kill him.

Nobody really left the ghetto for good. Oh, they slipped out for a short while from time to time. They did that because they had to eat. They would slip out of the crowd and go to one of the places where everyone knew you could trade a coat for some suet. Or some shoes for bread or medicine. But then they would put their star back on and return to the ghetto.

In other words, you could run but there was no place to hide.

My aunt Sonya was one of the very few who left the ghetto immediately. She was very personable and was able to get along on the outside. She had many friends and she relied on them to give her a place to live. She lived with her school friend and worked for her as a maid. They pretended she was a distant relative from the country. Since she was a very attractive, bubbly type of young woman, she was afraid men would be making passes at her all the time. So she pretended to be a *davatka,* that is, a highly religious Catholic. In the Lithuanian tradition there are very religious women who do not become nuns and live in a monastery, but who live in the world as if they were nuns. They always wear black clothes and a black scarf. They never look up and are constantly in prayer. They spend most of their time in church.

So my aunt pretended to be a *davatka* who worked as a maid in the home of her friend. Her friend's husband was a well-known architect who worked for the Germans, building whatever they needed. He was quite well off, and German officers would come to visit them. My aunt, as the maid, would bring their food and wait on them. She was the one who opened the door to let them in when they arrived.

There were some curious incidents. They would turn on the German Blaupunkt radio to listen to music. And the cultured Germans, visiting the home of a cultured Lithuanian, might say, "Yes, that is Beethoven's Third Symphony." And the voice of the country *davatka* from the kitchen would cry out, "That is Beethoven's Fifth Symphony!"

She had something of the actress in her. In school, although she was chubby, she took ballet lessons. She participated in theater clubs. She wrote poetry. She translated Russian poets.

So, she literally played the role of a country girl. She purposefully spoke Lithuanian with a country accent. She learned all the prayers she needed to know and she observed all the rituals. No one, not the neighbors nor the priest to whom she would go and confess, ever suspected she was an imposter.

Her situation was both dangerous and theatrical at the same time.

All Jews at that time were left-leaning politically. They believed in equality. So the idea of being someone's maid, to say nothing of serving Germans, was psychologically very difficult for her. She found it extremely humiliating. And, to let off steam, she would occasionally go out into the barn and speak French with the pigs. She did that to rehabilitate herself in her own eyes.

In the beginning, she would come to the ghetto and try talking my father into leaving. But father did not see how he could do that with a young baby — me — on his hands. She also tried getting her older brother to escape. He was alone and he could have joined the partisans. He was a healthy young man in his early thirties, he could have escaped. But he did not want to. Why?

That is a plot for a tragic anecdote.

I never knew my uncle Lev Gink. But judging by what I know, he was the most talented of my grandfather's six children. I have told about my artistically inclined aunt. My uncle was more attuned to intellectual pursuits, the sciences. All of his siblings considered him the most accomplished of them all. He never had anything but bad luck.

He was unlucky as a boy when he was returning home from the beach, and he came upon a house on fire. He ran in to put the fire out and climbed up on something that gave way and caved in. He whacked his head, broke his nose, and, maybe, suffered permanent damage. He was always a little disheveled. He was a brilliant mathematician and chess player. He got married, but it was a bad marriage and they divorced. He always suffered over that. Later he met a woman, fell in love with her and they were married. It was a wonderful love affair and a genuine, happy marriage. She was beautiful, energetic, and lively.

Evidently she was unlike him, because he was very reserved and closed. She was a swimmer. He taught at a school at Palanga, that is, at the seashore. And they used to swim way out to sea. If you take into account that this was an era when women were much less emancipated than now, she was really quite something. They had a son.

She was a dentist who worked at the military hospital. As soon as the war began, the hospital was evacuated. As an employee of the hospital, she had the right, with her year-old son and her husband, to be transported out with the other military employees. But my uncle ran back to say farewell to my father, my aunt, and other uncles. I do not know how long he spent with them — thirty minutes or two hours. But, by the time he went back, everyone had left. They waited for no one. This was all being done on very short notice.

My uncle perceived that as a sign of fate. Maybe it activated some psychological trauma. But for him, it was a blow of fate. Perhaps he thought his wife did not love him so much if she could leave so easily. He did not want to understand what happened. What he understood was that his life was over. He did not care anymore. He gave in so totally that when they said, "Go to the ghetto," he was the first to go.

He had never been religious. He was a progressive, as were all Jews at that time. Now he became a practicing Orthodox Jew. He observed all the rites. His sister tried to convince him to escape the ghetto but he said it was all in God's hands.

When everyone was driven out to work and people would sneak out to get something to eat, he would too. But you could not bring anything back into the ghetto with you. You had to hide things well to get them back in. Whenever he would come back through the gates, the guards would always find what he had hidden. They would take it away from him and beat him. Always.

Two years later, my parents finally understood that the executions were closing in on us. These executions were always conducted by profession, by age, or some other category. It was as if to say, "Nobody is being killed here, unless it is people with beards. People with beards are being killed." So everybody without a beard felt safe.

My father described this psychology very well in his book. Let us say they began executing old men. Well, everybody understood it was difficult to feed them. It was war time, after all. But they certainly would not shoot young, healthy people. Then they would shoot all those who were sick among the young people. And the remainder would think, "But, I'm healthy. It's no threat to me." Then they would begin executing people of certain professions. And so, someone like my father might think, "Well, those people aren't necessary for the war effort. But I am a doctor. They need me."

This was the psychological game of explaining to yourself how you were going to continue to live. The executions always began in the little towns and then spread to the big cities. When the action against children began in the villages, everybody in the cities knew that soon — in a month or in a week — the children there would be exterminated. This is when my parents resolved to escape. And they did.

My father went to say farewell to his brother. But he arrived at prayer time. Jews have certain prayers that cannot be interrupted. So, my uncle did not even respond.

When almost everyone in the ghetto had already been shot and there were only a few people left — their job was to burn the corpses — my uncle was not shot because he was one of those burning the corpses. When the ghetto was evacuated, he was not shot either. He was put on a train with the other surviving Jews and sent to Germany by way of Poland.

However, a couple of Jews fled the train. In retaliation, the Germans stopped the train and removed one or two people from each train car and shot them. My uncle was one. He was shot.

This is a tale that cannot be called an anecdote. Although it is an anecdote because it is so illogical, so paradoxical. A man lived out of sync. He could have escaped but he did not. Even so, he was not one of those who were shot. Then, when it would seem he was out of danger, he was selected at random and shot.

When my parents first slipped out of the ghetto, they lived in the home of Sofia Binkiene. She was a beautiful woman; for a short while she was an actress. She was the wife of the famous Lithuanian futurist poet, Kazis Binkis.

Picture this. Living in this small home or cottage was Binkis, who was then dying of tuberculosis; his wife; his wife's two daughters by a previous marriage, both of whom had just had children; and his son who had just had a child. Obviously all the respective husbands and wives were there, too. They all lived in this small house. And, since he was dying of tuberculosis, Binkis had to have a special room all to himself.

So, my mother, my father, and I also came into this household. True, my mother and father were there only a few days before moving on to other places. I stayed on there longer because it was harder to find places to hide children.

Did your parents know the Binkis family?

No. They knew who they were, because it was a famous family. But my parents were just common citizens. They existed on completely different levels.

How did you end up in their home, then?

It was quite simple. Sofia Binkiene was involved in sheltering people. This beautiful, elegant woman was a leader in the effort to save people. She was probably forty at the time, maybe younger. She was in contact with many different people in different places. She knew all the places where, right now, it would not be safe to send someone, but in a month it would be all right. Or, she saw to it that people were transferred from one place to another if necessary.

One of her sons-in-law, Vladas Varcikas, was a violinist. He would put on the yellow star, go into the ghetto, and talk Jews into escaping. He would say, "Not all Lithuanians are shooting Jews. Some are saving them, too. There are ways to safety." And then he would go back out and go home. He was one of the main connections in the chain.

In a bad Soviet movie, or even a good American one, Sofia Binkiene would probably be pictured as a very systematic, businesslike woman. Nothing of the sort. She was an elegant society lady who was busy saving people. She did it as naturally as she would busy herself with her own grandchildren or her dying husband. It is just something she did.

Do not forget, these were hungry times. And she had to feed her whole family plus all these Jews who were coming to her. I have no idea how she did it. Usually, Jews would stay with her until she could find another place for them and then they would move on. If that arrangement failed for some reason, they might come back for a while until she organized something else.

There are a lot of anecdotes involved in this.

One Jewish girl of seven or eight lived there all the time. They claimed she was the Lithuanian daughter of a relative in the country. Binkis, of course, knew nothing about any of this. He was busy staving off death. They told him that, because of the war, the house was full of relatives. Suddenly, he hears someone playing Grieg on the piano. And they tell him, "That's one of the relatives from the country." And he says to his wife, "Zosia, what are you deceiving me for?"

Or, here is another story. I had whooping cough, which is very contagious. And there were two very young infants in the house — one six months, the other just a couple of months old. And here I was among them with my contagious illness.

Or, still another story that we already touched on earlier. I'll put it in better perspective here. You know my character more or less. Just imagine that I am a thousand years younger, but with the same disposition. I was everywhere and into everything. I could not sit still for a second. I wanted to talk to everybody and find out about everything. So, when someone would knock, I would always be the first person to come running to open the door.

Binkienė's daughter was another beauty. She was also an actress, probably nineteen or twenty years old at the time. Men were constantly falling in love with her; she would marry one and then divorce him. If there is a curse of being too beautiful, she had it. She was living with her first husband then, Vladas, an alcoholic violinist. He could be so drunk he would not remember who was Lithuanian or German, let alone Jewish. He could forget his concerts. He was terribly jealous of his wife, and since she was such a beauty, perhaps he had reason to be. He would come home drunk out of his mind and throw her out of bed into the street half-naked, shouting, "You whore! Get out of my house!" He would slam the door and lock her out. She would be out there trying to get back in, and the German officers living in the neighboring houses would come out and gallantly offer their help. They would knock at our door and attempt to smooth things over with her husband.

Who do you think would run to open the door? I would.

There I was, this little black-haired, dark-eyed Jew who spoke nothing but Yiddish — I did not speak Lithuanian at all. And I would say, "*Vos!?*" That is, "What!?"

It was impossible to make me stop answering the door, so Sofia Binkiene taught me to say a few words in Lithuanian. She was the first to begin teaching me Lithuanian. Later I was in other places where I was taught Lithuanian, and I picked it up fairly quickly. Eventually, I forgot my Yiddish. But it took them a long time to cure me of my Yiddish pronunciation.

Another story I often tell concerns the moment after the Germans had already left, but the Russians had not yet arrived. My father ventured out of the place where he was being sheltered and headed to the last place I had been. This was a home for mentally retarded children where I was cared for by Antonina Vaiciuniene. I often slept in the same bed with children who would wet their beds or worse. He came to take me home. But when he arrived, there was no one there. A man explained that the Germans had taken everyone with them, the children and the workers of the home. Among them was Antonina. However, it turned out that one child had been left behind and hidden with a neighboring family. It was I. So my father went to get me. By that time, I had pretty much forgotten my father.

How much time did you spend in this home?

Maybe a week, maybe a month. I was constantly being moved from one place to another. As I understand it, I was hidden in various places for a period of about six months. This included the time with Binkiene and the time in the home for retarded children. I spent some time in a barn with pigs. I spent some time in someone else's home. In all, I probably spent time in four or five places.

I rarely saw my father. And since I was two years old, it only took me a couple of weeks to forget him.

Anyway, when he came to get me, I did not want to go with him.

He seemed a stranger to me. So he gave me a pair of shoes. I was barefoot at the time. These shoes had wooden soles. That was really something. That was better than a new Mercedes-Benz. It was something out of the realm of the impossible. For me to have a real pair of shoes. They were wooden and they click-clacked when I walked.

That made it worth going with this guy.

So I agreed to go with my dad. But when it came nightfall, I was afraid. My father asked why. I said, "Because I'm afraid the Yids are going to come kill us."

"Why do you say that?" my father asked.

"That's what everybody says," I answered. "That the Yids are going to come and kill us all."

Maybe people drilled that into my head so I would be less apt to stick out in the crowd. Or maybe they merely wanted to turn me into a common Lithuanian kid. The Lithuanians, indeed, did talk like that. Because they had been guilty of killing many Jews and they were afraid of the Russians coming in and avenging them for that. There were, of course, many Jews in the Red Army.

So, I said, "The Yids are coming and they're going to kill us."

My father began explaining a rather complex situation as best as he could. He said, "You know, I don't quite know how it happened, but the fact of the matter is, Kama, your father is a Jew, too."

That was a catastrophe for me. Because Jews were the ones who went around killing people. They were a terrible enemy. Horrible. Monsters.

In time, my father had to break the news to me that, by some curious coincidence, unfortunately — but there was nothing to be done about it — my mama was Jewish, too.

The worst news was still to come though: I was a Jew.

I was an extremely outgoing boy. In the ghetto I used to walk up to the barbed wire at the gate and try to talk with the guard. I was impressed by this guy with a gun whom everyone was afraid of. That is how I imagine it, anyway. I was too young to remember it, of course.

But my family told stories about it and I have worked out my own impressions based on those stories.

Anyway, I would try to talk to this guy, but he would chase me away. I remember his name to this day. He was a German named Gekke. My mother used to use him to frighten me. She used to say, "Gekke läßt nicht," which means "Gekke doesn't allow that." To this day I remember that phrase of taboo, a phrase forbidding something. "Gekke läßt nicht."

Evidently that phrase had special significance in my life. Because for many years there was much that was forbidden to me. I could not become an actor. I could not become a director. When I did become a director, I could not get work. When I could get work, I could not stage what I wanted. And on and on. For most of my life everything was forbidden.

"Gekke läßt nicht."

For me there was this mythical, magical Gekke who had the right to forbid me things. It was the exact opposite of "Open Sesame," when all the doors open for you. For me it was "Gekke läßst nicht" and everything was forbidden. It was ever-present for me throughout all my years in Lithuania. One way or another, this was the dominant theme in the conversations I heard between my parents and between them and friends. Some of the stories I tell are stories I heard them tell people who would come visit us. Usually, these guests were some of the rare Jews who had survived and who had had similar experiences. For that reason, they were willing to go over the same topics again and again.

From time to time, those Lithuanians who had sheltered us would visit. These people, essentially, had become our relatives. Whenever they would have christenings, we would attend, even though we were Jewish. We could not fail to be present on such important days in the lives of people we considered relatives.

When I was married I brought Henrietta to Vilnius to introduce her to my parents. Then, on the evening of the next day, I took her to introduce her to those who had sheltered us. It was only natural. These people were closer to us than many aunts and uncles.

I told you about the baby girl who was born in the Binkiene home when I was being sheltered there with whooping cough. Well, when this girl grew up and had her first baby, it so happened that she had Rh-negative blood. That meant a potentially fatal illness for both the mother and the newborn child. My father, who was a doctor, remained in constant attendance at her bed. Meanwhile, all of the local Jews wrote to their relatives in Israel — during this period in Soviet history, one simple letter like that could have dire consequences — and requested them to send medicines that were necessary for blood transfusions. All of these medicines began coming in almost immediately. Ultimately, the mother and her child were saved.

Nobody thought anything of it. It was the natural thing to do.

I still see these people from time to time — the mother who gave birth, and her daughter, who is now in her early thirties, I guess — and they still remember and love my father as if he were their own.

This brings me to the last major story I want to tell.

Somewhere around 1988 or 1989, shortly after I returned from a trip to Finland, I was told a letter was lying in wait for me at the Moscow Art Theater. By this time I rarely was at that theater, so I had not seen it. I went and picked it up and saw that it was sent to me by someone I did not know in Lithuania. I opened the envelope and a dried flower fell out. I pulled out the letter, which was written in uneducated Lithuanian, and began reading.

"Dear Kamushka, Is it really You, the little boy who used to hang onto the hem of my skirt? Is it You who has become so famous and highly respected?"

The letter went on in that vein, employing old-fashioned, high-falutin words and phrases. The author of the letter wrote that she had read about me in the newspaper and how she once had been a nurse in a home for mentally retarded children where she had sheltered me. She wrote about how my father would come and criticize her for loving me too much because I was so young I might become too attached to her. She wrote about how terrible the times were, about the fear and the lack of food that affected everyone. She wrote that she had heard times were difficult again in Russia — indeed, that was when food shortages were upon us — and she wanted me to know she had a garden and could send potatoes if I needed them. This was followed by a signature. I did not recognize the name.

It was very strange; I knew very well almost everyone who had sheltered me at one time or another. If I did not know them by acquaintance, I at least knew their first or last names. But I knew nothing about this person. I immediately sent her a telegram to let her know I had received her letter. I told her I would come visit her as soon as I possibly could get away. And, indeed, I left for Lithunania three days later.

I flew to Vilnius then traveled to Kaunas. And, by the address she had given me, I found her home in a section of the city where all the homes are little wooden structures with tiny gardens around them. The people here are considered city dwellers, — they do not live all that far from the center of town — but they essentially live a country life. Everyone has gardens, pigs, and dogs.

I approached the house, where a cat sat on the doorstep, and knocked. Nobody answered. There was an elderly woman, barefoot, working in the garden, up to her elbows in earth. She turned and asked, "Who are you looking for?" I named the name that was signed at the bottom of the letter I had received.

"What do you want?" the woman asked.

I told her who I was. You probably can imagine her reaction. And my reaction. It is not one I can describe, but it was a profound reaction. We walked to the house. Before entering, she wiped and washed her hands.

Calling it a house is overdoing it, perhaps. She occupied two tiny rooms that were little more than corridors to the rest of the house. And she also had an extremely tiny kitchen. All told, she probably occupied no more than twenty-five square meters, and, most likely, it was less. It smelled of cats and old age. The cat was old. Her clothes, although newly washed, had lost their freshness.

She began by restating what she had written in the letter. How I had followed her around and had clung to the hem of her skirt. How my father had criticized her. She had documents she wanted to show me that proved that, in fact, she had sheltered Jewish children. It was some brochure that had been published on the topic. She apparently feared I would not believe her.

Later I learned that she had been a nun who worked at that orphanage for mentally retarded children. Catholic monasteries often run such hospitals nearby and that was the case here, too. The nuns were the nurses — literally, the sisters of mercy — who worked there. This was her calling, to administer mercy to those who were in need of it. She worked primarily with infants, most of whom were doomed to die early deaths.

At the same time, she hid Jewish children among the patients at the orphanage. The ghetto was located not far away, just on the other side of the river. So people would make the short trip over the bridge and would bring children back to her.

Many years later I returned to this orphanage with a film crew who made a documentary film about this woman and me. It was a small, two-story building containing, perhaps, five or six wards. That was probably also the number of nurses who worked there. At any given time, they usually were sheltering at least ten Jewish children, sometimes more.

The first day I visited Antonina Vaiciuniene she pulled out pictures to show me. Among them were photos of her brother, who, himself, was a monk. He also was involved in sheltering Jewish children, only in another region in Lithuania. Her mother had been a simple peasant, illiterate. Antonina herself was only semiliterate.

She said, "Look, I was very thin." I asked, "Did you have no food?"

"Of course not," she replied. "First, there was a war on. Second, the little bit of food I did get I would give to the children. And even that food I had to divide up among the Jewish babies."

She gave up her own food to feed these children.

But hunger was not the main thing. Much worse was the fear. She could have been taken out and shot at any moment.

She told of one time when she became so overcome with fear that she went to the country to talk to her mother. She said to her mother, "Mother, I might be shot at any time. I am afraid. I am sheltering Jewish children."

And her mother said, "Then you will at least know what you are dying for."

It sounds like something out of a fantasy novel. Bad literature. A melodrama. But Antonina was not a two-bit writer. Not at all. She was a completely different cut of person. She was a simple, semiliterate, country woman.

From then on, we exchanged occasional letters. In truth, she wrote more often. I did not write frequently. As a rule, she would write once every two months or so, recalling how I had hung onto the hems of her skirt or how my father had criticized her. And in every letter she would add, "I hear you are having problems in Russia again. If necessary, I can send you potatoes or onions."

She had given me a set of amber beads and when I visited Jerusalem I brought her back a cross and rosary beds that had been blessed. I also brought her a clump of earth. She received these gifts as if they were holy relics. Her entire life had consisted of an active relationship with God. And all of her deeds had issued from her faith. She sewed a small sack into which she put the earth from Jerusalem and wore it around her neck next to the cross.

I have also heard you tell of a man called Broliukas who had you christened.

Yes, among those in Binkiene's organization — if you can call it that — was a man we called Broliukas. This is the diminutive of the Lithuanian word for *brother*. If he had been rather more imposing in some way, he would have been called simply "Brother." But he was not — he was Broliukas, "Little Brother." His real name was Gotautas. I do not remember his given name. He was not a real, ordained monk. Every church or monastery has its collection of people who live or spend most of their time there. These are very religious people; often they are not entirely well. So they do not work in the church; they have no official capacity. But they live there, observing all the services and prayers.

Broliukas was illiterate. He was a go-between in this "organization." He would go around, trying to encourage people to help in the effort to shelter Jews. He found places of shelter for those Jews who needed it. Naturally, he did this as an effort to try to convert the Jews to Catholicism. This was a perfectly natural thing for him; it could not possibly have been any other way.

The Catholic priests were often the ones to create fake ID papers. As a little child, I did not need that, but my mother and my father did. They were given new names, a new nationality, and even the particulars of a false biography. Since all Catholics were christened in the church, the priests would falsify the church records to make it appear that Jews were actually christened Catholics.

He would come to one of the churches where the priest was manufacturing false documents. They would give him three or four, which, of course, he could not read. So he would put women's IDs in one pocket; men's IDs in the other pocket. That helped him keep somewhat organized. He would come to a man, pull the documents out of his "male" pocket and say, "Your new name is thus-and-such. Take a look here and see if you can't find your new papers."

He did all this, of course, for the sake of God.

Sofia Binkiene, for example, did it for very different reasons. She knew perfectly well why she was doing what she was doing, and it was not for the sake of God. She used to say openly that the Lithuanian people had been stained with blood by the murder of innocent Jewish people. She wanted to prove by the very fact of her existence that Lithuanians were not only murderers.

What is interesting is that she was not even a Lithuanian. She was Polish with a little bit of Russian blood. But she was the wife of a great Lithuanian poet, was born in Lithuania, and so we can consider her Lithuanian even if she had no Lithuanian blood. She unquestionably was a Lithuanian hero. It is one of those amazing paradoxes. She considered herself responsible for the reputation of the Lithuanian people.

Broliukas did it for the glory of God. And not just for God, but specifically for the Catholic God. He did it for Jesus Christ as He is understood by the Catholics. As such, he wanted everyone that he helped to survive to be christened. Now, most of the people he was aiding were atheists and so they perceived it as a kind of formality. They could see that it meant a great deal to him, so they would go along with it. Perhaps they did it because it was a necessary component of survival; perhaps they did it out of respect to him. Although I do not think he was the kind of person who would elicit respect in anyone. He was something like the town fool. A bit of a holy jester.

In short, I was christened because that is what he wanted. I was taken to a church near Kaunas, I do not know which one. In attendance was my aunt who, as I have explained, was living under the guise of a *davatka,* a kind of nonconfirmed nun. Also there was a man who acted as my godfather. I do not know how they did it. I probably was not displayed naked because that would have given me away. As a Jewish child, I was circumcised. So there you have another of those comically horrifying moments.

That reminds me of a story I must tell about my father. He was sheltered as a *batrak,* a hired hand who worked for a landowner in the country. This was not a servant, but a man who hired himself out to do all the hard work for someone. One day my father fell ill with a high temperature. He lay on top of his bed, covered only with a sheet because he was so hot and sweaty from the illness.

Meanwhile, a German there was unhappy because no one would bring him horses. He raised a ruckus, shouting for the *batrak* who was nowhere to be found. He burst into the little niche inhabited by my father and was even angrier to see the lazy bum just lying there. He tore the sheet off of him and there was my father lying there — a Jew. Apparently the German was so angry he did not notice this little detail.

My biography as a creative artist began early. Shortly after the war, perhaps a year after, I discovered the actor in me. In our courtyard stood a two-story wooden house with a steep wooden stairwell leading to the second floor. The kids gathered on that stairwell, two to three on each step and watched theatrical presentations on the landing below. As a rule, I put these shows on with one of the neighborhood girls. I played the father and she the mother. Kids play parents all the time, but we were doing this for an audience. I liked that a lot.

I had heard a song on the radio that went something like:

Oh, back roads, dust, and mist,
Anxious cold and plains of grass.
You can't know what it is fate contains,
So just fold your wings and die out on the plains.

This song touched me very deeply. It was a beautiful song sung by a tenor with a military choir. I studied it for a long time so as to be able to sing it for my audience in the courtyard. These were about ten or fifteen kids aged five to seven, I guess.

I also remember being with my cousin, the son of my uncle Lev who was taken from the train and shot. My cousin and his mother had waited out the war in Russia and now had returned to live in the same building as we, only one floor higher. He spoke only Russian and I spoke only Lithuanian. But, as kids do, we quickly began understanding each other, and, as a result, he began speaking Lithuanian and I began picking up Russian. I was younger by a year, but I was the more energetic of us. He was like his father, somewhat lethargic, a great mathematician, chess player, and failure.

I would call him out to play what we called — or, I called, since it was all my doing — "our games."

We had an apartment that by the standards of those times, was simply luxurious. Three rooms and a corridor in a three-story building that had been built in the early 1930s. Its architecture was the so-called bourgeois constructivist style. It had a bathtub. True, most of the time it did not work, but it was a built-in bathtub like wealthier people might have, not a freestanding one. We had a big kitchen.

As soon as the Russians moved in, my father was made the head of the health department for the whole city of Kaunas. He was thirty or thirty-one years old at the time. Why was he appointed when he was too young to have learned his profession yet? Probably because the Russians could not trust the Lithuanians and, because, as a Jew who had survived the ghetto, he most likely was not of an anti-Soviet or nationalistic bent. Consequently, he became the top health man in town and that was the position he held for his whole life. Although he wanted to, he never did work as a practicing doctor. Life had something else in store for him.

So, he was given this apartment. One room was a bedroom in which mama and papa slept, and there were two small cribs where I slept with my brother, who had just been born in 1945. Another room was my father's medical study where, apparently, he still hoped he might receive patients one day. Then there was the living room with marvelous furniture in the severe constructivist style of the 1930s.

My father traveled to Konigsberg after the Germans left and brought back medical instruments, beds, linens, and other equipment for hospitals and clinics. There was nothing in Kaunas. Possibly he brought back some of our furniture from Konigsberg, I do not know. It certainly was not our old furniture. We had nothing left.

I remember the light gray, almost beige, striped rug in the living room. The sun would fall through the window on the windowsill and catch just a corner of the rug, the rest of which would remain in stunning, cool shade. For me, this image represents the absolute ultimate in domestic comfort and contentment. I remember badly but highly polished surfaces that were not marred by even a speck of dust. There was nothing extraneous on them. That severe constructivist style would not allow it.

My cousin and I — I was four or five at the time, he was five or six — would carefully open the glass door to this room. Sometimes we would do it with mother's permission, sometimes without it. We would sneak quietly into the room and play *our games*. There was a round table. And on the floor rug there was a stripe — for us it was a river — beyond which you could not go. If you did, you might be taken prisoner or shot by the Germans. We would narrate the stories to each other as we crawled on the floor. It was an on-the-spot improvisation of what was happening as well as of the manner in which we existed within our fantasy. Then it would come to the culmination.

The table could be unfolded if you unlatched these metal keys. We would take those metal keys and bang them. The awful racket that made was the sound of tanks or gunfire. When mother was home she would come in and forbid us to do that, but usually she was not at home.

She was at work, a food store where she was employed as a cashier. She found this job by chance, and it was a great job to have because in hungry times, when the lines to buy things were horrendous, we always had first access to whatever was delivered to the store that day. From time to time she would go to the bazaar and sell things we did not need so much. It was a terrible, hellish life.

My mother was fated to live a life other than the one she should have lived. She was a beautiful, personable woman. She could have been a society woman. She was elegant with great taste. She never had anything of what she should have had. She raised three children in the extremely difficult Soviet era. Her work was very hard. She was always on the receiving end of that long line of aggressive Soviet citizens who want to eat and had to stand in line for three or four hours to do that. They yelled at her, threatened her, accused her of making mistakes or showing favors to someone. Aside from her children, who were the reason for her existence, that was the life she lived. She was undoubtedly not without talent; she was good at languages and music. Most likely, however, hers was a feminine, motherly talent.

Then there were the games I engaged in without my cousin. He and I were different in character. I was more energetic, a leader, a director at heart, who, apparently, dragged my cousin forcibly into something he really was not interested in. So there were other games I called "our games" which I engaged in alone. Sometimes I would sneak into father's study. He had a white glass and metallic closet. On the glass shelves lay his sparkling medical instruments. Before the war, when he graduated from medical school, his father, who was a pharmacist, had bought those instruments for him.

I mentioned how my grandfather Zingman was a poet and writer who sold books on the side. My grandfather Gink was a pharmacist who sold kerosene on the side.

When the war came and my father took us to the ghetto, he buried his instruments in the earth. When the war ended, he dug them back up. Nobody ever used them, although he took them everywhere we moved and they always stood on display. Later, I understood that most of them were gynecological instruments. Why, I do not know. Perhaps his father thought it would be easier for him to make a living as a gynecologist. In any case, Father never had any use for them.

So, I would go into Father's study. There was a box in there with chess pieces. Like all Jews, Father played a little chess. It was an old set and, as I remember it now, the box was large and made of leather. I would put a candle in it, light it, and look at the shadows its flame would cast. I imagined seeing an old king and queen. And all around them, other kings and officers and pawns seemed to be walking about or dancing to music as the candle cast swaying shadows on the chess pieces and the rug.

At the same time I also took part in a real theater. This was in kindergarten or in school when I was five or six. They put on a play called *The Little Turnip*, based on an old Russian folktale. I played the title role — the turnip — and I sang a song in Yiddish. This is how it began, if I translate it from the Yiddish: "I am a turnip, the biggest one in the world . . ."

About this time a film crew came to shoot a story about happy Soviet children spending their time splendidly in a marvelous Soviet kindergarten. I guess it was because I was an especially active young kid who was constantly getting into things, but they shot several close-ups of me. Moreover, they put me behind one camera and filmed me as if I were shooting a film of the other kids at play. That is how I wet my feet as an actor.

And as a director.

Well, as a cameraman, to be more exact.

I entered a school that specialized in music when I was six. That was a year after I learned to read. My father had an inclination for music; he himself played the violin and taught us to play the mandolin. He had perfect pitch and a pleasant voice. Every cultured Jew is obliged to play a musical instrument.

My violin teacher was that very same son-in-law of Sofia Binkiene, Vladas Varcikas, who had been active in sheltering Jews. What do you think? He never taught us a thing. He was a member of the orchestra at the opera theater and he would play there when he was sober on occasion. But he was entirely incapable of working with us kids. When it was time for exams, he would come to our house for a few days in advance and do his best to give me a crash tutorial. I, not having the vaguest notion how to play the violin, would have to perform some simple melody. I could get out the first few bars, but after that it got pretty tough. The violin is not an easy instrument to play. You must hold the bow and move it lightly so that it does not make sawing noises. Then your arms get tired and you get a sore spot under your chin. For me, as a child, anyway, this was hell. I do not know how I got through the first half of the year. By the beginning of the second year I was kicked out of the school. But when that happened it was not because I played the violin so badly. I was kicked out because I hit a girl. I did that, I presume, because I was not indifferent to her.

Varcikas, as I have said, was like a member of the family, and he used to come to the store where my mother worked when he was dead drunk. He would walk to the front of the line and stand next to mother. He would demand she give him money for drink.

What could she do? She could not refuse him. You understand why that is. And it did not matter that she had no money. Or that all he was going to do was drink the money up. She had to give him money.

There were times when, late at night, we were all asleep and there would be a knock on the door. Very loud and aggressive. You must remember that when my father, Miron, was being sheltered, he had to change his name to Jonas. And so, following the heavy knock on the door we would hear a voice shouting, "Jonas!" The violinist and two or three of his friends had come to take father drinking. Or they would come to "visit." What are you going to do? You cannot say, "Go away." You can tell anyone to go away, but not this man. This man saved your life.

Father, then, even though he had worked late and had to be up early in the morning, had no choice but to get up in the middle of the night and receive his guests. With the rest of us sleeping in the next room, he would go into the living room and pull out liquor for this guest who was already so drunk he could barely stand. Moreover, he had to receive the other two or three people who had nothing to do with sheltering anyone, but merely were drunks. And they would behave like drunks there in our living room. My father had to sit there and take it all with a smile until they wanted to leave.

But I would like to bring this tale to a proper end. This drunken musician had been divorced by his wife; nobody could possibly live with him. He was just a plain old drunk who never knew a sober day. He was kicked out of the orchestra he worked in. One day he was riding in a truck with his drunken friends to some neighboring town. He fell out and temporarily went deaf. Although his hearing did return after a while, he could not play his instrument anymore.

And, you know what? He quit drinking. He was a liberal who in Soviet times clearly was no nationalist. He had helped Jews. He may even have become a communist. He was appointed the director of the musical theater. He is still alive. I last saw him in 1998.

After I was kicked out of the music school, my parents had trouble finding a school that would take a scoundrel like me. Eventually I was enrolled in a four-year Yiddish school. I rather suspect that if this was not the only Yiddish school in the Soviet Union, it was one of only a few that might have been located in Lithuania. All classes were conducted in Yiddish and, naturally, all the children were Jewish. There were four classrooms, a teacher's room, and a corridor. Next door was an orphanage. It was a Jewish orphanage occupied by children whose parents had been killed. These were kids who had been sheltered by Lithuanians.

After the war there were many serious incidents. Jewish people would be wandering the countryside looking for their children. But sometimes the Lithuanians who had sheltered them would not want to give them up. This happened for various reasons. Sometimes it was simply a matter of people becoming attached to the children whom they now perceived as their own. Sometimes the children were a useful workforce — shepherds, milkmaids, and the like. They were a form of cheap labor and people did not want to give them up.

Sometimes the Lithuanians simply did not believe the Jews who came to claim the children. There were incidents of Jews being murdered who had come looking for their children.

I have a photo from the second or third grade where you can see quite clearly which of the kids are from the orphanage and which are not. It is in the faces and especially in the clothes. I am dressed to the nines in some outfit we got through American relief — shorts, a sharp shirt, suspenders, a sweater. True, my head is shaved because there were lots of disease-carrying insects at that time. But you can see that I am a self-confident kid who was spoiled at home. Next to me stand children wearing pants, shirts, and dresses out of material so thin it really cannot be used for clothes. It is a striped material that reminds you of prison garb. The looks on the girls' faces are not the expressions you expect to see in a child. They are six, seven, eight years old.

Naturally, there were terrible fights there. This was between the orphanage kids and the kids who were not in the orphanage. I was always getting mixed up in fights. I would always go after kids older or bigger than me. I was always a little kid.

After about two years the school was closed. This was around 1949 when the legal harassment of Jews had begun — preparation for the Doctors' Conspiracy and the like. I remember very well how the hallways of our apartment were filled with bundles and packages of linens and other things. This was because mother was preparing for exile. The rumor was circulating that all the Jews were going to be moved to the autonomous Jewish republic of Birobidzhan. Nobody knew anything about it. All we knew was the Soviet film that told of the happy life lived by those Jews in Birobidzhan. What it really was, of course, was a concentration camp in Siberia. I remember Mother saying she did not fear it at all because nothing could be more terrifying than Hitler. She did not realize that Stalin could be no less terrifying than Hitler. And so they were ready to go.

Father was fired from his position. He was a doctor and a Jew. He was lucky, of course, that it went no further. He was not exiled, at least. He moved to Vilnius where he got another job. That is how it was done then; the men escaped exile by going to another city. Then Stalin died.

Maybe that is when it started — my desire to be an actor.

In Vilnius I joined a theater club at the Pioneer Palace. I had success playing in the kids' shows. It was an important period in my life. I participated in this theater club throughout my school years. I changed schools a couple of times, but I kept going to the drama club. Of course, when I was in the ninth and tenth grade, I played in school productions.

I remember well playing in a funny story by Chekhov. I dreamed up a series of comic tricks that helped me perform better. I never enjoyed more success as an actor than I had in that role. Later I would perform without success as an acting student, and even later I would perform in shows when I was studying with Tovstonogov to become a director. Also without success. But I was a big hit in that Chekhov story. I have forgotten the title, but it is a story about a man who comes to a store to buy something. Either the customer or the storekeeper is a German, I forget now. The man left his shopping list at home and he cannot remember what his wife wanted him to buy. Every time he thinks he has remembered something, it slips his mind again. That is pretty much the whole story. It is one of Chekhov's early newspaper feuilletons.

I now understand that I played that part so well because I concocted a gag for myself. I imagined that my character had already bought an armload of things, books, an umbrella, packages of things, and the like. So when I walked in the store, I was already loaded down. And when I started asking for something or looking for my grocery list, I would drop something. When I would bend over to pick that up, I would drop something else. When I would lean over to retrieve that, I would lose control of another object. It was a cascade of physical humor and all the school kids in the audience laughed like crazy. I felt as though my audience understood me, and I really felt great up there on stage. So when it came time for me to speak my lines, I was very much at ease. I performed my lines well, very much within the bounds of the genre. This was my best role as an actor ever. I think it was in the ninth grade.

I know that your father organized a puppet theater.

That is not all he organized. My father had a creative spark in him. Whatever he did he did with conviction and excitement. I do not mean he was given to flights of inspiration. That was not it at all. He would become fascinated by something and would investigate it thoroughly. Even if it were something that really did not require any great inquiry.

In Kaunas, for reasons entirely unknown to me, he organized and ran a male choir consisting of health service employees. In its first year, it won some prize in a big regional or national competition. It was a famous health service employee choir.

When he had to leave Kaunas for Vilnius and he took over the ambulance service there, his ponderous, exhaustive character once again made itself known. The ambulance service in Vilnius at that time boasted of two vehicles and two rooms. In one room a dispatcher slept and worked; the other room was occupied by the drivers and doctors attached to the two ambulances. When someone called for help, everybody leaped up and decided who would go out on the call. One team would go out and the other team would wait for the next call.

My father decided there was no point in everybody leaping up and racing to the next room to decide who would be going out. He installed a button on the wall that connected the two rooms electronically. With this button, the dispatcher could light up one or two lights in the other room. One light meant one team was going out, two lights meant the other was going out. This was a big innovation that required a creative approach.

He eventually developed this system to the point that he established radio contact between the dispatcher and the ambulances themselves. This was the first such system in the Soviet Union. Let us say the ambulance is out on call somewhere when a second call comes in. It is a terrible waste of time for the ambulance to have to come all the way back to the base to find out that it must go right back out again.

What is also important here is not only the fact that my father devised such a system, but that he had the ability to push new ideas like this through. This was crucial in Soviet times when you always had to convince higher-up bureaucrats to let you do anything out of the ordinary. In this case, only the military had access to radio communications. Civilians were not allowed to have it. So, my father not only came up with the idea, he was able to convince the bureaucrats to let him implement it. He got hold of some clunky old radios somewhere and had them installed in the ambulances. This provided an increased ability to respond to life-threatening emergencies.

Furthermore, he broke the ambulance brigades into specialized groups. This way, if some specific treatment was required — a heart specialist, a gynecologist, or a children's doctor — the doctor most suited to the need would be the one sent out.

When my father himself had a heart attack — and he had two — he began analyzing methods of using electrocardiographs. These machines were still very new and unwieldy. You had to come to the hospital to be treated. Only if you were a very important person would they load up an ambulance and bring the apparatus to you. So, while my father was lying in bed for two months, recovering from his heart attack, he studied the electrocardiograph. And when he went back to work, he resolved to establish a team of doctors who would take electrocardiograms. This was the first cardiac team in the Soviet Union. That is, a team of doctors specializing in heart problems who were able to come to the patient with the electrocardiograph machine. And he made all the doctors working for him learn to read the electrocardiograms.

My father was a man of tremendous will. I would even say of wrathful will. This was very much the way in the Stalin and post-Stalin periods. He made people do what he wanted. He did not care whether his doctors were interested in something or whether they wanted to do it. He made them do what he considered necessary.

He was the first man in the Soviet Union to begin keeping statistics about seasonal diseases and infections — what people were coming down with in the spring, summer, fall, and so on. He broke these statistics down into locations, showing that there were greater or lesser incidents of certain illnesses in certain areas. This allowed him to make the work of his ambulance group more effective. From time to time he would be invited to Moscow to deliver reports on the work he was doing.

This was in the era before computers, so he was doing all this with those old perforated cards. I do not know any of the details, but this is what I remember. Mother would get out her knitting needles and punch holes in the cards where Father wanted them. If he needed to know how many births there were in a certain location in a certain year, he would stick the needle into the stack of cards and all the appropriate ones would come up.

He did not devise this system. It is something he came up with by examining how other people worked on similar projects.

While he was doing all this, he bought mandolins and taught us kids how to play the mandolin. That was not enough to satisfy him, however. He also purchased mandolins for all his health service workers and he made them learn to play, too. So they were all sitting there plunking on the mandolin while waiting for emergency calls to come in.

Keep in mind, he did not bother to ask them if they wanted to learn to play the mandolin or not. He figured it was a waste of his employees' time to just sit there waiting for calls. He wanted them to be busy doing something because he felt that idleness is a form of degeneration and weakness. He did not want them playing cards, so he bought them mandolins.

When he resolved to teach his children to play chess, he also arranged whole chess competitions among various ambulance services. All the doctors, nurses, and drivers were involved. He took part himself, as the ambulance service director.

This now brings us to your question. At one point Father read a book by Sergei Obraztsov, the great Soviet puppeteer. He liked that book a lot and decided to make puppets himself. Somewhere he got hold of a play-dough kind of material that was very hard to find in the Soviet Union at that time and started making puppet heads. Then he became interested in papier maché. So, he investigated that craft thoroughly, learning that you rip off small pieces of paper and glue them onto your model, following that with a layer of newspapers and then another layer of clean, white paper and on and on. Then, when you have five layers, you cut it open and you have a form that corresponds exactly to the model. But of course, this is all very soft, so you have to wrap it in gauze. Then you take tooth-cleaning powder or chalk and mix it with carpenter's glue because it was especially strong. This would have to be boiled and our house used to stink to high heaven because of it! My mother was horrified. I remember the little candy containers he used because we did not have the proper instruments. The glue would boil up and bubble over the top and get all over the stove.

He did this by himself every evening although he made us stand by and watch. We did not want to, we were not interested. But Papa said we had to and so we had to. He was a strict man, but not only strict — when he got carried away with something he was unstoppable. He was capable of coming to a boil in a single second. And, as it is with me, his reactions were always physical first and only later would they be intellectual, verbal, or spiritual. In other words, he would whack you on the cheek first and only afterwards explain why.

I got my fair share of whacks because I was a wild kid and a bad student. When the door would open and my teacher would appear, my father would understand everything instantly and would come after me. I would run in circles around the table as he followed in a controlled manner. Finally he would catch me and I would get what was coming to me. Meanwhile, the teacher, who had come to say what a bad kid I was, would immediately take my side and plead with my father to leave me be because I was a good kid.

But let me come back to the puppet theater. Just as my father had discovered talented musicians and chess players among his employees, now he discovered some talented sculptors capable of making puppets. And all the ambulance crews were busy making puppets, costumes, and sets. Sometimes they did it while on the job, other times while at home.

The nurses who sewed the costumes knew nothing about making clothes for puppets. They knew how to make an overcoat, so they would just make a real one, only not your size, but in a little dinky size. That meant these things were hard to work with, because so many of the details a real overcoat needs are superfluous in a puppet's costume. But these women did not know that. They just did what they knew how to do. I still have a policeman's uniform from one of those puppets.

Then there were the rehearsals. Our apartment would be a madhouse. Dad nailing down boards and hanging a blanket to make the stage front. That is in one room. On the other side, in the next room, we the actors were gathered. This usually was my brother, a friend of mine, and I. Dad was the director, standing in the next room on the other side of the stage. He held a long stick with which he moved the puppets around. I do not know whether he had come up with that idea in his investigation of the art, or whether it was his own innovation.

But that was not the most important part of these puppet shows. The fact is that several of the characters had to sing. The music was picked up from popular songs of the time but the words were from, say, an Ivan Krylov fable. Or we would play something like Alexei Tolstoy's *The Little Golden Key*. The songs were a problem. I guess my pitch is not too bad, but to coordinate what I heard with what I actually sang was another thing altogether. And my father had no patience at all. He could not understand why I could not sing. He had perfect pitch and it made no sense to him. So I had to put up with him and his manner of directing me.

We would perform at home on our birthdays or at our friends' homes on their birthdays. The ambulance brigades would perform for each other at work on holidays such as the anniversary of the Revolution, New Year's, or May Day.

At some point, it became known that there had never been a puppet theater in Lithuania before. The puppet theater that my father had organized and in which my brother, my friend, and I were actors, was the first puppet theater in Lithuanian history. A journalist from *Pioneer Pravda* came all the way from Moscow to write an article about us. We were invited on tours and we performed once or maybe even twice at some community center for health workers in Minsk in the republic of Belorussia.

How old were you at this time?

I must have been thirteen or fourteen, which would mean my brother was nine or ten. We were almost grownups.

Of course, all the labor was done by my father's employees. They were all busy measuring and cutting and painting. It was serfdom in its purest form. Whatever the boss demanded was done.

I guess, then, that you had no trouble understanding Tovstonogov from the very beginning. You already had all the experience you needed with a "dictator director."

No, my father was not a dictator director. It was just something in his character that he had taken on from his ancestors. I do think there was something despotic, explosive, or hysterical in his family line. We all have it — my son Danya, I, my father, my grandfather Avram Gink. All our humorous and negative characteristics come from my grandfather Gink. You can see it in his photographs. He sits there like a king with his wife Liza and their kids around him. A very proud, very ambitious and very small figure. Evidently he was always giving out orders.

On the other hand, as I understand it, his wife Liza was a very wise, patient Jewish woman. She understood that when he yelled at her to do something that it was best not to argue but simply to do what she knew needed to be done. She supported in him his belief that he was the boss and the decision-maker. He was an educated man, of course. He was a pharmacist, after all. I do not know the extent to which my grandmother was educated. I suspect she was as educated as any young woman would have been in a small Jewish village of that time. She was obviously talented. She loved to read and her tastes were for relatively complex literature. I do not believe my grandfather read much. I think he was a somewhat limited person. Rather like my father, for that matter. I feel that in myself, those limitations that originate in the Gink family, those inborn limitations.

My father overcame them by the force of his will. When he took it in his head to do something, he did it. It did not matter if it was difficult, he did it. He was not at all inclined to the humanities. He had little understanding of literature and did not understand poetry at all, although he believed a person should read poetry. It was something one ought to read, so he read it. He had no feeling for it, but he read it.

My grandfather, Father's father, was even more limited than my father, of course. Despite his gold chain, his suit, and his proud pose in a photo, he was just a man from the local village. Although grandmother was larger and heavier than he, she looked smaller. She knew how to appear as if she were of secondary importance. Although it is obvious immediately that she was not of secondary importance at all. It is clear that she was the one who made all the decisions.

This is why the notion of my father as a dictator director is not quite right. It was simply a matter of his character, of his family genes.

I suppose it is true that if I had studied with some director whose character differed from that of my father, I would have understood that I must tame my character and be different. As it is, I saw that my given character was properly suited to the task at hand.

I finished school and dreamed of becoming an actor. Naturally, I knew where one must study to do that because the Vilnius Conservatory was a two-minute walk across the street from the building in which I lived. Whenever I walked by the conservatory, I could hear people singing or playing violins and cellos. Through the windows I could see people, some of whom, certainly, were not musicians, but those who one day would become actors.

When it came time for me to apply to the conservatory, it took the longest time for me to be able to actually open the door. It might have been as much as a month that I walked around and around that building. I could not imagine merely opening the door to paradise. How can you do that? It was not so much from fear as from the simple belief that I did not have the right.

But when I finished school, I allowed myself to go open that door. Even before that I had asked all around among friends about how one applies to acting school. Someone introduced me to an actress for whom I recited poetry and who gave me advice. I took my period of preparation for application very seriously. After the third round I was informed that I had been cut. The official reason was that my external appearance did not correspond to my inner capabilities. What does that mean? I was a very temperamental person, very emotional. I had a tragic, heroic manner. Meanwhile, I was a scrawny, dark little thing with a long nose. And no chin. I had a thin, high-pitched voice. My voice is a little lower now.

In other words, the more sincere and temperamental I became as I recited serious poetry or prose, the more comical I looked. I do not mean that in the sense that I was a potentially good comic actor. I mean I just had no effect. That is why they told me that my external appearance did not correspond to my inner capabilities.

It was a tragedy for me. I lost the meaning of my life. I had known since at least the fifth grade that I was going to be an actor. I went to the theater all the time; I knew everything about it and everyone in it. I participated in amateur theater and I read books about actors. I was a serious boy. I was like my father. It was not so much that I was analyzing things as he might have, but that I was seriously preparing myself for that big step. That is what I lived by. And suddenly it all fell apart.

I remember well that moment when I got the news. I went home and went to sleep. Then I woke up and, like any normal person, I got up and went to the bathroom to wash up and brush my hair. As I was doing that I looked in the mirror and asked myself, "What is the point of brushing my hair?" An actor must constantly be concerned with his appearance, his hair, his face. And I thought, "Why brush my hair now?" I remember this moment very well. It was a terrifying sensation to feel that everything was pointless.

My father had been skeptical about my desire to be an actor. He did not like the profession. He did not consider it practical, worthy of respect, stable, or lucrative. Being an intelligent person, he did not forbid me to pursue my dream, of course. But when I failed, he said, "Now you listen to me. Go to medical school." That is what was closest and most accessible to him. Moreover, he was in a position to have a talk with the necessary people to get me accepted.

All of my relatives had something to do with medicine. But I just plain did not like it. Plus it was a lot of work. You have to know chemistry well. I barely got through chemistry with C's in school. You have to know mathematics; I barely got a C in math. You have to know biology and I almost never did pass that in school. Then when you consider that a med student has to slice open cadavers, you begin to realize what a horror it all was. I was not interested in being a healer. No.

My father said in no uncertain terms: "You will go to med school." I said in no uncertain terms, "I will not."

My father and I had a difficult relationship not only because I was a bad student in school, but because we were too much alike in character. Basically we both would react to things at the exact same time, only in diametrically opposed ways. We had difficulties for a long time although later on that hardness softened.

So my father insisted I apply to medical school. That was still possible at that point because the exams for acting school were earlier than all the rest of the institutes. My father, trying to goad me, said, "Some of your classmates have even gotten into architecture school."

I remember that phrase very well, his attempt to puncture my pride.

Indeed, in Lithuania at that time the architect's profession was the most prestigious, the most respected of all. This was a time — 1957 — when people were finally beginning to be able to build something slightly different from that of the Stalin era. Particularly in Lithuania. It was a move away from the pompous Stalinist architecture toward an architecture made for people, an architecture that took into account comfort and lighting. Chairs began to have a design, not only a function. Specific chairs made for a specific café, for instance, with upholstery that matched that café only. Sofas took on smooth, loping lines. These were great people doing this. They were Europeans by inclination. The most talented members of the young generation, including two or three of my classmates, were getting into architecture. It was attractive because it was a mixture of the arts and the sciences — mathematics, drawing, imagination.

So, I said to my father, "I'll go to architecture school!" He said, "You?!" and I said, "Yes, me! I can draw better than my friends can."

That was true. I could. I did not draw well, but I drew better than they. I learned that they had spent a year preparing, studying classical drawing and the like. The upshot is that I refused to apply to medical school, and my father and I had a terrible falling out. But I began preparing for architecture school.

This was a turning point. That is the moment when I first began to develop my powers of will and concentration. I am not a person of great will, actually, but I am the kind of person who will succeed in accomplishing what I set out to do. It may take a long time — years, decades, even — but I will accomplish it.

At that time I was a weak, aimless young man. I was impulsive, hysterical, and pretentious. But I got a job at a drafting institute as a draftsman. I had done terribly at drawing in school, getting nothing but C's. I was too impatient and too clumsy. There were always blots on my drawings. But I got this job and began drafting. I did it very badly and very slowly. You were paid by the number of drawings you completed. I earned nearly nothing. Moreover, I was still a minor, sixteen or seventeen years old, so I did not have the right to work a full working day. I could only work for four hours.

That is where I learned to draw. I did plaster heads and plaster still lifes. That is where I learned to paint watercolors. That was the most difficult of all because you have to be extremely patient so as to keep the colors from running together. Every other day I went there to work and every day I took drawing lessons. But that was not all. When my lessons ended around 6 or 7 P.M., I would go home and bone up on my geometry, trigonometry and algebra. I had no idea what I was doing. But I kept at it, studying every evening until midnight. And then the next morning at 8 A.M. I had to be at work. When the time for entrance exams neared, I learned I could sign up for preparatory classes. So, on top of everything else, I attended tutorials in geometry, trigonometry, and algebra.

The time came when I applied to the architecture department of the most prestigious institute. This was a place where all the most talented, intelligent young people studied. They were not only future architects; they were painters, sculptors, and other kinds of artists. These were people who could have done anything they wanted but had chosen to come here. The institute was located in an old monastery next to the most beautiful old Gothic structure in Vilnius, the St. Anne Cathedral. This is the institute I applied to and I was accepted.

My father was stunned. My mother was thrilled. They said, "Well, you were accepted. Now you have earned a good rest. Take a small vacation in Palanga." All the Lithuanian Jews vacation in Palanga. I had been going there since childhood. So I went. Sun, sand, and sea. While there I met a former classmate, a young woman who was studying medicine. We had been close friends, and she knew how much I wanted to become an actor. The way I remember it now is that we were on the beach and people were sunning and swimming and playing around us. And she said, "You know what I just read in the newspaper?" I said, "What?" She said, "Here, read it yourself." She handed me the paper and I saw an announcement for auxiliary auditions for acting students in the Russian-language division of the Lithuanian theater institute. These were extra spots they had to fill after the initial admissions process had not given them a full class.

I made a beeline for the train station and bought a ticket for Vilnius. When I got there my mother said, "What are you doing here?" I had only just left for Palanga four days before and here I was back again. I said, "I was bored there. There was nothing going on."

Mom was busy with her usual tasks, doing shopping and cooking for the family and such. So she says, "You come along and help me." I could not very well say no, but this was right when the exams at the theater institute were being held. So I would run and bring her what she needed and then tell her I was going out for walks. In fact, I would quickly get dressed appropriately and go take my exams. In short, I passed them all and got as far as the third and final round. This is the point where, under the Soviet system, I had to turn over my high school diploma and other official documents to them if I intended to study there. Of course, I had already submitted my documents to the architecture institute.

I confessed that I had applied to the architecture institute when I originally failed to enter acting school. I explained that if I did not make the final cut at their theater institute, I intended to study architecture. But without telling my father, I took the risk of pulling my papers out of the architecture institute and placing them at the theater institute. And I was admitted.

I failed to tell about one aspect to this story. Back when I was going through the tragedy of having failed to enter acting school the first time, and was refusing to follow my father's advice to go to medical school, my schoolteacher had said, "You ought to study to become a director." I was taken aback. I said, "How could I do that? Directors are all so smart." I knew a little bit about literature and I knew painting pretty well, but I did not think I fit the mold. Moreover, it seemed to me that directors were people who knew exactly what they wanted and they knew how to go about achieving it. I, on the other hand, had no will power at all. Everybody had always said that about me in school.

Anyway, I was at loose ends because I had not been accepted anywhere. So, at that time, I decided to apply to directing school. I guess I got my father's permission or my mother's sympathy to do so, and I went to Leningrad. I chose Leningrad mostly because my aunt lived there and I could stay with her. I went through the exam process. The person giving the exams was a formidable type with the typical features of someone from the Caucasus — dark skinned, a large nose, and a rolling manner of speech. This guy was famous for something, although I did not know what. And he always arrived in a big fancy car, a Pobeda. The only people who had cars in those days were high-placed members of the Communist Party, dentists who had access to the gold used in tooth fillings, and rarely, the top managers of stores because they had opportunities to skim money off the top for themselves. But the notion of a man of the arts driving a car, and a prestigious Pobeda at that, was just unheard of.

I made it through the first three rounds of the entrance competition, which surprised me no end. I was not at all ready for those exams. I was not even seventeen years old. Eventually, this famous man summoned me and said, "Boy, go out and see life."

His point was this: I could have been admitted, but I still was wet behind the ears. I had to go out and get some experience. I was amazed

I had made it through the three rounds. I had never thought about directing before. I knew nothing about it. I was illiterate in the topic. And here I had made it to the final round. I was up against geniuses, real adults — some of them were even twenty years old.

When I got back to Lithuania I began reading about this famous man. His name was Tovstonogov. And I learned that he was the recipient of Stalin and Lenin Prizes, that he was a great director, and that he was the renowned artistic director of the Bolshoi Drama Theater. By this time, although I immediately began working to apply to architecture school, I knew I would one day study to be a director.

This detour was a crucial one for me because, later, even when studying acting in Lithuania, I had no expectations of actually becoming an actor. I knew that my time spent studying architecture had also been, in fact, more preparation to become a director. I knew that in four more years, Tovstonogov would be selecting students for a new course and so I had a goal to work toward.

By the time I applied to directing school the second time, I was ready. I had done sketches of my future productions, and I showed them during the entrance exams. They were amazed at what I had done. It was obvious from the very first minute that I would get in this time. When I came to talk to one of the professors — not Tovstonogov — he chatted with me as if we were old friends, as if he had finally found a colleague. He was a fan of Meyerhold, who at that time essentially did not exist officially. This man had even studied with Meyerhold in some way. We spent an hour talking about Meyerhold. We spent an hour talking about *Ivan's Childhood*, the film by Andrei Tarkovsky.

This was an official meeting when all the new students had come to meet the professors. All the students were lined up behind me and I was chatting with this professor on topics that were of interest to him. This was 1962, so I was twenty-one and he was probably fifty.

That is how I got into Tovstonogov's course.

Did he ever remember you were the "boy" he had sent off to see a bit of life four years earlier?

Of course not. And I never reminded him of it even though there was a certain closeness to our relationship. I was welcome in his home and was considered his favorite student.

You must understand that he would not attend our lessons for months on end. The day-to-day lessons were conducted by others. From time to time he would come unannounced to visit my nocturnal rehearsals. He also used to attend Henrietta's rehearsals. I did all of my intern work right there at Tovstonogov's Bolshoi Drama Theater. It was obvious he was proud of me. When he would ask questions and I would answer, he would lean back with a satisfied look and listen to what I had to say.

10

Joseph Brodsky and Crossing Borders

Joseph Brodsky was not only an important part of my life, but of my shared life with Henrietta. Strictly speaking, our friendship with Joseph did not last long and we never became extremely close. I cannot brag that Henrietta and I were his good friends. I am not even sure we were friends. We were acquaintances, close acquaintances.

But he played an enormous role in our lives because his poetry became a part of our lives. There are many things in our lives that Henrietta and I can describe only with the help of Brodsky's poetry. His words are the only words that fit certain circumstances.

The story of our acquaintance is this. I had always loved poetry, from my days as a youth. You could say I was brought up on poetic geniuses such as Mayakovsky, Pasternak, Tsvetayeva, Mandelshtam, and, later, Akhmatova. When I came to Leningrad to study directing, Henrietta said, "Listen, how would you like to read some poetry written by a kid of genius?" She gave me a few typed sheets. This was not published stuff, of course. They were the early poems "Fish in Winter," "The Blind Man Crosses the Square," "The Jewish Cemetery," and a few others I do not recall now.

The poems were good, though not works of genius. They certainly were a lot better than those of Yevtushenko or Voznesensky who, at that time, were considered marvelous Soviet poets. But they could not possibly be compared to anything written by Pasternak or Mandelshtam.

I said so and Henrietta was offended. She thought I just did not want to get caught up in the hoopla that was already beginning to accrue to Joseph's name in Leningrad. Among the intelligentsia and in artistic circles this twenty-one-year-old boy was already considered a genius. Everybody was talking about him.

A year or so later I heard about his trial after which he was exiled. Then there was the samizdat printing of the transcript of his trial and so on. This document was passed around among all of us.

None of this happened in a vacuum. There were other similar things going on, too. In that sense, there was nothing extraordinary in the fact that Joseph was tried and exiled. Shortly after was the Sinyavsky-Daniel trial. This kind of thing was an integral part of our lives.

By this time, Henrietta had begun passing on other copies of Joseph's poems to me. I found these much more interesting. Rightly so, because those first I had seen were really just juvenilia.

Henrietta had known Joseph since they were eighteen or so. They belonged to a homogenous intellectual-dissident-youth culture and they had crossed paths, probably in somebody's communal apartment where young people gathered to drink wine, recite poetry, and flirt. Henrietta was a famous beauty in these circles. Her admirable reputation was increased by the fact that she was intelligent, educated, witty, and personable. Nobody knew then that Henrietta was the future Yanovskaya or that Joseph was the future Brodsky. Just as no one knew that Tolya and Zhenya were the future poets Anatoly Naiman and Yevgeny Rein.

Henrietta introduced me to Brodsky after he returned from exile. By this time, I had a different opinion of him. I had seen more of his poetry and was interested to meet him.

I do not remember the chronology of it. It was just one aspect of our life in which the most important element was our studies at the theater institute, the scenes we were staging, the extracurricular work we were doing, and our own developing personal relationship. Henrietta and I had just married and we were two complex young people just beginning to live together in a communal apartment. There were all kinds of problems, not the least of which was that our workday usually did not end until the wee hours of the morning, say 3 or 4 A.M. We constantly had guests over in our communal kitchen — classmates from the institute, artists, photographers, all kinds of interesting people who craved company and talk. After they would leave, we would spend another hour or two cleaning up and discussing the evening's topics. Just about as we would begin falling asleep at 6 or 7 A.M., the doorbell would ring. Still sleepy and not very happy about the intrusion, we would open the door and see Joseph standing there. He always gave the impression he had not slept at all. He would barge into our single room rather unceremoniously, as though he had just been there and was coming back for something. Our bed would be unmade, and this infringement of an outsider on our private, personal lives was, frankly, quite awkward.

He would say, "I'll read you something now." Obviously, we would say, "Yes, yes. Go right ahead."

We would sit on our unmade sofa-bed, covering its embarrassing chaos with our bodies, and he would sit across from us. Then he would commence to shout. This was, say, eight o'clock in the morning. You could not call what he did reciting. He was shouting out his feelings. It was very rhythmic, very musical. He seemed to tumble over himself as he went. It was a kind of exalted, prophetic hysterics, really.

Most of his poetry was long by that time — even though he was still calling them verses, not yet long poems. His sentences were long and complicated, eight lines apiece. And he would become increasingly agitated as he worked his way through each one, his voice rising ever upward until the end when his voice would plummet downward. Then he would begin again with the next sentence.

This was quite trying, I must say.

I can sympathize with you to some extent. I attended a couple of his readings. Each time at the beginning I was enthralled. Each time by the end, I was exhausted. And I had not worked and rehearsed all day and night long before going to hear him.

Yes. It was not easy in part because it was early in the morning and we had not had any sleep. Second, his poetry by then had become very complex. These were things like "In Memory of T. S. Eliot," "A Talk with Heaven's Denizen" and such. Furthermore, the emotional intensity and energy that he brought to our sleepy room and sleepy souls was excessive. We could not keep up with him. We were not always able to make sense of the imagery he used in his poems. Frankly, it was quite an ordeal.

He would read one or two of his poems and then pause for a second or two. The assumption was that we were now supposed to say something. We usually would comment politely about how great the stuff was and how much we liked it. That was true, but it did not correspond to what we actually felt. We sensed that we were hearing poetry of genius. Certain segments made an incredible impression on us. But it was absolutely impossible to get a handle on it all. So we would utter some banalities and he would nod his head. He usually would get up before we finished saying anything and would often leave quickly without saying good-bye. Our heads would be in a muddle. We were left with the echo of his shouts and cries. We were left with his intonation, which has remained with us to this day. To this day we can pick up anything he wrote and remember his exact intonation as he read it, his utterly unique manner of recitation. Those, essentially, were our main meetings with him.

Once, we learned that the actor Sergei Yursky was a great admirer of Brodsky, and he wanted to recite his poetry on stage. Since Yursky was extremely popular in Leningrad, he was able to get away with more than most. He hoped that somehow, some way, he would be allowed to use a Brodsky poem for an encore at one of his literary performances. He knew we were friendly with Brodsky and asked us to introduce him. He wanted to hear Brodsky read in his own intonation and ask him some questions. We brought Yursky and Brodsky together there in our communal apartment.

Brodsky was a bundle of nerves when he arrived. In general, he was often upset when meeting someone new. He was shy and would clam up. I think he was especially unnerved by famous people. Evidently, Joseph perceived himself as a nobody, a kind of street person who was lionized by a very small, closed circle. On one hand, he was well known as the kind of person who always spoke his mind, never mincing words. He could be quite quarrelsome. It could be dangerous to lock horns with him. The other side of him, which I saw frequently, was that he often looked as though he did not belong when famous people were around.

Brodsky recited something for Yursky, and then Yursky said he planned on including his poetry in upcoming literary readings. He explained that he would read in a very different manner. Brodsky retorted, "Why read me differently?" It was a very curt, unexpected reply. A sense of awkwardness hung in the air. It was not just that Yursky was so famous, but also that he was a wonderful person. His desire to include Brodsky's poetry in his repertoire was an effort, of sorts, to "legalize" Joseph. Later they met at our place again. But what I remember most is Brodsky's brusque response.

Perhaps that is characteristic of writers. I once experienced something similar with the playwright Alexander Vampilov. We were in his hometown of Irkutsk, showing some of our shows from Krasnoyarsk. Vampilov at that time was known, but it was still a limited fame. (That was always a characteristic of Soviet life — people were famous in narrow circles.) I was a great fan of Vampilov. After one of our shows — I think it was *Fahrenheit 451* — we got to talking. He had liked the show, and so we started drinking and conducting a high-flying conversation about art. At some point I made the silly mistake of telling him how much I wanted to stage Chekhov's *Ward No. 6*. He became indignant. He said, "Why stage *Ward No. 6*? If Chekhov had wanted *Ward No. 6* to be a play, he would have written it as a play." Vampilov's eyes filled with blood and my character kicked in. We were both drunk by this time and it almost came to blows. The situation with Joseph never got quite so ticklish. But I remember the nature of his brusque responses.

Then there was a birthday once, either Henrietta's or mine. Among our guests were all of Henrietta's relatives, Joseph, and one very famous and very caustic theater critic, Zhenya Kolmanovsky. He allowed himself to write things that most people in the Soviet period could not get away with. For example, at a time when Tovstonogov was hailed by all as the greatest, most infallible genius of Soviet theater, Kolmanovsky allowed himself to criticize Tovstonogov. The result was that he was not allowed into the Bolshoi Drama Theater. Nevertheless, he was a friend of ours, although he was ten years older than we.

I remember now how strange it was — Joseph arrived carrying a gift. He had bought a big, fat book about theater designers of the Soviet era. It probably had a title like *Fifty Years of Soviet Theater Design,* one of those stuffy Soviet publications. Naturally, all the designers and shows represented in it were of the most orthodox Soviet kind. In short, a pile of nonsense. Very expensive nonsense, at that. A book like that was not cheap. But Joseph figured that since we were theater people, it was appropriate for us. In fact, it was of no use or interest to us at all. We kept it — and maybe still have it — only because Joseph gave it to us.

The get-together never quite got off the ground, in part because Kolmanovsky felt he had to make smart-aleck comments about Joseph every few minutes. I do not remember exactly what he said now, but let's say it was something like this: "So, how is the genius poet doing tonight? I hope our food does not attack his poetic taste?" Something like that, only more witty and more cutting. Joseph did not know how to respond. He just hunched lower and lower over the table, munching on the food in front of him. This continued for quite a while until I finally put an end to it. As a result we broke off with Kolmanovsky, whom we had loved and valued very highly. He had been a good friend for two or three years. Later we made up again before the final blowup, after which we broke off forever.

For Joseph, theater was something seductive and enigmatic, and there were times he would approach us in the common capacity of an author who would like to be staged. He once translated Brendan Behan's *The Quare Fellow.* It has different titles in Russian translation, including *Seven Seventy-Seven* or *The Death-Row Prisoner.* Joseph wanted me to stage it. It is a stunning play, I must say, about an Irish prison and the people who live there. Since nothing happens there at all, the entire prison is alive with the rumors that a new death-row prisoner is to be brought in. This prisoner, number 777, never arrives although everything that happens in the prison is connected with him. That is how the lives of these prisoners become known to us.

It is an excellent play, and Joseph's translation of it was phenomenal. It would have been a joy to stage a play like that. But how? Joseph could not understand that. He thought that since he had brought me

the play, I should just stage it. I do not think he had the vaguest notion that no one was willing to give me a job anywhere. He had no
idea that I was a total nobody.

Once a year I would travel to Moscow and make the rounds of
theaters looking for work. I would introduce myself to the literary directors and tell them I was a student of Georgy Tovstonogov. I would
explain how talented I was and do everything in my power to show off
my wit and erudition. Naturally, it was pointless. I never got any work.

During one trip, I ran into Joseph on the corner of Gorky Street
and Kamergersky Lane, right by the Moscow Art Theater. We must have
talked for a half an hour on various topics. But the main topic was when
I was going to stage the play he had translated. He was very offended.
He thought I had failed to appreciate the value of his translation. There
was nothing I could do to get it through his head. I told him flat out,
"I haven't staged a thing in three years. Anyway, there is no way anybody is going to let me do this play in particular. To say nothing of
the fact that it is your translation. If you translated the Soviet hymn,
they wouldn't let anybody sing it."

Did he ever attend any of your shows?

Never. First, he was not much interested in attending the theater. Second, our shows were performed rarely. We only rarely got a chance to
stage things and even when we did, they were always closed down
quickly.

Henrietta and I ran into Joseph one June as we were walking down
Liteiny Prospect in Leningrad. He invited us home for a visit. I had
been there a time or two; Henrietta had been there more often. You
must understand: Henrietta and I were what I would call "mutually
aging unemployed people." We spent much of our time waiting for job
offers that never came. We had no phone, so our lives were spent gab-
bing at the Actors House, the Saigon café, in our kitchen, or during
incidental meetings on the street. As such, when Joseph invited us home,
we had no other place to be and we were happy to go.

He told us he was just on his way home from the KGB's so-called
Big House or from the visa office — I do not recall exactly now. He

had just been given written permission to leave the Soviet Union. We did not know that he had been summoned by the authorities a month earlier and had been offered the option of leaving. He gave it some thought and made the necessary written application. That day when we ran into him on Liteiny Prospect, they had signed his sentence, so to speak.

That was shocking news. It really threw us for a loop. He himself was rather out of it at that moment. I do not remember what we talked about. We did not discuss the news at all, although it hung in the air.

We sat in the living room of the apartment where his parents lived. It was a typical large Leningrad room. A part of it was barricaded off by a dresser behind which was a cubicle that served as his room. The entrance to his "room," quite famous, now, thanks to his memoirs, was through the dresser. You would open the dresser door, walk in and come out on the other side. We stayed in the living room with his mother, who brought us tea and cookies and jam or whatever, while Joseph went into his room.

His mother said, "It's fate. It's fate. It's fate." This was a time when you knew you would never again see a person who left the Soviet Union. He would never come back, and you could not imagine having the opportunity of traveling to see him either. Joseph's father said, "Such upheavals! Such upheavals!" But in one wise, restrained phrase, his mother literally put her finger on Joseph's situation. She said, "Joseph's upheavals are here" — and she tapped her heart.

Joseph then came back out of his dresser and brought us an offprint of a Western publication of some of his poems.

Oh yes, this is from Ardis's *Russian Literature Triquarterly*. I recognized the format immediately.

Signed and dated April 18. Then he emigrated. We had no connection with him, although we would hear about him from time to time. He had become very close to one of my best friends, and they would talk by phone on occasion. We heard how he had gone to the United States. Through our mutual friend we would occasionally see his new poetry. We loved this work, and as I have said, it helped us to explain us to ourselves. Naturally, we always wanted to find a way to "legalize" him in some way in a show — even if that meant just sneaking a few lines in somewhere.

In one of the first interviews I ever did — this was with my friend Maria Sedykh — I ended up by quoting from "A Talk with Heaven's Denizen" and prefacing it with the generic phrase, "as the poet says,"

Inasmuch as pain is not a violation of rules,
suffering is
a capacity of bodies,
and man is an examiner of pain.

Naturally, I did not say who the poet was, although it was still cut out of the published text.

These lines lie at the basis of everything for me. They are capable of explaining everything. I have always believed that notion. All my shows have been about that. Moreover, the articles that have been coming out about me lately accuse me of this. One was just published that stated, "Most important in Ginkas's shows is suffering, not people." This is not, of course, because Joseph said it. It is just that he formulated it so well. I am never quite certain whether those are his words or whether they are mine.

Many years later Henrietta staged *The Nightingale*. Although this was during the perestroika period, the atmosphere was still heavily Soviet. In this show, Henrietta included poetry by Akhmatova, Pasternak, and Brodsky. We very much wanted to tell him that we had legalized him in some small way, but we had no contact with him. When he received the Nobel Prize for literature we sent a telegram but received no answer.

As time went on, I traveled often to Helsinki where I staged many shows. At one big arts festival there, Henrietta and I had been invited to bring three of our shows. When we looked over the festival program, we saw it was to open with a reading by Brodsky. Our shows were to open the theatrical segment of the festival. We were quite nervous that we were finally going to see him again after so many years. We did not know if he would remember or recognize us.

We went to the place where he was to give his reading. It was a large, grassy area in a park where a huge tent had been put up. In addition to the stage, there must have been seating for a thousand people. Alongside it was another huge tent of about the same size. There, people were walking around, buying food, eating, drinking, and talking. On the stage was Joseph, who, as always, shouted his verses. In another tent nearby the musical segment of the festival was getting underway — the jazz or rock coming from there was very loud. It was not easy to hear what Joseph was shouting. We knew what he looked like now from his photographs, but we saw a man who was much older than his years. He had a paunch and was bald — his former red hair was gone. He was visibly drenched in sweat, not because it was humid, but, I suspect, because he was so indignant at the conditions in which he was reading and at the way people were listening to him. Still, he shouted out a few of his poems, and then the Finnish translations were read. That was the end of that. The obligatory applause was not strong enough to drown out the music that was still playing.

We went to look for him in the backstage area. Quite a few autograph hounds, Russian-speaking women, young and otherwise, immigrants, students, and others had been able to get past the police guard to where he was standing. Joseph was drenched in sweat. It was obvious he was absolutely livid. As he signed each autograph he would make fun of the person he was doing it for.

If I remember correctly, we approached him and said we had sent a congratulatory telegram when he received the Nobel Prize, but that we did not know if he had ever received it. Pulling his eyes off the paper in front of him, he cast a glance at us. I do not know what that meant. But he went back to signing autographs. I told him that Henrietta had included his poetry in one of her shows, and that at least in that way we had tried to maintain contact with him. He muttered something and continued signing autographs.

This whole meeting was a disaster. We had irritated him by being witnesses to his unsuccessful reading. So we quickly said our farewells and left.

He knew who we were when we approached him, of course. Moreover, we had appealed to him in advance through the organizers of the festival. He was staying, I believe, in the nearby city of Turku at the time and we had sent messages that we would happy if he would attend our shows. He had answered through them that he would be unable to. Of course he recognized us. But the time was not right.

Not long after that, we learned he had died. Henrietta organized a memorial at the theater for him. Among the people taking part in the concert were Yevgeny Rein and Anatoly Naiman. For that evening Henrietta had a portrait of Joseph blown up, which stood on the stage. That enormous portrait now hangs in her office and I am extremely happy that it takes up so much space. It hangs among other portraits of people who are very dear to us — Tovstonogov, Anatoly Efros, Mikhail Bulgakov, Stanislavsky, and Andrei Sakharov.

I can add one more thing to finish off this long and circuitous story about Joseph. A day or two after I had heart surgery in Helsinki in 1997, I got a call from a friend, a Swedish radio journalist who lives in Finland. She was stunned by the news of my operation, and she wanted to know if she could visit me. I said I would be happy to see her. She always spoke in a certain state of excitement, and now that was even truer than ever. The reason, it turned out, was not only because she was worried about my health.

She explained that ten years before in New York she had done an interview with Joseph after he had had a heart operation. I asked if I could listen to it and two or three days later she brought me the tape. It was absolutely stunning. I put on that tape and listened to his voice. It was taped just as we are working now, in his apartment, and all the sounds of them drinking and eating were audible. Glasses were clinking, the phone was ringing, you could hear him lighting up his cigarettes, people would come by and you could hear him talking with them and then he ran next door to borrow some cigarettes from a neighbor because he was forbidden to smoke and he had run out. Amidst all of this he gave a brilliant interview.

It was like receiving a personal greeting from him, totally unexpected. All the intonations, all the expressions were so familiar that I had the sensation I was having a visit with him at home. Later, when I got back to Moscow, I offered the tape to the journal *Moscow*

Observer and it was published there.* At least for the present, that is how our story with Joseph ends.

You talked of breaking off with your friend Yevgeny Kolmanovsky. I have heard you had a spectacular break with the designer Eduard Kochergin.

No, there was never any break in our relationship. What happened was we had a spectacular altercation while working on *Resembling a Lion*.

Eduard had designed a wonderful set, which is hard to describe. It depicted a strange, stretched-out room. There were no corners in this room, which, because there are no fourth walls in the theater, was something like a huge open sea shell. There were a handful of realistic objects — a sink, a chair, and a door — but the walls were stretched out and painted a uniform silver color. In place of wallpaper, the walls were hung with lace, which was also painted silver. Everything was silver. The metallic sink was silver. This was Kochergin's idea. I had told him this would be a play about love, but specifically about Soviet love. It would have the aroma of Soviet monotony to it. The smoothed-out corners and the lace were a reference to the play's lyrical quality. But then Kochergin said, "Have you ever noticed that whenever anyone in our country wants to make anything look festive they paint it silver?"

Indeed, trash cans on the street, street lamps, and the like were always painted silver for May Day or the anniversary of the Revolution. If it was necessary to impart a false sense of monumentalism to something, you painted it silver. A dirty, nasty, crumbling wall, for instance. Paint it over in silver and there you have a Soviet holiday. An important aspect is that the color was never gold, always silver — silver had this kind of cheap, secondary quality. Moreover, in Soviet times, grave markers, the chains marking off grave plots, and even the plywood stands for the Soviet red stars over graves, were always painted in silver. It was never a fine, shiny silver, but always a crude, dull silver color. It was not exactly gray, it was a kind of deathly celebratory silver.

---

*"Iosif Brodsky. Golos 1987," *Moskovskii nabliudatel'*, no. 1 (1998), 91–97.

During the course of rehearsals, it became clear I was going to need a small soap tray by the sink. I was having an actor wash his hands. The show was close to opening and the set was almost finished. All that was left was to paint it. Now, whenever I worked with Kochergin, he always participated in the most delicate stage of painting his sets. I always admired that and I, too, would sometimes join in and help. At this point most of the set had been painted, but Kochergin was putting on the final silver touches and gluing on the last corners of lace.

I had been reminding him for quite awhile that a soap tray needed to be added. Every time I brought it up he would either complain that he did not want to hear about it or he would mumble that he would do it soon. But he never did. Finally, I told him once again that a soap dish had to be attached to the wall by the sink. He grabbed his bucket of silver paint and flung the whole thing at the wall he had just finished painting so carefully.

I stood below, by the footlights, in front of the stage. I gasped when he did it, but I never had time to react otherwise because he instantly grabbed the bucket and came running after me to hit me with it. He threw the bucket at me and missed. Then he leaned over the edge of the stage and began trying to kick me in the chest.

This was so unexpected, so ingenuous, and so amazing that I burst out laughing. He cut loose with a string of obscenities that I answered back in kind, and he stalked off the stage. An hour later he came back and quietly began fixing everything he had ruined.

That story got around, of course. A quarrel like that, which almost becomes a fight, is real grist for the mill. It was not long before the news reached the theater next door. This place was run by a person of my generation. He was one of those people who were willing participants in the status quo. He was very successful in his participation and, moreover, he was not bereft of talent. As a result I did not like him — you could even say I despised him. He knew that, and we had a very strained relationship. This director also worked on occasion with Kochergin, and so there were people who wanted him to hear as quickly as possible about our altercation. But this person was no fool. Reportedly, he replied by saying, "I am envious. I would like to have the kind of relationship with Edik where he would feel comfortable behaving like that with me."

This story says something about both Kochergin and me. You have to know Kochergin to picture it. He is extremely precise, pedantic, and careful in everything he does. The point is this: He felt that tiny soap dish violated the whole composition around the sink. He was categorical about that and I understood him. But there was nothing I could do about it.

The action made its own demands.

There was a whole scene built around it.

I recall you once telling the wonderful story of the first time you crossed the border from the Soviet Union into Finland with another of your designers, David Borovsky.

Actually, I had been in West Berlin one time before that. You must understand what going abroad meant to a Soviet person who had never been anywhere. It was unreal. We knew there were people living out there who were somehow different from us. Not that they had three hands, but there was something different about them.

Imagine this: When I was still a school kid, I thought all Americans had snub noses. And that they were all fat. That is the way they were pictured in all the caricatures. And caricatures were the only places I could possibly have seen an American. I was disconsolate about that, in fact, because I — or, at least, my father — had a nose like that, which meant that I was almost an American capitalist. Obviously, I was more sophisticated in my notions of foreigners when I took my first trip abroad, but, still, there was something of the fantasy world in it.

I once had a dream about taking an evening walk. At some point I crossed a line in the middle of town and realized I had found my way to the West. In this dream, I walked about the nighttime city in a state of fear and consternation. One second the world is familiar, the next second everything is totally different. I could not fathom it. That was an actual dream I had, about my traveling from one dimension into another.

Then it so happened that my production of *Five Corners* was invited to perform in West Berlin. First we flew to East Berlin. From there, we were to cross over to West Berlin. In the East Berlin airport, everything looked and smelled Soviet. The place smelled of sweat, sour cabbage soup, and toilets. It was noisy, plates were banging. It was only a little better than the typical Soviet scene. Rather like one of the Baltic states. The walls were not quite as dirty; they were almost presentable.

We were led to a door. It opened. We entered. We presented our passports and papers. They stamped them. And now all of a sudden everything was different. Everything. Absolutely. The interior was totally different. Empty and spacious. Clean. Nobody was banging plates. It did not smell of anything. You went into the toilet and it was clean and light. The toilet flushes. It was a total enigma. This was in the same place, the same building! But you opened a door and entered a new world.

Once we had walked through this clean, neat, beautiful, spacious, quiet interior, we descended an escalator and went outdoors. There, waiting for us, was a double-decker bus of the kind I had only seen in pictures. It, too, was neat and clean. Its windows were sparkling, not all splattered with mud. The tires, almost toylike, were so shiny it seemed they had just arrived from the factory. A friendly driver smiled and said, "Bitte!" We got in the bus, which set off on astonishing roads winding through gorgeous forests and hills.

Fantastic. It was as though we had gone through a magic door. A door into another world. The image for me was stunning. You open a door and everything changes. It was all the same building, just two halves of the same place. Fantastic.

So, I had already had that experience when I left for Helsinki with David Borovsky. The train headed out from Leningrad through Vyborg. We stopped there at the border, and they took us off the train for an hour to harass us with all the formalities of going abroad. The Vyborg Station, naturally, smelled like a toilet. Where it did not, it smelled of that thick soot that pours out of Soviet trains. People were lying around, waiting for local trains. The loudspeakers were barking. Everything was just as you would expect it to be.

This was around five o'clock in the morning. We were to cross the border in a half hour. When we all got back on the train, David said,

"Kama, don't go back to sleep." I said, "I'm sleepy." He said, "Don't go back to sleep. I want to show you the border." I couldn't figure out what he was talking about. How could you see a border? He made me stand by the window and we looked out at the landscape. We went flying by unkempt trees, broken bushes, falling-down barracks, ruined train cars, trash, abandoned piles of wood and coal, dirty snow. The woods we passed through were a mess, as if some tractor had come through and ripped half of it out. In other words, just what you would expect from a Soviet forest.

And then, suddenly, there was first one post and then a second. And the woods, as if miraculously, were neat and even. The snow was pure white. We came upon a well-groomed little house. It looked as though it had just been built and been licked clean. That was Vainnikalla, the first station in Finland.

Borovsky says, "Let's go hunt for Mercedes-Benzes. Every time I pass through here there are Mercedes-Benzes standing at the station." I said, "Come on. Mercedes-Benz is the best car in the world. This is some hick town in the middle of the night. There aren't going to be any Mercedes here." We went out into the parking lot and, sure enough, there were Mercedes-Benzes out there.

Ever since then — and over the course of some twelve years I traveled to Helsinki several times a year — I always got out of the train at Vainnikalla and looked in the parking lot to see if there were Mercedes-Benzes there. There always were. Until the last three or four years, anyway. They have disappeared of late.

They have now all moved over to the Russian side.

That must be right.

When I listen to your stories, I listen both as a foreigner and as a person who has lived in Russia for twelve years. And I must say, I find each side incredibly attractive — both the ragged, broken-down forest and the neat, clean woods. I remember you once telling about the differences in walls in Russia and abroad. I was amazed because your observation defined what I have long felt about what distinguishes life and art in Russia from life and art in the West. Incidentally, your walls here in your apartment are quite smooth and even. Not at all like Russian walls.

Because we just had a painstaking remodeling job done.

Be that as it may, you said that Russian walls are always crooked and bumpy. In them you can still see the human touch, the individual hand that made them as they are.

Yes. Yes.

In the West, walls are always perfectly flat and straight. There is no sign anywhere in them that any human has ever touched them.

They are always done there with that instrument, what is it called? A level.

They are beautiful, clean, and highly impersonal. The Russian wall, on the other hand, is curved and lumpy, bowed and uneven. You can see where the human hand moved along it . . .

Creating a wall that is alive.

You can see where a human actually worked . . .

Leaving behind a sign of his individuality . . .

Trying, but not quite succeeding in, getting it to come out even. I really love that.

Yes, but is impossible to live like that all the time.